The Bodhisattva's Brain

The Bodhisattva's Brain

Buddhism Naturalized

Owen Flanagan

The MIT Press
Cambridge, Massachusetts
London, England

For information about special quantity discounts, please e-mail special_sales@mit-press.mit.edu

This book was set in Stone Sans and Stone Serif by the MIT Press.
Printed and bound in the United States of America.

Library of Congress Cataloging-in-Publication Data

Flanagan, Owen J., 1949–
The Bodhisattva's Brain : Buddhism Naturalized / Owen Flanagan.
    p.   cm
"A Bradford Book."
Includes bibliographical references and index.
ISBN 978-0-262-01604-9 (hardcover : alk. paper)
1. Buddhism—Psychology. 2. Buddhist philosophy. I. Title.
BQ4570.P76F48   2011
294.3'3615—dc22
                                                            2010053617

10 9 8 7 6 5 4 3 2

To Betty Stanton, and the memory of Harry "Bradford" Stanton, who made comparative neurophilosophy, and much else, possible

Contents

Preface   ix
Acknowledgments   xv

Introduction: Buddhism Naturalized   1

I   An Essay in Comparative Neurophilosophy

1   The Bodhisattva's Brain   9

2   The Color of Happiness   37

3   Buddhist Epistemology and Science   59

II   Buddhism as a Natural Philosophy

4   Selfless Persons   93

5   Being No-Self and Being Nice   115

6   Virtue and Happiness   165

Postscript: Cosmopolitanism and Comparative Philosophy   203

Notes   209
References   237
Index   249

Preface

This book is the unintended consequence of an accident. In the summer of 1999, while on a working vacation in Costa Rica finishing *Dreaming Souls* (2000b), I received an email inviting me to participate in a weeklong discussion the following March in Dharamsala, India, with the 14th Dalai Lama and a handful of scientists and philosophers on the topic of "destructive emotions." Prior to the invitation I had some curiosity and a bit of knowledge about Buddhism, as well as a strong conviction of the worth of comparative philosophy, reasoning that either there was or wasn't wisdom about the human condition, and that studying different, and if possible unrelated traditions, would reveal which it was, and if there was any, what it is. The invitation to the Dalai Lama's compound in Dharamsala was, I was told, due to a positive impression my book on the nature of consciousness, *Consciousness Reconsidered* (1992), specifically its defense of the use of first-person phenomenology in a robust naturalistic theory of consciousness, had made on several of the Dalai Lama's scientific acquaintances (there was no reason then or now to think that the Dalai Lama himself had read any of my work).

The meeting, the Eighth Mind and Life Conference in the spring of 2000, led to a certain unexpected visibility for the participants, including myself, since ideas hatched at the meeting (not by me) led immediately to some widely discussed neuroscientific experiments attempting to determine whether, or possibly to demonstrate that, Buddhist brains revealed their owners to be unusually happy. Because I had been present at the original discussions of whether Buddhism—specifically certain kinds of Buddhist meditation practices—might produce positive changes in the hearts and minds of practitioners, I was immediately and frequently asked to speak and write about the results of these experiments, which according to the media, more than the scientists involved, showed that Buddhism, uniquely perhaps among the world's great wisdom traditions, might produce what

Aristotle said everyone wishes for, to possess eudaimonia, to be a happy spirit, to flourish. The publication of Daniel Goleman's bestselling book about our meetings, *Destructive Emotions: A Scientific Dialogue with the Dalai Lama* (2003a), helped establish the consensus that someone, somewhere, and pretty recently, had proven that Buddhists were the happiest people in the world.

By 2003, thanks to numerous chances to speak and write on the alleged connection between Buddhism and happiness, and by then serious immersion in the study of Buddhist philosophy (for the record, I am not a Buddhist), the idea for this book was hatched and writing began. Two aspects of my serendipitous situation were especially motivating, despite many interruptions, including an intervening book, *The Really Hard Problem: Meaning in a Material World* (2007), which contained a chapter engaging the Dalai Lama's views on astrophysics, evolution, justice (karma), and consciousness, a descendant of which is contained in this book as chapter 3. First, as a philosopher who has spent most of my life, not just my career, thinking about the nature of mind, the mind–body problem, how mind, morals, and the meaning of life connect, trying to make the world safe for a fully materialist view of mind, I was intrigued, delighted, and frequently bewildered by having an inside seat at one of those rare moments when science, specifically cognitive science, philosophy, and religion, or something like religion, come together, interact, and intersect. There were widespread discussions, and many published expressions, which continue, of the idea that neuroscience was actually in the process of empirically vindicating the claims of one lived philosophical tradition, namely Buddhism, to yield happiness and flourishing, or something in the vicinity, at a higher rate of return than the other contenders. The hyperbole was (and continues to be) jaw-dropping. I judged the desire expressed and embodied in the idea of vindicating scientifically the claims of a philosophical tradition to be uncommon and thus worth paying close attention. Here were people, Buddhists or folk who judge Buddhism as the correct answer to the question "How ought I to be and live?", who are not typically materialists about consciousness, looking at the brain for markers or correlates of a happy and good human life. I set myself this role—a sort of epistemologist-participant-observer from the planets of analytic philosophy and twenty-first-century cognitive science. It was interesting, to say the least, to watch a lived philosophical tradition interested in empirical evidence of its efficacy. I tried to watch the dialectic closely and now offer a report of the lessons learned.

The second motivating feature was this: I have always been a fan of comparative philosophy, long convinced that there are certifiably great non-Western philosophical traditions, such as Confucianism, Taoism, Hinduism, Jainism, and Buddhism, or for that matter extinct Western traditions like Stoicism, Epicureanism, and Cynicism, about which most Westerners, philosophers included, are ignorant. I've always thought that the study of these traditions might disabuse us of several related blind spots: ethnic chauvinism, the view that non-Western traditions are esoteric in a bad way, for reasons beyond their unfamiliarity; the idea that Religion (with a big "R") is inevitable for psychological reasons; and that it is required, true or false, to shore up meaning and morals. I thought this an opportune time to introduce my fellow philosophers, as well as the many scientific naturalists who like me are allergic to hocus pocus, to a suitably deflated secular Buddhism, what I call Buddhism naturalized. Buddhism, like Plato and Aristotle's philosophies, is a comprehensive philosophy. It contains a metaphysic, an epistemology, and an ethics—a way of conceiving the human predicament, human nature, and human flourishing—that is deep and not simply superstitious nonsense. Now some parts of Buddhism are superstitious nonsense, so there was also the prospect of asking this question: Is it possible to take an ancient comprehensive philosophy like Buddhism, subtract the hocus pocus, and have a worthwhile philosophy for twenty-first-century scientifically informed secular thinkers? It struck me that among the world's major spiritual traditions, Buddhism (I'd say Taoism and Confucianism as well, but that is a different book) isn't ethically or politically particularly dangerous and is, in its saner forms, philosophically extremely sophisticated, even credible. The history of the West has been and continues to be the story of bloodbaths rooted in part in preposterous faith claims, whereas Buddhism has been kindler and gentler despite being a proselytizing tradition like Christianity and Islam. In his 1966/1975 classic lecture, "The Buddhist Attitude to Other Religions," K. N. Jayatilleke writes:

The Buddhist attitude to other religions has from its very inception been one of critical tolerance. But what is significant is that it was able to combine a missionary zeal with its tolerant outlook. Not a drop of blood has been shed throughout the ages in the propagation and dissemination of Buddhism in the many lands to which it spread and religious wars either between the schools of Buddhism or against other religions have been unheard of. Very rare instances of the persecution of heretical opinions are not lacking but they have been exceptional and atypical. Buddhism has also shown a remarkable degree of adaptability in the course of its historical expansion.

One might object to the claim that Buddhism is a comprehensive philosophy that is peaceful, tolerant, and not particularly politically dangerous:

there are either no successful Buddhist states or the ones that are successful in the sense of being stable, still with us, and so on, are not exactly
exemplary. As I write, Sri Lanka, formerly Ceylon when Jayatilleke wrote
the "not a drop of blood" words above, has just emerged from a bloody
civil war. Myanmar is the longest-lasting Soviet-style military dictatorship
in the world (tied perhaps with North Korea). In Bhutan, famous for its
king's endorsement of the Gross Happiness Product (GHP), racist practices
against Nepalese are considered normal and acceptable. And many of the
very same Tibetan Buddhists who make Hollywood weep with nostalgia for
Shangri La, and who make the (other) Chinese angry, do so because they
long for the most undemocratic form of government conceivable, a feudal
theocracy where the leaders are reincarnations of reincarnations.

These facts might be disassociated from Buddhist philosophy, since in
each case, with the possible exception of the Tibetan one, the problematic
political regime is not itself Buddhist. There is also the possibility, which is
what I think really, that Buddhism is a comprehensive philosophy that is
very weak in the political philosophy department, overrating compassion
and underrating the need for institutions that enact justice as fairness. But
again that also is another story.

There are some excellent Buddhist scholars, but almost none of them
teach in philosophy departments at research universities in America that
offer PhDs (although many excellent ones teach and do research in religion departments at research universities and in philosophy departments
at excellent liberal arts colleges). This is strange given that Buddhism is so
philosophically rich, contains ideas about personal identity and the metaphysics of nature and causation that ought to appeal to contemporary philosophers, and especially given that as many as one in twelve people on
earth are Buddhists.

Most of my personal interaction with Buddhists over the last decade has
been with Tibetan Buddhists. Because of the 14th Dalai Lama's charisma
and visibility, certain aspects of this form of Buddhism are familiar, even if
not well understood in the West (similar to the situation with Zen in the
second half of the twentieth century). Although I do not (as best I can avoid
them) enter into sectarian debates that divide Buddhists, I have tried to get
a feel myself for the spirit that runs through the Buddhisms—there are only
Buddhisms, no Buddhism– by spending time in countries where forms of
Buddhism other than the Tibetan variant are lived, including Korea, Japan,
Taiwan, Hong Kong, China, and Thailand. I thank the many East Asian and
Southeast Asian Buddhists who helped this gadfly try to catch on to their
lived philosophy. What I learned in Asia as well as in travels throughout

America and Northern Europe talking to Western Buddhists who claim to be of Tibetan or Tantric or Thai or Vipassana or Ch'an (Zen) or Pure Land lineages is that all such souls (Eastern and Western) think they really know what Buddhism is, what the Buddha said, thought, and meant, when in fact they are inspired either by one of the many varieties of Buddhism or by something of a mix of the many varieties of Buddhism. In the East, most Buddhists take their variant as the right one, the true form. In the West, outside the small circle of scholars and serious Buddhists, the largest sects of Buddhists or the Budd-curious divide bimodally depending on what aspects of Buddhism they are most impressed by and interested in: either it is meditation and the personal soul soothing they see meditation offering or it is becoming nicer, more compassionate, and the soul soothing it (or thinking of oneself as nicer) offers. There is room I came to think for a book that introduces those interested in comparative philosophy, as well as the many Westerners interested in Buddhism only or mostly as a form of mental hygiene and/or moral self-improvement and self-indulgence, to the deep structure of the metaphysic, epistemology, and ethics of Buddhist philosophy.

As for by own understanding of Buddhism. Hmm. Once in Korea I was told on arrival that a professor friend had warned that I would be speaking on "Buddhaganism"—Flanagan's interpretation of Buddhism. This is not a bad way to think about my opinionated interpretation and examination of Buddhist philosophy and psychology offered here. Although I try to offer a credible primer on Buddhist philosophy, I am interested in Buddhism as a great philosophy, in the same sense that we think of Confucian philosophy and classical Greek philosophy as great. But, as in these other cases, I am interested in whether for us contemporary folk there is a useful and truthful philosophy in Buddhism, among the Buddhisms, that is compatible with the rest of knowledge as it now exists and specifically, because this is always a problem for spiritual traditions, whether Buddhism can be naturalized, tamed, and made compatible with a philosophy that is empirically responsible, and that does not embrace the low epistemic standards that permit all manner of superstition and nonsense, sometimes moral evil as well, in the name of tolerance, or, what is different, high spiritual attainment that warrants teleological suspension of the ethical in the hands of fanatics of all stripes. The demand for high epistemic standards is not only directed to Buddhism and other spiritual traditions, it is also intended to call to task those glib souls who claim that science, specifically neuroscience, can tell us, even that is has already told us, about what makes for human flourishing and for true happiness, and that it can reveal, even that it has revealed, how

Buddhism, or for that matter any other great comprehensive philosophical tradition, produces what we all want, to achieve eudaimonia, to flourish, to be happy. All such claims are scientifically premature, as well as philosophically naive. Flourishing and happiness are not in the head, at least not only in the head. These things—flourishing and happiness—might be in our hands if we pay close attention to which among the myriad experiments in living work well, and which ones not so well. History, sociology, anthropology, behavioral economics, comparative philosophy, even what I call comparative neurophilosophy are required, but also happily available, as tools to advance the projects of understanding better whether and how human flourishing is possible, if, that is, it is possible. Living well, finding meaning in a material world for finite beings is a really hard problem, the hardest problem of all.

Berkeley, California
June 2010

Acknowledgments

Many people, a strange mix of straight-arrow analytic philosophers, neurophilosophers, comparative philosophers, psychologists, neuroscientists, Buddhist laypersons, monks, nuns, and Buddhist studies scholars, helped me create this work: Roger Ames, Julia Annas, James Austin, Stephen Batchelor, Doug Berger, Pamela Buck, Troy Catterson, Arindam Chakrarbarti, Win Chiat, Patricia Smith Churchland, Robert Conrad, Robina Courtin, Richie Davidson, Ronald De Sousa, Georges Dreyfus, Paul Ekman, Jay Garfield, Carl Gillett, Jonathan Gold, Daniel Goldman, Charles Goodman, Alison Gopnik, Tenzin Gyatso (the 14th Dalai Lama), Sam Harris, Rob Hogendoorn, Marion Hordequin, P. J. Ivanhoe, Richard Jaffe, Tao Jiang, Thupten Jinpa, Christopher Kelley, Shian-Ling Keng, Damien Keown, Brian Knudsen, Joel Kupperman, Tim Lane, Donald S. Lopez Jr., Antoine Lutz, Tim McHenry, Matt McKenzie, D. K Nauriyal, Tom Polger, Elizabeth Price, Wayne Proudfoot, Matthieu Ricard, Alex Rosenberg, Richard Baker Roshi,Andy Rotman, Hagop Sarkissian, Robert Sharf, Nancy Sherman, Mark Siderits, Sam Sims, Walter Sinnott-Armstrong, Ted Slingerland, Tamler Sommers, Andrew Terjesen, Evan Thompson, Robert Thurman, Jeannie Tsai, Francisco Varela, Alan Wallace, Joyce Walworth, Jan Westerhoff, and David Wong. There are many others in audiences at universities in the United States, South Korea, Japan, Taiwan, Thailand, China, Ireland, United Kingdom, Holland, Brazil, and South Africa who helped me a lot. I am grateful to them all. Finally, I am grateful to Tom Stone who acquired this book for MIT Press and to Phil Laughlin who sheperded it to publication.

Introduction: Buddhism Naturalized

Anachronism and Ethnocentrism

Suppose we permitted ourselves this luxury: invite Confucius, Siddhārtha Gautama, Mohammed, Joan of Arc, Catherine the Great, Karl Marx, Thomas Jefferson, Sojourner Truth, or any other interesting or wise dead person with a view, or who is a representative of a tradition, into our conversations about our problems—poverty, heath care, capitalism, how to be a good person, how to live well, to flourish, to be happy—and listen to what they say. This is anachronistic. Some say anachronism is bad, even that it is not allowed. Allow it.

Next imagine responding to the anachronistic answers of our respected ancestors with our own reflective standards of cogency, wisdom, and breadth and depth, feeling free to judge their answers as helpful or inadequate for our problems in our time. This is ethnocentric. It is temporally different but logically identical to judging the ideas and ways of other contemporary peoples as well suited for us or not suited for us, as good for us or not good for us in our time. Some say ethnocentrism is bad, even that it is not allowed. Allow it.

Three Philosophical Styles: Comparative, Fusion, and Cosmopolitan

Next, consider three styles of doing philosophy. First there is *comparative*. Compare and contrast. Regarding ethics, Confucians say that filial piety (*xiao*) is a mandatory virtue. Aristotle doesn't mention xiao or anything in its vicinity as essential to morality. For Buddhists, compassion (*karuna*) is the first and highest virtue; for citizens of contemporary liberal societies, left or right, individual compassion is an optional virtue while justice or fairness, at both the personal and political levels, holds pride of place as a constraint on the exercise of otherwise unlimited freedom. Second, there is *fusion*. What do we get when we add Confucian xiao to Aristotle's list of virtues? Is it an interesting, appealing mix or not? Could such a mixture work to improve our culture, say, by making the youth more respectful and society more orderly?[1] Finally, there is *cosmopolitan*. Think of the exercise of reading and living and speaking across different traditions as open, non-committal, energized by an ironic or skeptical attitude about all the forms of life being expressed, embodied, and discussed, including one's own, but sensitive also to the demands of one's own way of being and living given its utterly contingent but nonetheless identity-constitutive role in making one who he or she is. The cosmopolitan is a listener and a speaker, an anachronistic and ethnocentric one, he or she compares and contrasts, is willing to try fusings of silly and safe sorts, but mostly likes living at the intersection of multiple spaces of meaning, waiting and seeing and watching whatever happens happen.[2]

Many Westerners are attracted to Buddhism because it offers one way to be "spiritual but not religious," the currently favored answer to the religion question on social networking sites. This is an interesting development. Historically Buddhism is atheistic or quietistic when it comes to a creator God. Siddhārtha put the creation question, as well as most other standard metaphysical questions, aside in one early sutra as impractical or beyond human understanding or both. But Buddhism is opulently polytheistic insofar as spirits, protector deities, ghosts, and evil spirits abound (Collins 2003, 104). Buddhists in East and Southeast Asia believe in rebirth in about the same proportions as most North Americans believe in heaven. Amusingly, many believers in heaven find belief in rebirth superstitious and thus silly, whereas from a reflective naturalistic perspective both are silly. Is a fully secular, naturalistic understanding of Buddhism possible? Are Quakers and Unitarians Christians? Are secular, naturalistic Buddhists really Buddhists?[3]

Naturalism comes in many varieties (Flanagan 2006), but the entry-level union card—David Hume is our hero—expresses solidarity with this motto: "Just say no to the supernatural." Rebirths, heavens, hells, creator gods, teams of gods, village demons, miracles, divine retributions in the form of plagues, earthquakes, tsunamis are things naturalists don't believe in. What there is, and all there is, is natural stuff, and everything that happens has some set of natural causes that produce it—although we may not be able to figure out what these causes are or were. Why be a naturalist? World historical evidence suggests that naturalism, vague as it is, keeps being vindicated, while the zones "explained" by the supernatural get smaller everyday. Naturalism is a good bet.[4]

Buddhism Naturalized

Imagine Buddhism without rebirth and without a karmic system that guarantees justice ultimately will be served, without nirvana, without bodhisattvas flying on lotus leaves, without Buddha worlds, without nonphysical states of mind, without any deities, without heaven and hell realms, without oracles, and without lamas who are reincarnations of lamas. What would be left? My answer is that what would remain would be an interesting and defensible philosophical theory with a metaphysics, a theory about what there is and how it is, an epistemology, a theory about how we come to know and what we can know, and an ethics, a theory about virtue and vice and how best to live. This philosophical theory is worthy of attention by analytic philosophers and scientific naturalists because it is deep. Buddhism naturalized, if there is or can be such a thing, is compatible with the neo-Darwinian theory of evolution and with a commitment to scientific materialism. Such a total philosophy, again if there is or could be such a thing that could be called credibly "Buddhist" after subtracting what is psychologically and sociologically understandable, but that epistemically speaking is incredible superstition and magical thinking, would be what I call "Buddhism naturalized," or something in its vicinity. Such a theory might shed light on the human predicament, on how finite material beings such as human animals fit into the larger scheme of material being. Because such a theory would speak honestly, without the mind-numbing and wishful hocus pocus that infects much Mahayana Buddhism, but possibly not so much early Theravada Buddhism, Buddhism naturalized, if there is or can be such a thing, delivers what Buddhism possibly uniquely among the world's live spiritual traditions, promises to offer: no false promises, no positive illusions, no delusions. False self-serving belief, *moha*, is a sin for Buddhists.

"Buddhism naturalized" is in the declarative mode, thus inviting being read as a moniker for a kind of Buddhism that already exists, and indeed I think it does. But one might think, and think rightly, that even if naturalistic Buddhism does have some advocates, it is definitely a minority movement. Almost every university professor and college-educated businessperson I interviewed in 2009 in Thailand claimed to believe that one can purchase, by donations or by good acts, "merit" that will be counted toward a better rebirth; the Dalai Lama consults oracles; and Alan Wallace, a prominent American Buddhist scholar, speaks for the majority in insisting that Buddhism is incompatible with "neurophysicalism"—the view that mental events are brain events—of the sort that I, like most other philosophers of mind and neuroscientists, defend. Perhaps it would be more appropriate to speak or write "Buddhism naturalized!" as an imperative, which would make it clear that this is a work of advocacy for something that doesn't yet have any traction, at most a tenuous foothold, but that I think ought to exist, something worth fantasizing about like the "the best chocolate cake in the history of the universe that is also not fattening!" A better way of putting the topic, the issue, the problem might be neither declaratively nor imperatively, but more humbly in the form of a question, "Buddhism naturalized?", which conveys that what I am up to, or what I should be wondering about, is the question of whether there is or could be such an item as naturalistic Buddhism. This is the way perhaps that a true cosmopolitan would engage in my project.

Even if there is a minority movement that fits the bill of naturalized Buddhism in the sense that it dissociates itself from beliefs in supernatural and nonphysical phenomena, it does not follow that it really deserves to call itself Buddhism. Actually it doesn't really matter to me whether the philosophical theory I am interested in talking about here is called "Buddhism," "buddhism," or just the philosophical theory—the metaphysics, epistemology, and ethics—that remains after you subtract the unwarranted nonnatural beliefs in Buddhism from Buddhism.

It might be claimed that "naturalistic Buddhism" is possible because it once was, or is now, actual. The original Buddhism of Siddhārtha Gautama from 500 BCE, and possibly some kinds of less metaphysically extravagant Theravada Buddhism of the first few centuries of the common era, as well as contemporary secular Western Buddhism(s) come to mind as candidates. Still one might wonder whether such a thing as Buddhism naturalized as I conceive it, and thus even the Buddhism of Siddhārtha himself, is or could really be Buddhist, as opposed to some twisted sister of the real thing. There is fool's gold but it isn't really gold. Gold is the substance with atomic number 79. Good imitations of gold are not gold. Could a tradition like Buddhism be like that? Specifically, could it be that if you subtract the hocus pocus about rebirth and karma, and bodhisattvas flying on lotus leaves, and Buddha worlds, and nonphysical states of mind, and deities (although not a creator god), and heaven and hell realms, and oracles, and lamas who are reincarnations of lamas, there is no Buddhism left? Could this suite of supernatural beliefs be to Buddhism what the atomic number 79 is to gold, such that whatever it is that is on offer under the guise of Buddhism naturalized, it isn't, can't be a bona fide Buddhism without these nonnatural, supernatural beliefs?

Perhaps Buddhism naturalized would be a weird or dangerous doctrine, or at a minimum and more credibly, as I've said, it might not really be

Buddhist. Think of it this way: Can one be a Jew, Christian, or Muslim without heaven or hell or without God, say Yahweh, God, Allah, conceived as one and the same or different conceptions of God; Or with one (either one—God and heaven and hell) and not the other (God but not heaven or hell, say)? Because what is actual is possible, some secular Jews would seem to be proof that some such credible and stable Judaism naturalized exists. Perhaps some secular humanists from Britain or the United States or Iraq or Turkey can make the same claim for themselves—that is, that they are Christians or Muslims without the supernatural stuff. There are now, in the West at least, wise persons educated in the tradition who claim to be nonbelieving Buddhists, something akin to what we would call agnostics and atheists if we were inside the Abrahamic traditions. Stephen Batchelor (2010), a former monk in both a Tibetan (Gelug) and Korean (Zen) lineage, calls himself a Buddhist atheist.[5]

Scientific Naturalism and Analytic Philosophy

Naturalists believe that when it comes to saying what there is, or might be, we should stick close to the facts. And when it comes to explaining how things that happened or are happening happened, stick to causes that have revealed themselves both to exist and to possess actual causal powers that could explain the phenomena. Despite the fun provided, tooth fairies are not candidates for what gets done when a child loses her tooth and hides it under her pillow. Mommies and daddies are. Sometimes how things happened, say the Big Bang, are cloaked in mystery. Naturalists endorse quietism or neutrality on such mysteries, awaiting in this case the experts, the astrophysicists, to say something deeper than that, which is now known. It is not just a matter of opinion to which everyone has an equal entitlement to speak (and have us listen) about how things happened or are happening, when what happened or how it happened is puzzling or obscure.

Analytic philosophy is a style of philosophy that prefers care in argumentation, and that favors strong inductive and/or valid and sound arguments, where possible, for its conclusions. Poetic, purely evocative discourse is welcomed, as long as its truth claims, if there are any, can be put into arguments. Nietzsche and Kierkegaard are stunningly great analytic philosophers who write poetically but meet this standard. Pure poetry, artistic expression, is preferred and/or privileged when it comes to expressing how things seem; more direct modes—scientific and analytic ways of speaking, writing, and arguing—are preferred when describing the way things are.[6]

The anachronistic, ethnocentric, and cosmopolitan discussion that follows has two parts, which can be read independently of each other. Part I, "An Essay in Comparative Neurophilosophy," is devoted to extending a contemporary discussion that crosses boundaries between neuroscience and philosophy and pertains specifically to the question of whether Buddhism produces flourishing or, what is different, happiness, and whether neuroscience can study such things as flourishing and happiness. The very public discussion about the alleged connection between Buddhism and happiness gives me a chance to wear the only two hats I own. With my philosopher-of-mind hat on, I write a cautionary tale of excessive enthusiasm for what brain science alone can reveal about what we want most to know about: in the present case, the causes and constituents of human flourishing and happiness. With my comparative philosopher cap on, I try to isolate what claims a naturalized Buddhism might make on behalf of itself as an embodied philosophy that produces its own kind of flourishing and happiness; and I try to explain what kind of flourishing and happiness that is, what I call eudaimonia[Buddha] and happiness[Buddha]. At present, there is no basis for the claim that Buddhists are the happiest people in the world, even that they are happier than average. I explain a host of reasons for skepticism that any evidence for such a claim exists or is in the offing, ever. Part I ends with a chapter on Buddhist epistemology, which I claim is staunchly empiricist, and thus science friendly and potentially attractive to naturalists. Because Buddhist epistemology is empiricist, it has I claim the tools internal to itself to naturalize. Buddhism naturalized can be achieved without a hostile takeover.

Part II, "Buddhism as a Natural Philosophy," takes up the feature of Buddhism that makes it most interesting to this philosopher, namely, Buddhism claims that there is a powerful conceptual and possibly motivational link between being an empiricist epistemologist, gaining metaphysical insight into the impermanence of everything including one's self, and being a good person who flourishes and possibly is happy. Part II is devoted to explaining more thoroughly what, assuming now there can be such a thing, a naturalized Buddhism would look like, and how it might be an interesting conversation partner to those of us who are scientific naturalists and analytic philosophers, and who are still trying, after all the years, to better understand what there is, how we can know it, and how best to live given all the uncertainty. It might seem odd to say this, but I will: among the world's great still living spiritual traditions, Buddhism naturalized offers, along with Confucianism, which was always pretty naturalistic, an interesting, possibly useful way of conceiving of the human predicament, of thinking about meaning for finite material beings living in a material world.

I   An Essay in Comparative Neurophilosophy

1 The Bodhisattva's Brain

BUDDHISTS LEAD SCIENTISTS TO THE "SEAT OF HAPPINESS"

This is my favorite extravagant headline from among numerous hyperbolic ones that appeared in the third week of May 2003. To my chagrin the source was an article I published that week in *The New Scientist* magazine that reported on two preliminary studies on one meditating monk (Flanagan 2003a). News agencies such as Reuters, the BBC, and Canadian and Australian Public Radio were the first out of the gate with reports on the research, and I did (too) many media interviews. *Dharma Life* magazine, in an amusing headline of its own, called the scientists, Richie Davidson and Paul Ekman, who performed the early studies on the meditating monk, "Joy Detectives." I had described their preliminary results as "tantalizing" and said that we were positioned to test the hypothesis that long-term Buddhist practice might produce happiness. This is very different of course from saying that studies on Buddhist practitioners had, in fact, led scientists to the Holy Grail of the "seat of happiness"!

"C'est la vie," as the cheerful French-born meditating monk, Mathieu Ricard (the fellow whose frisky brain caused the media stir), might have said. "Que sera sera!" The hypothesis that there is a connection between Buddhism and happiness is now out there, and research designed to test the hypothesis is advancing. So now several years after my initial article appeared I take a deep breath and ask, is Buddhist dharma the path to "true happiness"? The question is interesting because Buddhism is first and foremost a philosophy that promises awakening and enlightenment. Is it possible that awakening and enlightenment bring happiness in their trail? If so, what kind of happiness?

Happiness Hypotheses

What is the evidence for the claim that there is a connection between Buddhism and happiness? The claim that there is some such connection is out there. The first point or observation is that there are several different claims that, to my eye, are being conflated but should be kept apart.

• There is a connection between being a Buddhist (What counts as being a Buddhist—monk, nun, layperson? What are the membership properties?) and being happy (which kind and how defined?).
• There is a connection between meditating (which way among the thousands of different types?) in a Buddhist way and feeling good (does feeling good = being happy, and if so, which kind of happiness?).
• There is a connection between being in a Buddhist frame of mind and being good. (What is the nature of this connection? Is it causal or correlational? How are being in a Buddhist frame of mind and being good conceived, and what, if any, connections are each, being a Buddhist and being good, alleged to have to happiness as opposed to each other?)
• There is a connection between being a Buddhist and physical heath and well-being. (What is the connection between health and happiness; how are health and happiness conceived?)
• There is a connection between being a Buddhist and possessing certain kinds of unusual autonomic nervous system control such as being able to control the startle reflex. (What is the connection between happiness and this sort of autonomic control?)
• Experienced Buddhist practitioners are very good face readers. (What is the connection between face reading and happiness?)
• Experienced Buddhist meditators have lots of synchronized global brain activity. (What is the connection between such synchronized global activity and happiness, well-being, good mood, physical or mental heath, and so on?)

There is more, but these seven hypotheses provide a sense of the distinct claims being bandied about and conflated as if they express some well-founded scientific consensus that Buddhists are unusually happy.

Kinds of Happiness

Philosophers East and West agree that humans seek pleasure and that not all pleasures are equally worth seeking. There are debates about the relative worth of sensual versus intellectual pleasures (which is worth more, great sex or contemplating the impermanence of everything?), quantitative versus qualitative pleasures (how many ice cream cones are worth literacy), and so on. Aristotle pointed out that everyone he asked, "What do you want for its own sake, for the sake of nothing else," said "eudaimonia," literally to be "happy spirited." The trouble is that people in his sample disagreed about both its causes (money produces it, money doesn't produce it; virtue produces it, virtue doesn't produce it; sex, drugs, rock 'n' roll produce it, etc.) and its constituents (eudaimonia involves feelings of contentment or joy or bliss or ecstasy or none of these).

The word *eudaimonia*, like our word *happiness*, is polysemous. It is a theoretical term that pretends by its unity of sound to have a unity of meaning. But it doesn't. Aristotle argued for a certain normative conception of eudaimonia as the right one, the philosophically defensible one. This conception—eudaimonia^{Aristotle}—was not necessarily the popular conception; it was, however, by his lights, the best conception. For Aristotle, eudaimonia involved an active life of reason and virtue. The life of the Aristotelian eudaimon was a happy life, a good human life, the life of a person who flourishes. It was contrasted with the lives of the hedonist, the hermit or recluse, the most famous or popular person, and the pure contemplative (leaving aside *Nicomachean Ethics* bk. X, where Aristotle celebrates the contemplative life that earlier he says is suited only to the gods). Even if those who live these other kinds of lives claim eudaimonia, it is not eudaimonia of the right sort, namely, eudaimonia^{Aristotle} = an active life of reason and virtue, where the main virtues are familiar ancient Greek ones—courage, justice, friendliness, and generosity. If such people—the hedonist, the hermit, and the rich person—are happy, they are not happy in the right kind of way (perhaps this involves a certain kind of phenomenal feel, perhaps not; perhaps this involves a certain kind of causal history, e.g., good upbringing versus a pill). One can say one is eudaimon, one might even be eudaimon by the lights of a certain conception, eudaimonia^{Hedonist}, for example, but not be eudaimon as conceived and endorsed by a philosophical theory such as Aristotle claims to provide and defend, by the lights of eudaimonia^{Aristotle}.

I've said eudaimonia, in Aristotle's hands, refers to a happy life, but here I need to be careful. The reason is that it is not quite right to say this since eudaimonia does not quite mean happy in the normal sense(s). Eudaimonia^{Aristotle} is usually translated as flourishing or fulfillment rather than as happiness, and the reason is this: a great and noble life of reason and virtue might not (always, sometimes, or at the end) be pleasant or abound in good results. Why? The slings and arrows of outrageous fortune, luck, might keep one unhappy in the subjective sense, while having lived well, done one's duty, and so on. One might know one has lived well, nobly, but not feel or be happy in one familiar sense.

The lesson from Aristotle generalizes. *Happiness*, like *eudaimonia*, is a theoretical term. Before we can assess what an ordinary person's claim to be happy or to seek happiness means, or what a neuroscientist who claims to be looking for happiness in the brain means, we need a thick description of what each speaker means by *happiness* and cognate words. For contemporary Americans, happiness names a subjective mental state. For Aristotle, eudaimonia involves, first and foremost, being and living in a certain way—living an active life of reason and virtue. In fact, it may be that there is no necessary connection between being eudaimon, flourishing, living a good human life, and being happy in our colloquial sense. Aristotle says that a person cannot be declared eudaimon until after one sees the downstream effects of the person's life, how the grandchildren turn out, as it were.

To keep the polysemous character of the concept(s) of happiness and related concepts such as flourishing, fulfillment, and meaning in view, I deliberately use the word *eudaimonia*—a vaguely mysterious ancient Greek word—as a cipher, an uninterpreted marker, a variable, designed to indicate that I aim to speak about a conception of flourishing, or happiness, or fulfillment, as conceived by a particular tradition. Often this will require superscripting: eudaimonia[Local Hedonist Club] versus eudaimonia[Aristotle] versus eudaimonia[Buddha], or relatedly but not equivalently, happiness[Local Hedonist Club] versus happiness[Aristotle] versus happiness[Buddha]. When I revert to talk of happiness, or flourishing simpliciter, the context will normally mark the theory-specific conception in play. Usually when I use a term like happiness[Buddha] or happiness[Aristotle] rather than eudaimonia[Buddha] or eudaimonia[Aristotle] I am marking the subjective feeling state (happiness) that accompanies (normally results from) a certain lifestyle, the life of a eudaimon, an individual who is a true practitioner of a philosophy. In the cases of both Buddhism and Aristotle's philosophy the subjective feeling state, the happy part, may not be the main reward promised for living a good Buddhist or Aristotelian life, for being a eudaimon[Buddha] or eudaimon[Aristotle].

The Nihilist, the Hedonist, and the Eudaimonist

There is an objection, which, if true, would stop the inquiry into whether and how Buddhism produces happy souls at its very first step. The objection is that Buddhism first and foremost among all the great wisdom traditions tells us that seeking happiness of any kind is a futile, Sisyphean aim. What there is and all there is, is suffering (dukkha). This is what the first noble truth says, and all that is promised in the three remaining noble truths is some relief from suffering, not happiness.

In his brilliant book about the nineteenth-century European reception of Buddhism, *The Cult of Nothingness: The Philosophers and the Buddha* (2003;

orig. French 1997), Roger-Pol Droit explains that it was precisely the nihilistic, even annihilistic—"crash, suffer, and burn"—aspects of Buddhism that attracted nineteenth-century philosophers like Schopenhauer and Nietzsche. And indeed such aspects are there. At the same time, or perhaps I should say at a different time, in America from the Beats of the 1950s through the hippies of the late 1960s and early 1970s to the New Age metaphysics of the 1980s and 1990s there lies an interpretation of Buddhism (with a fair dose of Taoism and local coloration) that is more hedonistic than nihilistic. "Follow your bliss," "Love the one you're with" ("For tomorrow you die"), and so on. Recent, late twentieth- and early twenty-first-century attraction to Buddhism in the West involves emphasizing aspects of the tradition that are eudaimonistic (with a fair dose of narcissistic leftovers) rather than straightforwardly nihilistic or hedonistic, and that key in on possibilities for personal growth, goodness, social progress, and happiness of some yet to be specified, but not simple hedonistic, sort. Thus the Dalai Lama (although he is not the spokesperson for all Buddhists) pitches a conception of eudaimonistic happiness in his bestseller aptly titled *The Art of Happiness* (1998), (coauthored with Howard Cutler, a U.S. psychiatrist), where they write such things as these: "Now, we are made to seek happiness. And it is clear that feelings of love, affection, closeness, and compassion bring happiness" (p. 52), and "For our life to be of value, I think we must develop basic good human qualities—warmth, kindness, compassion. Then our life becomes meaningful and more peaceful—happier" (p. 64). The first quote suggests that happiness is the summum bonum, the highest good, the ultimate aim (telos). The second quote equates happiness with peace of mind and meaning and says that warmth, kindness, compassion produce happiness, so conceived. The points expressed here are complex: happiness can be said to be the highest good we seek, but it is happiness interpreted as a peaceful, tranquil state that comes from a sense that one is living a worthy human life, specifically a life of compassion.

This is the message—especially the promise-of-happiness part—that is being heard or emphasized now by Western Buddhists, so I will work here from the premise that there is a eudaimonistic—neither nihilistic nor simplistically hedonistic—interpretation of Buddhism available. The difficulty is working out the details of that conception in such a way that the conception of flourishing in the positive sense is differentiated from other conceptions of flourishing. This presupposes that it is intended to be distinctive, different—for example, from its close relations among other Indic traditions such as Hinduism and Jainism, or from other contenders for the right conception of the good life, like Judaism, Stoicism, Christianity,

Islam, Confucianism, Taoism, hedonism, consequentialism, communism, Kantianism, and contemporary Western liberalism.

One other point: the word *sukha* (which exists in both Pali and Sanskrit and is the antonym of *dukkha*) occurs frequently in ancient Buddhist texts and arguably comes closest to our colloquial term *happiness*, although sometimes it seems best translated as "pleasure" or "pleasant feeling." But other terms like *ananda*, *harsha*, *priiti*, *saubhagya*, and *kushala* are also translated as "happiness," or again, sometimes as "pleasure." Many usages of *sukha* (and its cognates) depict it as a state with illusory features. We seek sukha that is permanent when nothing is permanent. We seek to feel sukha come what may, but this would involve wishing to be deluded (moha) since what will come will include dukkha (sadness and things that cause it). Both sukha (happiness) and dukkha are impermanent. This line of argument would lead to the conclusion that whatever it is that Buddhism promises, it isn't happiness (sukha), although it might be happiness[Buddha].[1]

Other evidence suggests that Buddhism does have a concept of happiness, even if sukha does not precisely capture it. For example, one very plausible analysis of the difference between compassion (karuna) and lovingkindness (metta or maitri in Sanskrit) is that compassion involves the disposition to alleviate suffering, whereas lovingkindness involves the disposition to bring something like happiness (sukha), or better, happiness[Buddha] in its place.

Buddhism, Happiness, and Contemporary Mind Science

Following Aristotle, (1) happiness means different things to different people; (2) not all kinds of happiness are judged to be good or worthy; and (3) not all methods of achieving happiness, even of the multifarious worthy sorts, are thought to be acceptable or, what is different, effective.

When a worthy sort of happiness is claimed to be among the goods produced by embodying a practice, two requirements must be met by social scientists, psychologists, or neuroscientists wishing to study the connection between that practice and that kind of happiness. First, we must specify precisely what kind of happiness we are looking for; presumably bliss and serenity are different kinds of happy states. More importantly, not all aspects of the kind of happiness promised may involve states that are "in the head." If part of being a good Buddhist person involves regularly performing acts of compassion, these—the acts—are not "in the head." Actions are in the world. Whether and how the components, antecedents, and effects of actions show up in the head is a very complicated matter.

Second, we must have a clear conception of what aspects of the practice are thought to be key to attaining that kind of happiness—whichever kind it is. Even if Buddhist practice is said to result in certain purely subjective, and thus truly in-the-head states of happiness, Buddhist practice is too general to play an interesting role in a scientific explanation. Which aspects of Buddhist practice, meditation, ethics, metaphysical beliefs, diet, haircuts, and so on are being claimed as causal contributors? One can immediately see that drawing interesting cause-and-effect generalizations is not something that psychology or neuroscience alone is remotely equipped to do. Buddhism, like every other lived tradition, has a history, a (set of) sociology(ies), and beings in the world(s) who live as Buddhists (according to their own lights)—and none of these things or aspects of living as a Buddhist is "in the head."

One problem in trying to explore the connection between Buddhism and happiness is that there is a large variety of Buddhisms. Thus it will be helpful for present purposes if I can extract an "ideal type," a common core conception, from what is, in fact, a multifaceted tradition. Certain core principles do seem to be espoused and preserved across Buddhist sects. Walpola Sri Rahula, a Theravadan Buddhist, remains an excellent source on these shared core beliefs in his book *What the Buddha Taught* (1959/1974). That said, there are also distinctive practices and beliefs that, for example, distinguish Theravada, Mahayana, and Tibetan Buddhism (Vajrayana); Zen (Ch'an); Japanese Pure Land Buddhism; and Socially Engaged Buddhism. To some degree, these differences are based on differences in the choice and interpretation of key texts—for example, some Theravadan monastics read the entire Pali (original) canon, Tibetans less of it. But they are also due to philosophical interpenetrations, as in the case of Buddhism meeting Taoism in China, resulting in Zen (Ch'an), which, of course, took on a certain Japanese flavor as it migrated East. Buddhism in North America and Europe is not a sect or a coherent tradition. It is a syncretic blend of Buddhisms. Zen Buddhism first caught North American attention in the 1950s among certain members of the Beat generation. In the last four decades Socially Engaged Buddhism (Thich Naht Han 1987, 2004) and Tibetan Buddhism (Tenzin Gyatso, the 14th Dalai Lama, 1998; 1999) have become at least as influential as Zen. Meanwhile, Pure Land Buddhism remains to this day the most popular form of Buddhism among Japanese Americans. If there is anything distinctive added to the mix by Westerners (both in North America and Europe) it comes from a certain secularism, so that, for example, the doctrine of rebirth is sometimes rejected, reconceptualized, considered optional, or understood as a quaint but instructive piece of mythology.

I call the shared core conception of flourishing across the Buddhisms, eudaimonia[Buddha], and claim that it provides such a plausible analysis of flourishing, Buddhist style. The meaning of eudaimonia[Buddha] will receive elaboration as we proceed. On the first pass we can say the following.

Eudaimonia[Buddha] involves two aspects:

1. A stable sense of serenity and contentment (not the sort of happy-happy/joy-joy/click-your-heels feeling state that is widely sought and often promoted in the West as the best kind of happiness).
2. This serene and contented state is caused or constituted by enlightenment or wisdom and virtue or goodness and meditation or mindfulness as these are characterized within Buddhist philosophy.

The first condition specifies the subjective aspect, the "happy" part of eudaimonia[Buddha], and the second condition points in the direction of the form of life, or the aspects of the form of life, a Buddhist way of being in the world, which causes or normally produces the happy state, happy[Buddha]. That is, no. 1 specifies what kind of mental state Buddhism offers; no. 2 states that this state, perhaps it could be called happiness[Buddha] is caused by living a life of wisdom, virtue, and mindfulness, being eudaimon[Buddha].

I sometimes use the terms *enlightenment* and *awakening* (bodhi) and wisdom (prajna; panna, Pali) interchangeably—often as enlightenment/wisdom. For parallelism, I use virtue/goodness, or just one or the other, to refer to a life of good conduct (sila), especially a life of great compassion (karuna), as well as a character that embodies eventually, the divine illimitables or abodes (Brahma-vihara), compassion, lovingkindness, sympathetic joy, and equanimity. Such a character would be a saint, an arahant, a bodhisattva, possibly a Buddha.

Regarding meditation or mindfulness, I make this interpretive recommendation. Think of meditation as an equal requirement with wisdom and virtue, or if not quite of equal status, as a tool or ingredient that is useful, possibly necessary, to attain enlightenment/wisdom and virtue/goodness. A purely instrumental view of meditation would be one where it is conceived just as a means to, say, make one feel more relaxed, or centered, where these help make a person healthier, or happier, or nicer. If meditation is instrumental for bona fide Buddhists, it is not merely instrumental in this way. Georges Dreyfus, in his marvelous philosophical anthropology and biography, *The Sound of Two Hands Clapping* (2003), explains that contrary to Western assumptions, most Tibetan monks meditate very little, being much more involved in chores, in ritual performances for patrons, and in loud memorization and recitation of texts. But there are some virtuosi who are meditators: "More often than not, meditation's role is normative, it is the means through which the ultimate goals of the tradition are realized. . . . It is important to be able to point to some people as practicing meditation. They are the virtuosi who authenticate the ultimate claims of the tradition, but their numbers are small. Meditation is a difficult practice, and not everybody will equally succeed in it or even benefit from it. . . . Why engage in meditation unless one feels a special call and ability to do so?" (Dreyfus 2003, 169; also see Sharf 1998 for a wise assessment of the overblown status of meditation in the West compared to the reality inside the Buddhisms).

If the role of virtuosi meditating monks is instrumental, it is not instrumental in the way meditating for a positive mood is. The function of meditation among the virtuosi is to keep some hearts and minds in states such that they can be counted on "to authenticate the ultimate claims of the tradition."[2] One plausible way to understand authentication is that meditation can certify, possibly only for these virtuosi, the Buddhist conceptions of wisdom and virtue as "true." An even stronger claim for meditation is that nirvana, a state of release from all unwholesome attachments, can be achieved in only three ways: in meditation, in death (if death is final), or in achieving Buddhahood after eons of rebirth, after which comes permanent release. On this view, meditation is the only way enlightenment can be achieved while alive.

The point is that there is a range of views of meditation. Westerners often think of meditation as a stand-alone practice or set of practices. But at present I am interested in the role it plays within Buddhism(s), in achieving eudaimonia[Buddha]. And there, inside Buddhism, meditation or mindfulness is usually seen as a necessary instrument to gain wisdom and virtue, as the only way to gain wisdom and virtue, or as partly constitutive, part of the makeup, in the form of vigilance against unwholesome attachments, of realized, enlightened Buddhist persons. To picture the relation between wisdom, virtue, and meditation, it helps me to think of a New York City street pretzel where all parts are woven together and no part is independent of another, or obviously comes first.

Until recently, claims that Buddhist practice produces eudaimonia[Buddha] were based on first-person phenomenological reports of practitioners and behavioral assessments by third parties—either fellow practitioners or nonpractitioners—about how Buddhist practitioners seem to be or, what is different, claim to be, for example, serene or compassionate. In recent years, psychologists and neuroscientists aligned with affective neuroscience and positive psychology, as well as psychiatrists and therapists of various stripes, economists, and evolutionary psychologists have begun to examine the social and psychological bases of positive affect, positive mood, non-destructive emotions, and their connection to happiness. This pure and applied scientific work is motivated in large measure by a commitment to improving the quality of human lives by empirically confirming which ways of being and living yield genuine meaning and authentic happiness (Seligman 2002 Keltner 2009). I call such inquiry "eudaimonics," inquiry into the causes and conditions of well-being (Flanagan 2007), which I prefer over "positive psychology," because the latter but not the former tends to focus on feeling states, whereas the main focus needs to be on lifestyles. Some of this research, but certainly not all, seeks to examine the connection between Buddhism and happiness, or more usually, between certain Buddhist practices—mainly meditation—and positive affect, mood, and judgments of subjective well-being.

Regarding the current state of research, there are in fact no scientific studies yet on Buddhism as a lived philosophy and spiritual tradition, in any of its forms, and happiness. None, zero! The most famous study on Buddhist practitioners by Davidson's group (Lutz et al. 2004) in the prestigious *Proceedings of the National Academy of Sciences* (PSNA) shows that there are significant and unusual oscillatory patterns in the brains of experienced meditators compared to controls. But there is no claim made in that study that these unusual oscillatory patterns subserve differences in mood or affect. What we do have are a few scientific studies that involve examining meditators—mostly experienced Tibetan Mahayana practitioners from France, America, and Northern India, which shows better-than-average mood (Lutz et al. 2004), or individuals new to the practice of Zen and mindfulness meditation (Kabat-Zinn 1994 Davidson and Kabat-Zinn et al. 2003; Rosenkrantz et al. 2003), which show small improvements in mood after meditation. But in the latter case especially, one needs to beware of the "Hawthorne effect," the finding that any intervention (usually in business) improves what one claims to want to improve (productivity, morale, etc.). Assuming—which I am not sure of—that we will eventually succeed at measuring the effects of different types of Buddhist practice on happiness, we need to be clear about what sort of happiness, if any, the practice aims at or promises. This requirement is a general one for doing good science in this area. If one wants to study ordinary Americans, Aristotelians, utilitarians, Trappist monks, secular humanists, scientific naturalists, or members of the local chapter of the hedonist club, one will want their experts to specify the kind of happiness they claim to seek or to achieve. And one will want information on what aspects of their form of life they think lead to attaining their theory-specific form of happiness. Thus the recommendation that when we aim to speak precisely about the connection between some set of practices and happiness, we specify whether we are using their conception of happiness (the Trappists, the Buddhists, the hedonists) or ours (or, what is different, their concept or ours of flourishing or eudaimonia), and use the happiness[superscript] and eudaimonia[superscript] technique for carefully marking usage. Only with such information at our disposal can scientists construct experiments to evaluate (there will be no simple "look sees") if the kind of happiness sought is attained and whether the practices thought to produce that kind of happiness are in fact causally implicated in its production.

In these cases, as well as in the case of studies specifically designed to examine the connection between Buddhism and happiness, certain guidelines will lead to well-designed experiments that might yield revealing findings, one way or the other. For example, in cases where experienced practitioners are studied, we will want to know which kind of Buddhism they are committed to and what type of happiness, if any, that kind promises. I claim that eudaimonia^{Buddha} as depicted above captures a common core conception shared across all or most forms of Buddhism, and that it contains or embeds a conception of happiness^{Buddha}—a stable sense of serenity and equanimity. However, there are various more nuanced types or subtypes to be depicted and studied if one wishes to examine a specific Buddhist sect.

In cases where certain Buddhist practices—such as Tibetan Buddhist compassion meditation or the Japanese Pure Land practice of calling on Amitabha's presence (the Spirit of Life and Light) by chanting "Namu Amida Butsu" —are extracted from the kind of Buddhism in which they are typically embedded and are then taught to individuals who have no personal commitment to (possibly no knowledge of) any form of Buddhism, this will also need to be carefully marked. The reason is that such studies, no matter what they reveal about the efficacy of that particular practice in producing some good, even if it is some kind of happiness, have no clear relevance to what many think is most important and interesting, namely: What goods do long-term commitment to (a form of) Buddhism produce? Some people say they are Buddhists because they meditate (which kind?). But the fact that meditation techniques that have their original home in Buddhism are now used to control high blood pressure or to calm type A behaviors or simply to feel more relaxed reveals nothing about what goods Buddhism produces. Meditating Buddhist-style requires absolutely no knowledge of Buddhism, let alone commitment to its philosophical tenets and moral beliefs. Indeed, in my experience, it comes as a big surprise to Westerners (invariably followed by denial that it could be true) to discover that many, probably most, real Buddhists, whether they are in Thailand or Japan or Tibet, meditate—in an extended on-the-cushion way—very little, hardly ever (Dreyfus 2003).

Wisdom and Virtue and Meditation

Buddhism advertises itself as a form of life that will result in serenity and contentment if one allows into one's blood and bones three or four pieces of Buddhist wisdom, and if one also consciously and consistently embodies conventional morality, as well as the distinctive Buddhist excellences of great compassion and lovingkindness. The wisdom part consists of the recognition that everything is impermanent (annica), that I am among the impermanent things (anatman or no-self; annata, Pali), that everything that happens is caused to happen by prior events and processes and will yield other events and processes (dependent origination), and that if you try to find where things bottom out, you will be led, Zen-like, to find that they don't bottom out, analytic deconstruction never comes to an end (sunyata, emptiness). Buddhist wisdom says that everything is becoming. What there is, and all there is, are events and processes. Things and substances insofar as they exist at all are simply slow-moving events and processes. Compare: many scientists think that glass is a slow-moving liquid.

Meditative practices play two roles in the threefold chord: meditation can reveal the warrant for commitment to wisdom, revealing, for example, the ephemerality of all experiences, and virtue, tapping into one's desire to relieve suffering wherever and whenever it exists, as well as providing practice in overcoming the poisons—egoism—that contribute to the production of suffering.

Buddhism is a distinctive normative theory, spiritual practice, and/or practical philosophy whose First Noble Truth, its very first insight into the nature of life, is that suffering is abundant. The First Noble Truth of dukkha is normally stated this way: Everything is unsatisfactory and is, or involves, suffering. But this is implausible since some events, experiences, happenings—sunrises, sunsets—are satisfactory and do not involve unhappiness. The principle of charity in interpretation recommends trying to understand what is being said by the First Noble Truth in a plausible manner. I recommend this: There is a lot of suffering/unsatisfactoriness in the world; suffering is abundant; no good experience remains satisfactory forever—either the source of the pleasure becomes stale as when the bloom is off the rose or it remains pleasant and desirable but disappears as when a loved one dies. There is human-caused suffering, everyday lying, cheating, and stealing, and there is natural-caused suffering, tsunamis, earthquakes, plagues, and so on. We can do something to reduce the amount of human-caused suffering by behaving better. But natural suffering, including the eventual death of our loved ones and our self, is not in our control (or if it is in our control, it is only within the limits of healthy living practices and of medical and technological achievements). The question is: What can we do to keep the cycle of suffering (samsara) from defeating us? The answer is: Control whatever part of reality we can control that contributes to suffering—initially our own suffering and then that of others. What part is that? Essentially, the only things we can control are our own attitude and our own behavior insofar as they contribute to suffering.

We are now at the Second Noble Truth, which asks us to focus on features of our shared human nature that cause suffering for ourselves and for the others with whom we interact. The features of our human nature that contribute to suffering are false belief or delusion (moha), as when we think that the bloom will never fade, that our lover is with us forever; thirst or avarice (lobha or raga), as when we think we need to possess everything we want and that this will make us happy; and covetousness, anger, and resentment (dosa) at others for what these others have and we lack or at others for what they have done that we think affects our happiness. This is a lot since when in the grip of egoism, life is a zero-sum game. You win, I lose, you get, I don't.

The Third Noble Truth tells us that relief from the suffering our nature causes is possible if we work to tame or eradicate these three poisons— the tendencies toward false self-serving beliefs, toward acquisitiveness, and toward anger, hatred, and resentment that are rooted in our imperfect nature. The three poisons in our nature depict universals of human psychology, the Buddhist analog of original sin.

The Fourth Noble Truth provides the antidote to neutralize, possibly eliminate, the poisons.[3] This is the Noble Eightfold Path and it is the recipe for living that holds promise as the way (dharma) to release from suffering, and the achievement of liberation from all attachment (nirvana). The path is to cultivate, practice, and eventually embody:

1. Right view
2. Right intention
3. Right speech
4. Right action
5. Right livelihood
6. Right effort
7. Right mindfulness
8. Right concentration

We will need to explain what exactly these directions mean. They are not to be interpreted as particularly onerous, since the Eightfold Path is for everyone. On a first pass the directions can be divided into three sorts of instructions. Right view and right intention (1 and 2) pertain to wisdom; right speech, right action, and right livelihood (3, 4, and 5) pertain to virtue, and right effort, right mindfulness, and right concentration (6, 7, and 8) pertain to meditation. The interpretation of Buddhism as a New York City pretzel or as a threefold chord is supported by the Eightfold Path, which is espoused across all, or almost all, Buddhisms.[4]

What about Nirvana and Rebirth?

So far I've depicted eudaimonia[Buddha] with almost no mention of nirvana or rebirth. This is intentional. I am trying to provide a picture of Buddhism that could appeal to scientific naturalists, and both concepts are notoriously unscientific, nonnaturalistic. It is well known in anthropology and psychology that humans relish positive illusions and death-defying myths, especially ones that involve afterlives where karmic justice is doled out—and this despite the utter incredibility, the complete epistemic unrespectability of such beliefs. I am also trying to provide a conception of flourishing, Buddhist style, that scientists could study by tracking its appearances in the hearts, minds, and behavior of individuals and communities in this world, not in fantastical netherworlds. But these concepts must be analyzed since they are central to most Buddhisms and seem resistant to naturalization and demythologization. Furthermore, nirvana is typically offered as the ultimate end, the summum bonum, in Buddhism. Can you deduct the summum bonum from a philosophical theory and still be talking about that theory?

There are tame and untame conceptions of nirvana and rebirth. A tame view of nirvana would be this: nirvana involves release from unwholesome attachment and suffering. If I can overcome (or work to overcome) the three poisons in my nature, accept that all things, including myself, are impermanent, and live a life that is unselfish, that is maximally compassionate, then I am released (to whatever extent I approximate the ideal) from unwholesome attachment and the suffering it brings. I have reached the state of nirvana or I am in the process of reaching nirvana. Understood in this naturalistic way, the claim that nirvana is the ultimate end of Buddhism just means that enlightenment/wisdom and virtue/goodness and meditation/mindfulness that provide release from unwholesome attachment and suffering are the ultimate end (Conze 1951/2003).[5] Rebirth then can be straightforwardly interpreted as having achieved a new beginning by having succeeded at achieving enlightenment (understanding imperma-nence, no-self, etc.), being compassionate, and being mindful.

Nirvana is subject to more interpretive complexity and controversy across the different traditions of Buddhism than the concepts of enlight-enment/wisdom and virtue/goodness and meditation/mindfulness, some of which I'll discuss later in the book. Two familiar untame conceptions involve postmortem states that are either pleasant releases of my current attached consciousness into another world akin to some sort of heaven, or my complete dissolution and release from all attachment when I am even-tually and permanently released from all being, in either case as a reward for eons of rebirths that have succeeded finally in my achieving full enlight-enment. The dissolution view is akin to the way naturalists conceive death on the "one life and you are out" rule. But on the naturalists' view the dissolution of consciousness that results from or constitutes death is not a reward for anything. It is just the way things work.[6]

This interpretation according to which enlightenment/wisdom and vir-tue/goodness and meditation/mindfulness are the ultimate end is thought by many contemporary (but not all) Buddhists to state the ultimate end claim in a plausible and accessible manner. Wisdom, virtue, and medita-tion are or yield nirvana = release from unwholesome attachment, if any-thing does. Furthermore, such release after achieving enlightenment is the best state a human can achieve, and involves (if one wishes to speak this way) a kind of rebirth. First nature contains the poisons. The development of second nature can involve crossing a self-control, self-management, self-cultivation threshold, at which point I am positioned to control, possibly to overcome, some say to eliminate the poisons in first nature.

Thus, Buddhism as I understand it here claims that enlightenment/wis-dom and virtue/goodness and meditation/mindfulness are the ultimate end. Wisdom and virtue and meditation copenetrate and co constitute each other. You can't have one without the others. Following the dharma path so conceived will lead to overcoming the natural poisons or common human afflictions that lead to suffering, dis-ease, and unsatisfactoriness, if anything will.

What Do Nirvana and Rebirth Have to Do with Happiness?

Once again we ask, does Buddhism also promise happiness? In addition to all the promises of various releases from desire, passions, attachments, from Dasein itself—Will it feel good? Will I be happy? Is the promise of eudaimonia[Buddha] a promise of some kind of happiness or not? Among the kinds of Buddhism practiced by or, what is different, most familiar to contemporary Westerners, the best answer is yes. We saw this in the quotes above from the Dalai Lama's bestseller *The Art of Happiness*. But the situation is complicated. One confound is due to the psychosocial fact that Westerners are unlikely to be attracted to any complex philosophical practice that does not promise happiness. Thus, it is very appealing to the Western ear, whether he who wears the ear is already attracted to Buddhism or not, that the current Dalai Lama says, as he does repeatedly, that "the very purpose of our life is to seek happiness," even though how he describes happiness deemphasizes feeling happy and emphasizes possession of a sense of meaning and purpose. Read one way, the claim by the Dalai Lama could be understood as claiming that happiness is the ultimate end. Indeed, such an interpretation would be very appealing in the West. But it would be a misinterpretation. The dharma path involves a basket of goods, which contains all the goods that Buddhism endorses, all the ends, aims, or goals that are deemed as worthy by Buddhism. Happiness, understood colloquially, is arguably among these ends, but not the ultimate end. Enlightenment/ wisdom and virtue/goodness and meditation/mindfulness are the ultimate end. Living an enlightened, mindful life of virtue and attaining peace and tranquility is the aim.

That said, Buddhism acknowledges that humans are all over themselves trying to achieve happiness in the colloquial sense. If there is some core universal motive that humans are possessed of, and driven by, it is the motive to attain happiness, possibly just personal happiness, possibly happiness for close kin and those whose unhappiness would affect one and one's kin's happiness negatively. The trouble is that typically we seek types of happiness that once attained are transitory and thus unsatisfactory, or we try to attain wholesome types of happiness in all the wrong ways. Santideva, the eighth-century Indian Mahayana Buddhist sage, writes:

Although we wish to cast off grief,
We hasten after misery;
And although we long for happiness,
Out of ignorance we crush our joy,
as if it were our enemy.[7]

The trick is to direct our natural urge to happiness to the right sort of happiness and then to work with reliable methods to achieve it. The right sort of happiness, happiness[Buddha], is a component of or an outcome of achieving eudaimonia[Buddha]. It comes, if it does come, from practices that aim at enlightenment/wisdom and virtue/goodness via meditation (see Bodhi 2000, SN 4.223–229, SN 4.235–237). There are plenty of texts in the Pali canon where the Buddha distinguishes between types of happiness that are desired and chased after by the common person, the happiness of the path to liberation, and the happiness of liberation. He asks this: "What bhikkhus is happiness more spiritual than the spiritual? When a bhikkhu whose taints are destroyed reviews his mind liberated from lust, liberated from hatred, liberated from delusion, there arises happiness. This is called happiness more spiritual than spiritual" (SN 4.235–237; in Bodhi 2000, 1283–1284). Thus, not surprisingly, stories of "happy" arahants and "happy" bodhisattvas are abundant across various classical traditions (Bond 1988; Lopez 1988).[8]

It is only by living a life of wisdom and virtue/goodness and meditation that a sense of meaning, purpose, and happiness can be secured. It is a Zenlike paradox that if we seek simply to attain happiness we won't, whereas if we aim for wisdom and virtue and mindfulness, initially setting our undisciplined pursuit of happiness to the side, we might begin to achieve true happiness—happiness^{Buddha} that comes, reliably but not necessarily, from eudaimonia^{Buddha}.

It is a core feature of the human psyche, across all environments, that each individual is designed to seek happiness of a kind, or kinds, they-know-not-what. Happiness, taken as the name for the multiplicity of states that fall under the folk-psychological concept, might thus be said to be the sole universal aim. But happiness so conceived is not eudaimonia^{Buddha}. Still something in the vicinity of happiness so conceived might normally result from being eudaimon^{Buddha}.

Assuming there is some universal desire to be happy, are there similar core universal human propensities to attain enlightenment/wisdom and virtue/goodness, and to meditate or be mindful, propensities to be delivered from ignorance, to know the truth, and to overcome selfishness? The virtually unanimous consensus across the world's wisdom traditions is that if there are such propensities they are at best partial, and require considerable communal encouragement to become fully engaged. And even if we possess the seeds of fellow feeling, egoism needs to be modified, suppressed, or rechanneled for the seeds to grow. And even if there is some wisdom required for everyday life, some things we need to know for practical reasons, there is abundant evidence that humans relish certain comforting delusions.[9]

According to the interpretation on offer, Buddhism claims that enlightenment/wisdom and virtue/goodness and meditation/mindfulness alone

constitute the ultimate end of an excellent Buddhist life, the life of a bodhisattva, for example. No kind of happiness, conceived as a subjective feeling
state, is the ultimate end. However, achieving the ultimate end, eudaimoni-
a[Buddha], is a necessary condition for happiness[Buddha] and so long as external
and internal psychic conditions cooperate, eudaimonia[Buddha] reliably brings
"a lasting state of happiness and fulfillment"—true happiness, happiness-
[Buddha]. Is happiness[Buddha] a guaranteed result of achieving eudaimonia[Buddha]?
Given the vagaries and particularities of human psychology and the ways
the external world can fail to provide some other necessary conditions, the
answer, I have been insisting, is no. If Buddhism abides truth-in-advertising
norms, it can say that, allowing for the fragility of our natures and our
worlds, happiness[Buddha] normally and reliably comes from being eudaimon-
[Buddha]. True, authentic happiness is a great good and it comes, if it does
come, from diligent practice that both involves and yields enlightenment/
wisdom and virtue/goodness and meditation/mindfulness. One does not
become happy and then enlightened and virtuous. One who lives in an
enlightened and virtuous and mindful way—if luck is on his side—gains
true happiness, happiness[Buddha].

It should be clear enough that if there is such a thing as happiness[Buddha]
that normally accompanies eudaimonia[Buddha] it is not happiness as colloquially understood. One problem with commonsense folk psychology is that
it permits attributing happiness to unenlightened and nonvirtuous adults.
Indeed, folk psychology allows that such people might not just feel or think
they are happy but might actually be happy. But such people cannot be
happy[Buddha] because, whatever exactly happiness[Buddha] feels like first personally (something along serene and contented lines), it comes with or from
eudaimonia [Buddha], which is a state of enlightenment, virtue, and mindfulness. The latter is not a semantic stipulation, in which case it would be
uninteresting and simply beg the interesting question. It is a claim based
on 2,500 years of the development of Buddhist philosophical psychology.
The wisdom of the tradition as understood and interpreted by experts and
as "tested" by practitioners engaged in self-scrutiny of their way of life not
only confirms a certain picture of what true happiness is (it is some form
of happiness[Buddha]), but also what ways of thinking, feeling, and living,
namely, eudaimonia[Buddha], lead to happiness of this kind.

The convictions of practitioners, even as supported by keen interpreters
of the tradition, might not settle the matter in the minds of scientists who
want independent confirmation that Buddhism produces the kind of happiness it claims to produce and furthermore, that this kind of happiness is
in fact produced by features of the practice (wisdom, virtue, meditation, or

just one or two of these, etc.) that practitioners claim reliably produce it. To establish such things, we would need very careful operational definitions of the meanings of eudaimonia[Buddha] and happiness[Buddha], which among other things would specify, if we are talking about neuroscientific measures, what aspects of these phenomena are in the head and which not. For example, acting compassionately is not in the head—it is in the world; feeling in a good mood might be in the head; but the location of believing that every-thing is impermanent is puzzling since it is an intentional state and thus about something, about the way the world is, which again does not seem to be a matter only of what is in the head. As for illuminating items that are not in the head, neuroscience has very limited resources.[10]

Imagine that we find ourselves in this situation: the world's richest and not-very-virtuous person's brain lights up "happily" in the same way as an enlightened and virtuous Buddhist practitioner. In both cases happiness sector ø lights up to degree ß. Should we say they are both very happy, and, furthermore, that they are happy in exactly the same way? This would be odd if we have, as we do, good reason to think in advance that they experi-ence qualitatively different kinds of happiness with very different causes and constituents. We might want to say that the evidence suggests that they both experience the same level of happiness as understood quantita-tively, they both feel "happy 10" on a scale from 1 to 10, and the part of the brain that reveals the raw feel of happiness lights up in both brains. But this would be compatible with saying, as I think we ought to, that we do not yet see or detect whatever deeper brain activity subserves the different cognitive and conative aspects of their distinctive experience of happiness. On the credible assumption of neurophysicalism, if there is an experiential difference between two mental states, or a difference in behavior caused by two mental states, it had better show up as a brain difference. The fact that it might not show up using any extant technologies is irrelevant.

The general point is that only if we perform experiments using well-defined conceptions of the kind(s) of happiness we are looking for and trying to detect will we be in a position to judge whether our scientific techniques are sensitive enough to detect these states and to distinguish them from simulacra.

Analyzing Flourishing, Buddhist Style

Eudaimonia[Buddha] is, or comes from, commitment to and embodiment of Buddhist philosophy understood as a normative theory and practical philosophy of enlightenment or awakening and virtue or goodness and mindfulness. If it produces a kind of happiness, it is a type of happiness born of achieving wisdom (prajna), by becoming free of the standard mental afflictions that come with being human, and finding one's way to deep compassion (karuna) and lovingkindness (metta or maitri) for all sentient beings. Although I have claimed that enlightenment, virtue, and meditation or mindfulness co-constitute the ultimate end, we can analytically separate the three components:

Enlightenment/wisdom   Buddhist enlightenment requires that one come to understand (1) that all things are impermanent (anicca) and (2) for this reason I am not possessed of a permanent self, ego, or soul (atman; Pali, anatta). I am anatman, a transient being constituted only by certain ever-changing relations of psychological continuity and connectedness (MN 1.138, in Nanamoli 1995; Siderits 2003). Furthermore, (3) everything is in flux and everything including myself is impermanent because every state of affairs has its coming to be and its ceasing to be in the overarching process of dependent origination (pratītyasamutpāda; paticcasamuppāda, Pali). Mahayanans add an additional component to enlightenment/wisdom, (4), the belief that all things are empty (sunyata) in the sense that everything is lacking in an intrinsic or immutable essence (often put as lacking a self, because each thing is decomposable into its components, which are decomposable into their components, and so on ad infinitum). This is what Marks Siderits (2003) calls "Buddhist reductionism," something that would make contemporary scientific reductionists and eliminativists proud.[11]

Virtue/goodness   Buddhist virtue/goodness requires moral conduct (sila) and thus conformity to the third, fourth, and fifth of the steps on the Noble Eightfold Path. True virtue, of course, requires more than moral conduct. An individual, such as a bodhisattva, overcomes the three poisons of greed (lobha or raga), hatred (dosa), and delusion (moha), and positions herself to embody the four divine illimitables—compassion (karuna), lovingkindness (maitri; metta, Pali), empathic joy (mudita), and equanimity (upeksa; upekkha, Pali) (Sāntideva, eighth century CE; Lopez 1988).

Meditation/mindfulness   This component comprises a set of techniques as well as a general orientation to experience that is first and foremost attentive. A mindful Buddhist person learns to pay attention to her experiences. At Vipassana retreats eating is done in silent community. Why? To pay attention to the taste and texture of the food and to the activity of eating. Attention to one's own breathing, one's posture, one's mental states is paying attention to one's being in the world, and allows a more embodied, less cognitive sort of self-knowledge, than, for example, Socrates encouraged. Paying attention to experience provides first-personal verification, authentication, of Buddhist wisdom. All sensations, perceptions, and thoughts are impermanent, and so am I. Finally meditation is used for moral insight and training. Imagined scenarios of myself—in, for example, a Humean sensible knave situation, where I can take what I want and not be caught—allows me to rehearse how I want to be at my best. In this way mindfulness can help secure considered affiliation of myself (which is a no-self) with my better side.[12]

One reason to say that the latter characterization of wisdom and virtue and mindfulness involves an analytic distinction of three aspects of one phenomenon is because, as I have said, they are in fact codependent—a threefold cord, a New York pretzel. The Noble Eightfold Path reveals this. Although the Noble Eightfold Path is commonly thought to provide instruction for moral conduct (sila), only right speech, right action, and right livelihood (3, 4, and 5) pertain directly to sila. Right effort, right mindfulness, and right concentration (6, 7, and 8) pertain to mental discipline, samadhi (concentration meditation), and are designed to support both wisdom and goodness. And the first two steps on the path (1 and 2), right view and right intention, fall under wisdom (prajna)—for example, coming to see the truth of impermanence (annica, Pali; anitya, Sanskrit) and no-self (anatman; annata, Pali).

Despite general acceptance of the codependency thesis, different Buddhist traditions place differential, but never exclusive emphasis on enlightenment/wisdom and virtue/goodness and meditation/mindfulness. The type of Pure Land Buddhism that developed in medieval Japan—versions of which remain the largest sects in Japan today and among Americans of Japanese descent—has a certain proletariat flavor (Hattori 2000). Thus a Pure Land practitioner might, as it were, be said to "feel his way" into the doctrines of impermanence and no-self by chanting Namu Amida Butsu ("Homage to the Buddha of Infinite Light")—and starting to behave well (stories abound of prostitutes and criminals going this route). One starts by wishing to be less selfish, and then being less selfish. It does not seem as if Pure Landers must comprehend the metaphysics of impermanence and no-self in a deep and/or articulate way, although they may well come to act as if they do, and perhaps that is enough.

The Bodhisattva

Gaining deep understanding of eudaimonia[Buddha] is essential for those who wish to attain it, as well as for scientists who seek to detect, study, or measure it. To understand better what eudaimonia[Buddha] is, or is like, consider a bodhisattva. Setting Buddhas—omniscient and perfectly realized Buddhist beings—aside, the bodhisattva, like the arahant, is an exemplary Buddhist person who achieves eudaimonia^{Buddha} or is on the way to becoming eudaimon^{Buddha} . The bodhisattva realizes forms of enlightenment and goodness and mindfulness that can be embodied, in principle, by any person through devotion to the relevant ideals and by diligent intellectual, moral, and meditative practice.

The bodhisattva ideal on both classical and contemporary views is a developmental one. Achieving full enlightenment and the "marvelous qualities" of extraordinary virtue (Lopez 1988, 200) takes time, and thus how deep or complete the wisdom or virtue achieved by a particular bodhisattva is will admit of degree. To keep things simple, as well as congenial to a defensible naturalistic Buddhism (Batchelor 1998, 2010; Flanagan 2000a, 2002, 2007), which is also consistent with a form of twenty-first-century Socially Engaged Buddhism that many Westerners find attractive,[13] conceive of the bodhisattva in this metaphysically minimalist way.[14] She is enlightened insofar as she understands the causal interdependence of everything (pratītyasamutpāda), the impermanence of all things (annica), and the nature of herself as anatman, as possessed of no immutable essence that is her self. She conscientiously stays on the Noble Eightfold Path, overcomes the common mental afflictions (egoism, avarice, hatred, and the like), eventually embodies the four divine abodes, the six perfections (incredible patience, great mental acuity, extremely subtle perceptual sensitivity to the needs of others, and so on). Armed with compassion, lovingkindness, sympathetic joy, and equanimity, she takes her battle for happiness and against suffering into the world.[15] The bodhisattva is a courageous and virtuous moral activist, a warrior. She lives an active life of virtue, having become sufficiently enlightened to understand that in so doing she attempts to realize her full humanity and to achieve whatever excellence lies within the human range. She is flawed, incomplete, unsettled in her own skin and in her world in all the normal human ways. Being human, her being, her relations, her existence are fragile. She works to live without illusion, but like most persons is prone to comforting hopes, expectations, even beliefs.

The metaphysically minimalist conception is to be contrasted with a metaphysically extravagant conception according to which the developmental progress through all ten or eleven stages of bodhisattvahood takes "innumerable eons"—Buddhist eons are unusually long even as eons go—and an indeterminate number of rebirths. (Mark Twain once commented that "the problem with progress is that it takes so long.") The essential difference between the minimalist and extravagant conceptions is that the minimalist conception forgoes literal commitment to the doctrine of rebirth, character development that takes uncountable lives, as well as such powers as being able to fly in lotus position or to see "a number equal to the particles of ten million billion worlds" (Lopez 1988, 203).

The idea that there might be a one-lifetime track to enlightenment is thought to be a recent development, but the idea is available in the classical Pali canon (DN, Mahasatisatipatthama Sutta: "The Greater Discourse on Mindfulness," in Walshe 1987/1995, 335–350). The naturalist will require that whatever excellences of wisdom or virtue are achieved or achievable by the bodhisattva can't take longer than this one lifetime, because, well, that's all we have.

Next I want to claim that the bodhisattva, so conceived, can serve as a model for the kind of person all Buddhists can embrace either as a worthwhile state of being, or even—although this is not required—as the highest form of human life. That is, I use the bodhisattva as an ideal that—I hope—all Buddhists, as well as non-Buddhists, can perceive as noble and worthy, even if some might think achieving Buddhahood or being a more contemplative arahant is better, or on the other side, that Buddhist saints, like other kinds of saints, miss out on a lot of fun, albeit for a worthy set of causes. Any serious Buddhist practitioner who is enlightened and is motivated by enlightenment and compassion to alleviate the suffering of all sentient beings, and especially one who takes the vows to do so, is somewhere along the bodhisattva's path.

Some Complexities and Perplexities

The bodhisattva starts on the path to perfecting wisdom and virtue and mindfulness when she takes the familiar vows to achieve enlightenment and to liberate all sentient beings. The bodhisattva ideal is developmental. If, as I have argued, being seriously and sincerely engaged in the process of perfecting virtuous enlightenment is sufficient for being eudaimonia[Buddha], then the bodhisattva is eudaimon[Buddha], at least to some significant degree. And if achieving eudaimonia[Buddha] is necessary but not sufficient for achieving happiness[Buddha], then the bodhisattva has a better chance than most at being happy in that sense. One might have two legitimate questions. First, does attaining wisdom and virtue and meditating in the way the bodhisattva does typically cause her to be happy[Buddha], or do the wisdom and virtue and mindfulness constitute happiness[Buddha] so that she experiences her happiness as born of, related to, or made up of wisdom and virtue and mindfulness? Second, assuming happiness[Buddha] is achieved, is it the same at every stage in the development of the bodhisattva's wisdom and virtue and mindfulness, or might we need to parse both eudaimonia[Buddha] and happiness[Buddha] into, say, the ten subtypes depending on where the bodhisattva is along the path?

The correct answers are: (1) Happiness[Buddha] is caused not only by achieving enlightenment and virtue (and meditating), but enlightenment and virtue and mindfulness help constitute it. The bodhisattva experiences her happiness, if she finds it, as partly constituted by the trio of enlightenment and virtue and mindfulness. But even though wisdom and virtue and mindfulness are sufficient for eudaimonia[Buddha], they are not sufficient for happiness[Buddha]. The latter requires something additional including the luck of living life above a certain misery threshold, one internal threshold having to do with subjective feelings, the other external having to do with such things as food, clothing, shelter, and friends. (2) Yes, there almost certainly are subtypes of the general types eudaimonia[Buddha] and happiness[Buddha] whose subtle character depends on where the bodhisattva is on the path as well as on distinctive personality traits, temperament, and life circumstances of particular individuals found among saintly types.[16]

At this point we are able to state a defensible interpretation of eudaimonia[Buddha] that fills out the initial characterization. Eudaimonia[Buddha] is the name for a settled state of living that involves following the dharma path, overcoming the mental afflictions (egoism, avarice, hatred, and false view), abiding the Noble Eightfold Path, eventually embodying the four divine abodes, and living an active life of virtue so conceived. People who reach the bodhisattva stage have wisdom (prajna) and virtue (sila) of the sort that involves, among other things, the wisdom of knowing that and remaining mindful of the fact that all things are impermanent, including themselves, and thus that they are a psychophysically continuous being (anatman; annata, Pali) rather than an immutable self or ego (atman).

A person who is eudaimon[Buddha] lives well and flourishes. Being and living in the way just described is necessary for some type of happiness[Buddha], although not perhaps for happiness as conceptualized in any ordinary language. A person who is eudaimon[Buddha] will experience self-esteem and self-respect as well as a sense of pride in her character and actions.[17] Depending on how happiness[Buddha] is described, feelings of self-esteem, self-respect, and pride may be all that happiness[Buddha] consists in, or more likely happiness[Buddha] may involve or require other features as well, like serenity and contentment. I claim agnosticism here on the matter of whether a person who is happy[Buddha] and thus who by everyone's lights has a set of positive feelings toward herself and her life necessarily satisfies the ordinary language standards to be dubbed "happy" by those standards.

The Bodhisattva in Botswana

Suppose a bodhisattva works for Médecins Sans Frontières (Doctors Without Borders) with HIV and AIDS patients in a country like Botswana, where the epidemic is out of control. She is energetic and dedicated to her work and sees that she is doing good, but she sometimes misses her friends, her home (in his original autobiography, the Dalai Lama (1962)—in exile in India—expresses just such feelings), and is sometimes overwhelmed by the sorry state of things, the disease, poverty, promiscuity, indigence, widows, orphans, and so on. She doesn't fall apart but she does feel the pain of her charges. She speaks to her friends about feeling a bit low. Is this impossible? It is if she is a bodhisattva and the virtue of the bodhisattva necessarily brings about or is constitutive of happiness, where whatever else happiness means, it means "not low." Yet it seems possible that such a person might exist. This virtuous person, we might want to say, is a bit down; at least she is not extremely happy, gleeful, or joyful (Sāntideva 1997, ch. 6).

Bodhisattvas are often described as experiencing a kind of bliss (although it is noteworthy that the state of bliss is most commonly associated with entering the path). Must a bodhisattva always experience bliss? Can't a bodhisattva have nonblissful periods? Yes. Psychological realism, as well as canonical Buddhist texts, suggests that it is implausible to attribute ever-present bliss to the bodhisattva.[18] What about a temperamentally low bodhisattva, a bodhisattva who is committed to dharma, and who is thus eudaimon^{Buddha}—who flourishes Buddhist style—but who is depressed at the state of the world and whose compassion and lovingkindness are impotent against the suffering of her people in their time? Again, it would be odd to think that a life of wisdom, virtue, and mindfulness could not feel bad, even miserable, from the inside. To be sure, bodhisattvas have tools, meditation,[19] chanting, and so on, to moderate and to modify negative emotions so they do not become afflictive or destructive, but happiness, even happiness^{Buddha}, is only contingently related to being a bodhisattva.[20]

What I have just said is important for the conversation about Buddhism and happiness. On any given day a bodhisattva, an exemplary Buddhist person, might not be extremely happy, or very happy, or even just plain happy according to ordinary language standards. She might not even be happy^{Buddha}.[21] Even over long patches a bodhisattva may suffer the Buddhist form of certain familiar states of human being: doing what she believes is right, but not feeling contented or serene or hopeful about the state of things. She will, however, be eudaimon^{Buddha}. If some scientist is measuring her happiness using ordinary language standards she will not provide a first-person report that leads to the ascription of happiness, nor quite possibly will her brain light up in the normal "happy" or "very happy" way, and not even the happy[Buddha] way. And even for persons who are happy[Buddha], the state the neuroscientist needs to be looking for is theory specific—although we must allow that even a non-Buddhist could be happy[Buddha] by accident or due to the fact that some other form of life also produces happiness of that kind. Happy[Buddha] involves close causal relations, possibly constitutive relations, to beliefs, or belieflike states of mind, that form the core of Buddhist wisdom—impermanence, no-self (anatman), dependent origination, possibly emptiness. It also involves practical commitment to the specific virtues of the Eightfold Path and to the four illimitables, compassion, lovingkindness, sympathetic joy, and equanimity, as well as whatever feelings or abiding states of contentment and serenity are born of these beliefs, commitments, and mindfulness for keeping one's eyes on both oneself and on the prize. Any mind scientist interested in the connection between Buddhism and happiness better be looking for that state, or more likely, those states. But it is not clear what it would mean in the current state of brain science to see such a complex interactive state as this, or these, in the brain. One reason is that not all the components of eudaimonia[Buddha] are in the head. Eudaimonia[Buddha] involves doing things in the world, and since happiness[Buddha] is some sort of product of, or is constituted by, eudaimonia[Buddha], it may not be all in the head either. Even if happiness[Buddha] is characterized mostly in subjective, and thus mental, and thus in-the-head ways, it is not clear it is completely so. If I am happy when I am actually in excellent relations with my grown children and not simply imagining that it is so, these relations—if they are normal and healthy—involve real interaction with particular human beings. Neither the relationships nor the people are in my head. If this is right, then my happiness supervenes on happenings, events, and doings of the person I am, all of which essentially involve the others I am in relationship with.

I take the interpretive stance that the kinds of contemporary Buddhism(s) that appeal to Westerners do promote and promise happiness, best interpreted as (some form of) happiness[Buddha] or, possibly sometimes, intentionally or not, as some other kind of happiness favored in, say, twenty-first-century America, perhaps the "I am happy because I am so nice" kind of happy. What is usually absorbed and maintained from classical Buddhism, at least, is the crucial idea that achieving true happiness—assuming it can be achieved—requires overcoming various common mental afflictions and destructive emotions and that the search for happiness as popularly depicted and applauded then and now takes us on a fool's errand.

One final point before turning to a discussion of the empirical work that exists on the connection between Buddhism and happiness. Logically, "not suffering" does not entail "being happy"—even by the lights of common-sense folk psychology. Happiness, on every construal, requires more than not suffering. You have a headache, I give you aspirin. Are you happy? No. I have helped you not suffer. I have not made you happy. Happiness, whatever it is, would take more work, more generosity, than involved in giving you the aspirin. Was the Buddha happy? Was Jesus happy? Was Confucius happy? Were they trying to make others happy? The answers do not seem obviously "yes," according to common contemporary usage of the term "happy." Does it matter? Is it—happiness of any sort—the most important thing?

2   The Color of Happiness

"The Colour of Happiness" was the title of the article I published in the British magazine *New Scientist* in May 2003 that caused the media stir about happy Buddhists with happy brains. At the beginning of the previous chapter I listed several widely discussed claims to the effect that there is a connection between Buddhism and happiness, specifically that Buddhists are especially happy and that it is Buddhism (rather than say the weather where Buddhists live) that produces the happiness.

Now that we are clearer about what eudaimonia[Buddha] and what happiness[Buddha] are and how they are perceived as connected by Buddhists, we are in a better position to understand the empirical claims being made. Consider again several distinct claims that are often conflated, but should be kept apart.

• There is a connection between being a Buddhist (What counts as being a Buddhist—monk, nun, layperson? What are the membership properties?) and being happy (which kind and how defined?).
• There is a connection between meditating (which way among the thousands of different types?) in a Buddhist way and feeling good (does feeling good = being happy, and if so, which kind of happiness?).
• There is a connection between being in a Buddhist frame of mind and being good. (What is the nature of this connection? Is it causal or correlational? How are being in a Buddhist frame of mind and being good conceived, and what, if any, connections are each, being a Buddhist and being good, alleged to have to happiness as opposed to each other?)
• There is a connection between being a Buddhist and physical heath and well-being. (What is the connection between health and happiness; how are health and happiness conceived?)
• There is a connection between being a Buddhist and possessing certain kinds of unusual autonomic nervous system control such as being able to

control the startle reflex. (What is the connection between happiness and this sort of autonomic control?)

• Experienced Buddhist practitioners are very good face readers. (What is the connection between face reading and happiness?)

• Experienced Buddhist meditators have lots of synchronized global brain activity. (What is the connection between such synchronized global activity and happiness, well-being, good mood, physical or mental heath, and so on?)

Happiness and the Brain

At the time I wrote "The Colour of Happiness" (Flanagan 2003a), the only completed brain study that existed on the connection between Buddhism and happiness had an $n = 1$—that is, one experimental subject had his brain imaged by an fMRI. This is not ordinarily considered a good sample size. However, this first exemplary individual, Mathieu Ricard, was an experienced Buddhist monk (born and bred in France by very cerebral and classy parents) and his left prefrontal cortex, the area just behind the forehead, an area well established to be reliably correlated with positive emotion, lit up brightly (thus the editor's choice of "colour" in the title).[1] Indeed, his left side lit up brightly and more leftward than any individual tested in previous studies (approximately 175 subjects). However, none of these prior studies involved people meditating while the scanning was underway (in the meditating monk's case most meditation was on compassion and lovingkindness). These scientific problems did not prevent various media sources from announcing that scientists had established that Buddhist meditation produces (a high degree of) happiness. I do not know whether the "Joy Detectives" who, unlike me, were actually doing the preliminary studies cautioned the neurojournalists or not

Fortunately for science, prior to the study of the meditating monk that the 14th Dalai Lama—using his given name, Tenzin Gyatso—first alluded to in an op-ed piece for the *New York Times* on April 26, 2003 (Gyatso 2003b), that I reported on in the *New Scientist*, and that Dan Goleman (2003b) wrote about in the *New York Times* on February 4, 2003, there had been a number of excellent studies on positive affect and the brain (Davidson and Irwin 1999; Davidson 2000; Davidson, Kabat-Zinn et al. 2003 Davidson and Hugdahl 2003. These experiments revealed that when subjects are shown pleasant pictures like those of sunsets, scans (PET or fMRI) or skull measurements of activity (EEG) reveal increased left-side activity in the prefrontal cortex, whereas when subjects see unpleasant pictures (say, a human cadaver), activity moves rightward. Furthermore, people who report them-selves generally to be happy, upbeat, and the like, show more stable left-side activity than individuals who report feeling sad or depressed, in whom the right side of the prefrontal cortex is more active.

Positive mood, we can say, has two faces. And this makes a neurophe-nomenological approach possible. Subjectively, phenomenologically, or first-personally, positive mood reveals itself in a way that an individual feels and that she typically can report on. However, subjects commonly report difficulty describing exactly what the positive state is like or seems like beyond being "positive" or "good." Objectively, the subjective feeling state is reliably correlated with a high degree of leftward prefrontal activity (the neuro-part). Thus we can say that if a subject is experiencing happiness or, what is different, is in a good mood (both as conceived by American common sense), then the left prefrontal cortex is or gets frisky, or bright, or even colorful depending on whether you use EEG, fMRI, or PET.

It is important to emphasize that the prefrontal cortices are involved in more than emotion, affect, and mood. The prefrontal lobes are relatively recently evolved structures (in ancestors of homo sapiens) and have long been known to play a major role in foresight, planning, and self-control. The confirmation of the fact that the prefrontal cortices are also crucially implicated in emotion, mood, and temperament is exciting because it lends some insight into where—one place where—a well-functioning mind coor-dinates cognition, mood, and emotion. How exactly the coordination is accomplished is something about which little is known at this time.[2]

Davidson found that in a normal population (of undergraduates), pre-frontal lobe activity is distributed in a bell-shaped curve fashion. If the curve were entirely normal and assuming that the undergraduate population is representative, we would expect 67 percent of the population to be inside the top-hat middle bulge, with roughly 16 percent showing predominantly left-side activity and 16 percent showing predominantly right-side activity. If the curve were normal we might use alleged neurophenomenological background knowledge and say one-fifth of ordinary Americans are "very happy," three-fifths feel mixed or average, "okay" as we say, and one-fifth feel "on the low side." However, Davidson's bell curve was not quite nor-mal. It bulged some toward the happy side, a left-leaning parabola. This is consistent with data that claims that 30 percent of Americans are very happy (= say so), 60 percent are okay, and 10 percent are "not too happy" (Flanagan 2007, 150–159).

Given these data about a normal population, I take it that any find-ing to the effect that Buddhist practitioners are happier than most would be a statistical finding that significantly more than 30 percent are in the first group. A representative sample of Buddhist practitioners with 40 percent in the first group would be statistically astounding. A somewhat lower percentage would still be impressive. No such data exist—not even data showing that Buddhists hit the average (American) population score of 30 percent. There is an entirely separate but serious worry about the fact that almost all psychological science is based on the study of a WEIRD (white, educated, industrialized, rich, developed) sample of college students, the most anomalous population in the history of the earth (Henrich, Heine, and Norenzayan 2010).

Putting these two important points aside, first, about the hoopla involving happy Buddhists, given the evidence, and, second, about base-rate data gathered using WEIRD samples, we might still wish to ask this about the one meditating monk studied: Was the meditating monk who was "off the charts" the happiest subject ever tested? Saying yes is tempting, and many of my interviewers assumed that this was part of the message, as if being leftmost is like being the tallest. But this is crazy. At best being leftward is correlated with being happy or with, what is different, being in a good mood. There is no evidence that for everyone who measures leftward, the more left = happier (i.e., it is not the case that $(x)(y)(L)(H)$ $Lx>Ly$ then $Hx>Hy$). Nothing that is known about brains and the ways subjective states are realized or subserved neurally would make the hypothesis that the meditating monk is the happiest person ever tested worth taking seriously even if he was the most leftward subject ever tested.

Consider this sort of familiar example: Suppose two people think [that patch is red] in response to the exact same red-patch stimulus. Assume that both are having the exact same experience or thought, although it must be said even this assumption is controversial. We might after all experience red a bit differently; perception of red things might cause different associations, "the Proust effect," and so on. Bracket these worries. Assume that whatever else goes on when each of these two individuals think [that is a red patch], both think that much, and each thinks the thought in the same way as far as that red patch goes. If so, there will be brain activation in each individual that is that thought or is the neural correlate of that thought. But no one expects two different brains to have exactly the same thought in a way that is subserved by perfectly identical neural activation. The consensus is that the exact same thought can be realized (indeed is likely to be realized) in different brains in somewhat different ways. We expect the same for phenomenologically identical or very similar emotional states. There is always a level of grain at which (or so most think) some nontrivially different set of neural conditions will, or at least can, realize or subserve mental states that are functionally and/or phenomenologically indistinguishable. The basic rule of thumb is this: if there is an experiential difference then there is/must be a brain difference; but the converse is not true. Differences at the neural level need not show up experientially. In fact, one would expect that at some level of grain what might seem to be the exact same experience intrapsychically (i.e., to me at t1 and t2) or interpersonally, between us, will involve various differences in speed of neuron firing, neurochemistry, atomic structure, and so on.

One upshot is this: for all we currently know, the subject who tests twenty-fifth or thirty-fifth from the leftmost point so far plotted might be, according to all the evidence taken together—phenomenological, behavioral, hormonal, neurochemical—the happiest person ever tested. Left-side prefrontal activity may be a reliable measure of positive affect, but no respectable scientist has asserted, let alone confirmed, that among lefties, the further left you are, the happier you are.

There are some other problems. First, the concepts of "positive mood" and "positive affect" and "happiness" are not the same concepts. So running them together is not permitted. Furthermore, none of these concepts are fine grained enough, nor sufficiently well operationalized by the scientists who use them, for us to know what specific kind of positive mood or emotional state is (allegedly) attached to a lit-up area.[3] A second problem is that there is little effort being expended to distinguish among the neural realizer(s) of happiness and its content and causes. For all anyone knows at this point, a happy life—assuming we have a genuine case—whose causal source is family might light up the brain in the same way as a happy life whose source is virtue or money. And for all anyone knows a state of happiness whose contentful character is a meditation on nothingness may light up the same way as the state of happiness whose contentful character involves solving quantum mechanical equations. On the other side, one might wonder why we should seriously expect phenomenological states as different as hedonistic happiness and Buddhist happiness to be realized the same way in the brain. Consider the fact that many contemplatives—for example, Christian Trappist, Cistercian, and Carthusian contemplatives—believe in and meditate on a personal deity. Personal faith and a relationship with God are almost certainly thought to be constitutive of the kind of happiness—happiness[Trappist, Cistercian, Carthusian] —they seek. This difference in the content of their mental states—from Buddhists, for example, who unlike most of these others do not base their happiness on belief in a creator God—is one that ought to (it better) reveal itself when and if brain scans reach a point that they can deliver fine-grained understanding of different kinds of mental states, including happiness. Scientists can look for mental states that take a deity as their focus (mental content) without believing that there really are deities. But if thinking starts to go in this credible direction, then the fact that the happy hedonist and the happy Buddhist brains light up the same way might make us think that the lit-up stuff isn't really illuminating what we want to see more clearly. That is, in addition to the subjective, mood aspect of happiness, one should expect to see some brain differences that would be, or correlate with, the different constituents, components, and contents of kinds of happiness that might (or might not) be equivalent moodwise, but that can't be identical all the way through. Why? Because one person is happy because she believes [God is love] and another person is happy because [she is no longer in the company of the person who goes on about God being love], and so on.

Buddhist Happiness

These difficulties about the concepts being used and about content and causes suggest that anyone who aims to study the relations among a life form such as Buddhism and happiness ought to look carefully at the concepts of flourishing and happiness—eudaimonia[Buddha] and happiness[Buddha]— that the tradition claims to offer. Familiarly, classical Buddhism doesn't say much about happiness. It says a lot about suffering and its causes. But not suffering is not the same as being happy. You have a headache. You are suffering. I give you aspirin. Are you happy?

Buddhism claims, first and foremost, to offer a solution, so far as one is possible, to what it claims is the main existential problem faced by all humans: how to minimize suffering. According to one common reading of the First Noble Truth, happiness is not much, or at least not the main thing, on offer in classical Buddhism, at least not until one has lived uncountable lives, at which point—if happiness is conceived as "reaching" nirvana—one becomes happy in a very unusual way, by becoming nothing, nothing-at-all.[4]

Even if this was once the case, this situation has changed. The 14th Dalai Lama says repeatedly in recent writings that happiness is the sole universal aim of humans, which most, but not all, Buddhologists tell me is certainly not what Buddha taught. And he and several Western collaborators have been charting approaches that might help us overcome suffering—this is the aspirin part (Flanagan 2000a; Goleman 2003a)—and then to help us find the way to true happiness, as conceived in a Buddhist way, what I call happiness[Buddha] (Dalai Lama and Cutler 1998; Dalai Lama 1999; Flanagan 2006, 2007).

So we might wonder, given the hoopla over happy Buddhists, (1) what kind of happiness, if any, does Buddhism offer? Happiness[Buddha] I claim, but what is that?; and (2) is there any reason to think that Buddhists are happy in the same first-personal, phenomenological way and neural way that Trappist monks or hedonists or University of Wisconsin undergraduates are happy? Or is it that many more Buddhists are happy in some presumably neurally shared way? But then again given that Buddhists seek the kind of happiness Buddhism promises and not the kind that Trappist monks, hedonists, or Wisconsin undergraduates seek, it would be odd to think that happiness across these traditions or life forms would show up in the same way in brains.

Like every other moral tradition, Buddhism distinguishes between worthy pleasures and base ones, between things we ordinarily think bring happiness and things that really do bring happiness. Money doesn't bring happiness, at least not true happiness (although it might help some), but wisdom and virtue and mindfulness do. Buddhism is, at a most fundamental level, a practical philosophy that claims that being wise, virtuous, and mindful brings its own reward. Wisdom and virtue and mindfulness are necessary for, possibly sufficient for, liberation (nirvana), for eudaimonia[Buddha], for flourishing Buddhist style.[5] And they are necessary but not sufficient—remember the bodhisattva in Botswana—for happiness[Buddha]. By living a life of wisdom and virtue and mindfulness we overcome suffering and unsatisfactoriness and gain (maybe) happiness[Buddha]. What is happiness[Buddha]? And how is it related to eudaimonia[Buddha]?

I have tried to answer this question from several different angles, each time emphasizing that these are difficult questions. Here's a more extended answer. A person who is eudaimon[Buddha] is conventionally moral, so she doesn't lie, steal, cheat, gossip, or work for nonpacifist organizations (the Noble Eightfold Path). In addition, she works to develop four virtues: compassion (karuna), the disposition to alleviate suffering; lovingkindness (metta; maitri, Sanskrit), the disposition to bring happiness in its stead; sympathetic joy (mudita), the disposition to be joyful about the successes of others even in zero-sum games; and equanimity (upekkha, upeksa). The conventional virtues such as those listed on the Noble Eightfold Path as well as the latter four illimitable virtues are necessary for happiness[Buddha], but they are not sufficient. Happiness[Buddha] also requires wisdom where the wisdom consists of knowing such truths as that everything is impermanent and that I, being one of the things in "the everything," am impermanent too. This is wisdom. Meditation or mindfulness is either a good in its own right or is essential as an instrument for wisdom and virtue. Taken together, the four great virtues and a wise and mindful assessment of the nature of reality and oneself make one eudaimon[Buddha]. This much will alleviate some suffering. One might think that this makes one happy[Buddha] as well on the grounds that if one is not suffering then one is happy. But we saw earlier that there is no implication from not suffering to being happy. Another strategy would be to say that sympathetic joy (mudita) and equanimity (upekkha) are components of happiness[Buddha], or even that they are all there is to happiness[Buddha]. Maybe, maybe not. But even if these two states are the only kind of happiness Buddhism promises, or what is different, endorses, how consistently and to what degree they are experienced by an individual on the bodhisattva path will be variable. More importantly, no matter how we fill out the concept of happiness[Buddha], it is not the same sort of happiness the hedonist seeks, or the same sort of happiness sought by a Jewish mystic or a liberal twenty-first-century American. It would be odd to think that it is since each of these conceptions of happiness claims for itself very different feelings, as well as different causes, and insofar as it has content, different content. It is logically possible that everyone in fact seeks the same kind of happiness but it doesn't seem likely. If this is right then there would be a major but unnoticed conceptual problem facing the happiness researchers. If "happiness" is polysemous, if there are multifarious conceptions of what happiness is, what kind of state it is like phenomenally to its owner, and if, in addition, different kinds of happiness have distinctive causes and constituents, then the assumption that they can be measured against each other by looking at or for a single type of brain activity is problematic, or better, it is seriously misguided, confused.

There are really two distinct problems with any scientific work that advertises itself, or is advertised by journalists, as showing that Buddhists—or for that matter, any other group of individuals—are unusually happy. First, if there is a simple brain measure of happiness it must be a measure of some neural feature or set of features—blood flow, neurochemical x, y, z —that is perfectly correlated with all the kinds of happiness. There could be such a marker, a necessary condition, for each and every kind of happiness. But if so, great care must be given to specifying both what the shared phenomenological feature that marks every conception of happiness feels like and what its brain correlate is. If the necessary condition is something like positive mood (which seems to be the favored candidate in the literature for the shared phenomenological feature), then we need those who understand the form of life—be they

Trappists, Buddhists, hedonists—to explain whether their conception, promises positive mood. It is not clear whether happiness[Buddha] necessarily promises or involves positive mood, and, if so, what kind of positive mood it requires, promises, or involves.

Second, the search for "happiness" in the brain assumes that that is where it is. Eudaimonia[Buddha] is clearly not completely in the head. The virtues that comprise eudaimonia[Buddha] involve actions and actions are not in the head. Eudaimonia[Buddha] is a necessary condition for happiness[Buddha], which as I have been describing it, could be conceived narrowly, as in the head, or widely, as caused and constituted by a settled state of feeling and being, which is at best only partly in the head. My feeling and being are fully embodied and involve being in relation with the natural world and with other sentient beings. But my feeling and being in the world are in the world, not in my head. If my life is only or even mostly in my head, there is a problem, a serious psychosocial problem.

What Does Happiness Have to Do with It?

Even if this problem of looking for a univocal marker for what could seem to be a unitary phenomenon (one could imagine someone saying: "It's happiness we are talking about!"), but isn't, can be solved, there are other matters about the interpretation of the research. Specifically there is research that is interpreted by the "Buddhenthusiasta" (some neurojournalists but some of the researchers too) as reinforcing or confirming the happiness hypothesis, but that doesn't.

Consider Paul Ekman's work with a few Buddhist adepts. Before the meditating monk's brain was scanned in Davidson's lab in Wisconsin, he spent several days with Ekman in San Francisco. Ekman is the world's leading authority on the basic emotions (fear, anger, sadness, surprise, disgust, contempt, and happiness), as well as on the universal facial expressions that accompany them (Ekman 2003; Ekman, Campos, and De Waals 2003; Flanagan 2000a, 2003b, 2009). With his longtime colleague and collaborator, Robert Levenson, who works across San Francisco Bay at UC Berkeley, the two set to work studying the effects of long-term Buddhist practice on evolutionarily basic emotional responses and on individual differences in ability to read emotions off faces. One study focused on the startle response, which is thought to be essentially a mental reflex (that is, virtually automatic). The other looked at face reading.

When I tell people about this research there is often a presumption that Buddhist practice is known to result in unusual abilities, such as the ability to control anger or to read faces more sensitively than normal. But this is not known. It is what Buddhism sometimes advertises about itself, or better and more accurately, what some Buddhists or Buddhaphiles advertise for Buddhism. It hasn't been tested systematically to this day since Ekman and Levenson's experiments were only pilots and thus it could be, still might be, premature, hyperbolic claims. I was initially too naive in interpreting the results I here revisit, and was not always careful enough to mark the paucity of evidence for the happiness hypothesis (Flanagan 2000a, 2002, 2003a, 2006).

As I report on the Ekman and Levenson pilots ask yourself this question: What does this research on face reading and the startle response have to do with testing the connection between Buddhism and happiness? The right answer is that although the pilot studies were done on a small number (n = 4, as I recall) of Buddhist practitioners, what they test has nothing obvious to do with the happiness hypothesis. Nothing.

First the startle results. The amygdala, twin almond-shaped organs, as well as adjacent structures in the forebrain beneath the cerebral cortex, are part of quick-triggering machinery for fear, anxiety, and surprise. I see a fierce, snarling wolf and—without any forethought—head for the hills in fear. Lightning is striking in my vicinity—I am scared and anxious and seek lower ground. The amygdala and associated structures in the paralimbic system are key components of this affective response system. It is likely, but not yet confirmed, that areas in these very old brain structures (fish have amygdala-like structures) are involved in other evolutionarily basic emotions such as anger and, more controversially, in certain pleasant feelings associated with good meals or good sex. Although the amygdala lie beneath the cerebral cortex, they require cortical processing for activation. I need to see the bear (visual cortex) or hear the thunder (auditory cortex) before I feel frightened.

Much of what we know about the amygdala is due to pathbreaking work by Joseph LeDoux (1996) at New York University, who instigated work throughout the world on these structures. We know, among other things, that a person, via her amygdala and thalamus, can be classically conditioned so that things that really aren't worth being scared of or anxious about can become fear or anxiety inducing. We also know that although the prefrontal cortices and amygdala interact, what the amygdala "thinks" and "feels" is extraordinarily hard to override simply by conscious rational thought.

Ekman found some confirmation in the pilot study for the hypothesis that experienced meditators don't get nearly as flustered, shocked, or surprised as ordinary folk by unexpected sounds, such as a gunshot or a backfiring car. Indeed, there is some reason to believe that one subject, our old friend the meditating monk, in addition to not showing signs of being flummoxed, did not even move the five facial muscles that always move (at least a little) when the startling sound occurred. According to the standard protocol in such experiments, he was told that a loud noise would occur when the count backward from 10 reached 1. He chose one-pointed concentration (instead of letting the mind roam, imagine focusing on a single phenomenon, e.g., one's breath, for a sustained period, allowing no leakage of other thoughts) in one test, and "open-state" meditation (sit quietly, allowing whatever thoughts and sensations that leak in to do so, while avoiding judging these mental phenomena as odd, moral, immoral, attractive, unattractive, and so on) in another. The monk reported the biggest experienced effect in the open state where he "moved" the expected loud noise far away so when it came it seemed a faint noise.[6]

Interestingly, it was during one-pointed concentration mediation that the most interesting physiological surprise occurred. The monk's heart rate and blood pressure, contrary to all expectations and unbeknownst to him, actually decreased. Of course, these results need to be replicated with larger populations, but the preliminary findings are really interesting because gaining control over autonomic processes is thought by some to be well nigh impossible.

Next consider the face-reading results. The face-reading system is very complicated brainwise. It involves the amygdala, visual cortex, frontal cortex, and more, and is not reflexive in the way that the startle response operates. We may be innately biased to accurately read the basic emotions off faces. But proficiency at doing so takes time and experience. Children of severely depressed and/or alcoholic parents confuse angry and sad and scared faces. However, because the facial muscles move in essentially the same ways across all cultures (modulated by local "display rules"), most of us become pretty good at detecting the emotions expressed facially for the emotions they are. This is especially so when we are presented with photos in which various emotions are displayed or in simple one-on-one conversational settings.

At first it looked to Ekman's team as if no one who had ever been studied ($n > 5,000$) was any good at the following task. First show a fleeting image of a person displaying a basic emotion for long enough that it is detected and processed in the brain (between 1/5th and 1/13th of a second), but not long enough so that the person looking at it can report what she saw. Then ask the subject to pick out (i.e., "guess") which face from an array of pictures matches what was just flashed. The normal score is at random—that is, one in six correct answers/guesses. This is somewhat surprising because the literature on implicit memory or subliminal perception often shows that people respond above chance with similarly short, below-threshold stimuli in other domains, but not with faces. However, to everyone's great surprise, the meditating monk and two other experienced meditators scored at two standard deviations above the norm, getting three or four out of six right. Ekman hypothesizes that some combination of meditative work on empathy and concentration explains these unusual results. Maybe. But if so, we have no clue as to how meditation causes such remarkable powers. Before we try to answer how the remarkable power is caused, we need to replicate the very small sample evidence that such powers reliably exist among experienced meditators. That has not been done.

But there is reason to worry about the hypothesis. The word was that no one had ever done as well as the adepts. This turns out to be false. There were a few others in the big database Paul Ekman had who achieved similar scores. There is no way to know whether these individuals were skillful face readers or just lucky. That aside, Ekman has now developed techniques that can train anyone to be as good as the four adepts at reading microexpressions. (I have the one-hour training CD. You can purchase it at http://www.paulekman.com/training_cds.php if you have the proper certification and $175.)

What remains very interesting is this: Why, if it is so easy to learn this skill, hasn't everyone done so? After all, there is an arms race to detect liars and cheaters. Ekman (personal communication) has no answer yet. The fact remains that the adepts naturally developed the skill, but not as far as we know by trying to do so for faces. My best guess is that what is called insight (Vipassana) meditation, where concentration and skills of analytic attention are honed (often primarily on one's own sensations, mental states, etc.), results in good analytic skills in interpersonal situations. Ekman's first surmise was that it might have to do with skills that come from metta (lovingkindness) meditation, where empathy and compassion are honed. We both might be right. But as of now, no one knows why/how these adepts developed the skill or in fact whether they are unique in possessing it.

Returning to the question "What does this have to do with happiness?", it is worth emphasizing that Ekman's own work on Buddhist practitioners, aside from his collaboration with Davidson on the left prefrontal cortex study, has nothing directly to do with measuring happiness—either happiness as understood in ordinary language or happiness as defined by Buddhism or some other ethical or spiritual tradition. Perhaps being unusually calm when a loud noise occurs relates to feelings of well-being. For now, the most we can say is that certain kinds of meditation can be used to screen off the effects of normally unpleasant stimuli. Regarding face reading, no evidence exists relating the ability to read below-conscious-threshold facial stimuli and good feelings, happiness, let alone happiness[Buddha]. If the results are replicated, then the enhanced-empathy hypothesis (probably combined with the enhanced-attentiveness hypothesis) is a contender, but again empathy can, in certain individuals, be a source of some distress. In fact, Buddhist practitioners have long recognized this problem, so that there are techniques to ward off being afflicted by negative emotions that are not one's own (most of these involve rituals rather than meditation). At this point there are no data on the effectiveness of such techniques. A final concern is this: most Buddhists, the world over, meditate very little. The identification of being a Buddhist with being, first and foremost, a meditator is a Western invention, a fetish.[7] Furthermore, many forms of meditation seem to be used to good effect independently of any Buddhist commitments, Jon Kabat-Zinn's MBSR, most famously. These two facts beg this question: Even if meditation that originates in India is good for you, what does this have to do with Buddhism as a comprehensive philosophy or comprehensive form of life being good for you?

Buddhism and Influenza

Several other studies examine potential links between Buddhism and things other than happiness. A group at Emory University, led by Giuseppe Pagnoni, compares Zen meditators with at least three years experience and controls with no such experience to measure attention, concentration, and problem-solving ability. If Zen meditators are better than the controls at these tasks, then perhaps Zen meditation techniques can be used on persons with attentional disorders, ADHD, for example, and possibly even for persons in the early stages of Alzheimer's disease.

Meanwhile a collaboration between Richie Davidson and Jon Kabat-Zinn (2003; Rosenkranz et al. 2003), with an $n = 25$, found that as little as one hour of daily mindfulness meditation for eight weeks and three hours of weekly training produced positive effects on mood (as measured by leftward movement in prefrontal cortical activity) in the meditators (all of whom worked in stressful high-tech jobs), as well as increased immune function as measured by the number of influenza antibodies in meditators versus the nonmeditating controls, where both groups had taken the flu vaccine.

The important point for now is that the Davidson and Kabat-Zinn study (Davidson et al. 2003) examined the link between Buddhism and both positive affect and positive immune system effects. Measuring changes in the immune system and changes in cognitive performance among those who practice one-pointed meditation and those who do not is easy to study using existing psychophysical tools—one just measures time meditating, gives subjects brainteasers, and counts the number of influenza antibodies in the blood. However, studies allegedly establishing links between meditation and positive affect are not sophisticated enough to tell us much about the kind of positive affect experienced and whether and how, if it does, positive affect connects with the kind of happiness, happiness^{Buddha}, that is alleged to come from wisdom and virtue and mindfulness. Our way of measuring brain function in a fine-grained manner that correlates activity with specific and various types of mental states is in its infancy. Note, for example, the debate over whether, and if so how and where, the amygdala processes positive basic emotions (left or right, anterior or posterior). In 1999 Davidson and Irwin pointed out that resolving this question requires more powerful fMRI magnets than existed at the time. Now sufficiently powerful magnets exist, but they are being used on scientific issues other than whether Buddhist brains are particularly frisky in the happiness department. It is simply too expensive to chase such poorly formulated hunches. Even now with magnets powerful enough to plot activity in the prefrontal cortex, we understand almost nothing about how to distinguish among the myriad of specific states that fall under the very general categories of positive affect or good mood. That said, the meditating monk did show different kinds of neural activity when he was engaged in different kinds of meditation. It is way too early to know, however, whether the brain processes involved, say, in his meditation for compassion, correspond to the brain processes of other meditators also engaged in compassion meditation and whether, and if so how, these are the same or different from the neural activity of nonmeditators who experience or embody compassion.

In either case, it is completely unclear at this time whether and in what ways better immune function and better capacities to pay attention link up with happiness. They obviously link up to better health (a lower chance of catching the flu) and possibly with better school and job performance. It is easy to see how these might lead to a better life than the alternative. But what link if any these things have with happiness as colloquially understood or with happiness in the relevant sense—that is, happiness^{Buddha}, remains obscure.

I don't mean to be understood as saying that the scientific work just described is not interesting. It is. Nor do I mean to be understood as being overly skeptical. If there are interesting differences in the lives and experiences of Buddhists as compared to the members of other groups, then on general naturalist—physicalist, neurophysicalist, subjective realist—principles, these differences should eventually reveal themselves in neuroscientific experiments for the stuff in the head, and in empirical observations and generalizations about how Buddhists and these others live and fare in the world, in their work and love relations, and so on, for the stuff that is not in the head. My main point is to emphasize that the extant research on Buddhism and happiness is heterogeneous in terms of what states of body or mind are studied. The work just discussed connects Buddhism to effects on the immune system or on attention, concentration, and cognition, or on suppression of the startle response, or on face reading. This work is not about the effects of Buddhism on happiness, let alone on happiness[Buddha]. Even the work that claims to be about happiness is not, in every case, at least obviously, about happiness. This is because positive mood or positive affect does not obviously equal happiness even in the colloquial sense(s). The tools we currently use are simply not powerful enough to yield fine-grained descriptions of the mental states of subjects that would enable us, for example, to say: "Look, there is the joy; there is the compassion. Notice how the joy looks different from bliss, and how compassion looks different from lovingkindness." Combining various existing technologies, including doing assays of neurochemicals, might enable us to make such assertions after studying large populations of subjects. But that is a long way off. Meanwhile the only meta-analysis that has been done so far on the good effects of Buddhist meditation on mental and physical health over the last fifty years (through 2002) by Ospina et al. (2007) for the U.S. Department of Health and Human Services claims that the results are inconclusive.

What's Metaphysics of Mind Got to Do with It?

Now that we have examined an array of research that claims to measure a variety of states of the mind and body produced by Buddhist practice, I can express more clearly the problem that concerns me about brain studies of happiness. To make the concern as clear as possible it is necessary to say something about the metaphysical background assumptions that guide this work.

Almost all neuroscientific work proceeds on either of two assumptions. The first view, identity theory, assumes that all mental states are in fact brain states. We access the surface structure of our minds first-personally, in a phenomenological manner, in terms of how a particular state seems or feels to us. But first-person access fails to get at the neural deep structure of our mental states. Only impersonal, or third-person, techniques can do this. Suppose I see [a red patch]. According to identity theory, my brain will reveal activity in the visual cortex in areas that specifically compute "redness" and "patchiness." And there will also be some set of computations that marks, or is, the "I see." Then there will be some activity that is where the components are bound—in psychology this is known as "the binding problem"—or come together to produce my unified perception. Many think binding is done by temporal wave synchrony of activation in different areas rather that through a merger of information at a particular location. But either way there is identity between perception, my seeing [a red patch], and a certain distinctive set of brain events. The complete neuroscientific picture of my perception of the red patch will reveal everything that is true of my subjective perception, including causal and constitutive features of the perception that I am clueless about first-personally, such as which neuronal populations are involved in producing that very perception.

The second view, the neural correlate view (NCV), can be understood as quietistic or agnostic as far as commitment to metaphysical physicalism goes (the view that what there is, and all there is, is "physical," that is, matter and energy transfers). Although NCV claims that each and every mental state has certain distinctive neural correlates, it need neither endorse nor condemn the view that the subjective properties of every experience are reducible to or exhausted by the neural underpinnings of that experience. Perhaps subjectively experienced mental states have sui generis properties that are nonphysical.

Although proponents of the neural correlate view usually assume, as do proponents of identity theory, that there will be neural property correlates for all the features of mental states as detected first-personally, the view doesn't actually entail this. Since identity is not claimed, it is possible that mental states might be caused by or correlated with brain states, but that the neural correlates do not contain specific matches (correlates) for each and every property revealed at the mental level. It is even possible on NCV that there are no neural correlates for some rare and special mental states. NCV can be used in this way to reintroduce various mental will-o'-the-wisps that will please those with dualist hopes, aspirations, or tendencies.

In a piece titled "On the Luminosity of Being" (Gyatso 2003a) that appeared alongside my "Colour of Happiness," the Dalai Lama expressed doubt that, at least in the case of states of "luminous consciousness" (on some interpretations identical to achieving nirvana in this life), any neural correlates will be found for this extraspecial type of conscious mental state. Luminous consciousness is a pure state of mind that involves getting in touch with one's purest essence, one's Buddha nature, whatever that is. The Dalai Lama's argument rests, first, on the rarity of this state; second, on the fact that luminous consciousness seems so very nonphysical; and third, on the fact that Buddhist philosophy claims that destructive mental states, afflictions, and poisons (such as the three poisons, delusion, avarice, and hatred) do not penetrate luminous consciousness. Or better: these three poisons penetrate all material nature and thus the brain. But we can overcome the poisons so we must have a part of mind that has no commerce, not even correlative commerce, with the material world. This is luminous consciousness (see chapter 3 of Flanagan 2007 for a discussion of the Dalai Lama's views on testability and the nature of consciousness). This sort of expansive use of NCV is driven purely by antecedent commitment to a view that is antimaterialist, not by any features of the evidence; as such it is nonnaturalist.

Mental Detection: Content and Causes

Whether one is an identity theorist or holds the weaker neural correlate view, NCV, one will need to use what I call "the natural method," or what Varela (in Petitot 1999) more charmingly and memorably calls "neurophenomenology." In simplest terms, neurophenomenology is the strategy of trying to explain the activity of the mind-brain by gathering sensitive first-person phenomenological reports from subjects and then utilizing whatever knowledge and tools we currently possess in cognitive psychology and neuroscience to locate how the brain is doing what the subjects report experiencing.[8]

Neurophenomenology, or something like it, is the only game in town because when we explore the conscious mind we must always use two kinds of probes. First, there is the subjective or phenomenological method of gathering first-personal information about what an experience seems or feels like. First-personally, we often know and can report what mental state we are in (belief versus desire; happy versus sad) and what the content is—"I am happy because [my son graduated from college today]." Second, we make surmises about the causes of the states with particular contents, or about what behaviors or performance effects being in a certain mental state has. In the example, the cause might be identical to the content: "I'm so happy because my son graduated today." But often content and cause come apart. Suppose taking Prozac causes a person's mood to improve to the point that she finally appreciates good weather again. She says, "What a beautiful sunny day!" That [it is a beautiful sunny day] is the content of her mental state. But the cause of her positive mental state is due in some measure to the Prozac. Amphetamines are used to get kids with ADD to pay attention. Why? Because if a child pays attention she performs better in school than if she doesn't. Amphetamines might cause improvement in solving arithmetic problems, but amphetamines are not of or about numbers, addition, and subtraction.

Do current techniques and technologies for studying the brain reveal any fine-grained details that correspond to what I call the content and the cause(s) of mental states as revealed first-personally? The answer is no. Even if we grant that current techniques can detect positive affect, there is no technique that can distinguish contents of propositional attitude states—states like I believe that [p], I expect that [q], I am happy that [r], where p, q, and r are the propositional contents of the states.

My brain may light up happily, but no brain technology can reveal at present or in the foreseeable future that the content is that [my inheritance has arrived] as opposed to that [it is a cool and sunny day]. First-person phenomenological reports or behavioral observation can lead us to distinguish between two individuals, one who is happy that [she is working for Médicins Sans Frontières] and the other who is happy that [he just made a million dollars on insider trading]. Supposing, as is possible, that their happy centers light up in the same way and to the same degree, neuroscience can reveal no such content difference. So content is a big problem—terra incognita for contemporary brain science.

Similar problems arise regarding the causes of contentful mental states. When the cause of a mental state lies in the past, say in one's upbringing or in many years of practicing meditation, brain scans can't reveal the actual distal cause(s) because these lie outside the brain and in the past. Even supposing, as is plausible, that distal external causes leave neural traces, these are probably global and no one has a clue as to how to study or detect them.

How Much New Light Is Being Shed?

One lesson from reflecting on neurophenomenology and the study of happiness is that happiness[Buddha] is characterized as having a certain cause (or set of causes) and a certain content (with constituent structure—for example, the four required virtues of compassion, lovingkindness, sympathetic

joy, and equanimity). If there is such a thing as happiness[Buddha] it is produced by distinctively Buddhist wisdom, virtues, and mindfulness, or better by a life that abides and enacts such wisdom, virtues, and mindfulness.
First-personal detection, very humble detection, that one is enlightened
and virtuous and practicing mindfulness, is or could be part of the content
of the happiness.

Assume that we gather a group of Buddhists of the same age, with
the same amount of training, committed to the same kind of Buddhism,
and so on. Can brain scans detect the belief states that help constitute or
underpin their enlightenment/wisdom, which are required components of
eudaimonia[Buddha]? No. The problem could be due to current technologies or
current psychoneural theories of how, what, and where belief states are, or,
most likely, both. In either case, we cannot see or measure or distinguish
among such states. Can we distinguish among the virtues in the brain? No.
Can we detect virtue, in general, in human brains?[9] No. At present we are
utterly clueless and without resources to do any such fine-grained analyses
of the neural underpinnings of states of character. Furthermore, it will only
be the underpinnings that we can look for in the brain, and perhaps they
are not even underpinnings, but only neural aspects of virtue (or wisdom
and mindfulness), since a person's actual character is a state of being, and
thus not simply or only in the head. Maybe the subjective state we call
happiness[Buddha] is mostly in the head. But if it is, it has its own distinctive
character as a type of happiness, which needs to be specified precisely at
both the neural level and the phenomenological level for the kind of happiness it is. And this would require neuroscientists to engage in comparative
philosophy and psychological anthropology, which is a good idea—it is
the program of comparative neurophilosophy—but it is not happening yet.

Here is the good news: if there is any prospect for seeing or measuring
the neural states that are (if identity theory is true) the phenomenological
states that people experience, or are correlated with them, if NCV is true, it
will come from using the method of neurophenomenology, and integrat-
ing its findings with information from philosophy and the other human
sciences, at the same time that we are developing more sensitive methods,
technologies, and theories for studying the brain.

It amuses me to think of Siddhārtha Gautama looking down from
nirvana, heaven, the True Pure Land, or wherever, and observing all the
activity attempting to study, confirm, or disconfirm the relation between
Buddhist practices and various goods. I think he would be pleased both that
Buddhism has so many advocates and that the hope it brings to alleviate
suffering and, if it does promise this, to bring true happiness, is being taken

seriously. I picture him a bit befuddled by all the new gadgets being used to measure all sorts of mental and bodily states, as well as by a Zeitgeist that so relishes empirical confirmation by way of scientific instruments. But that aside, I like to think of Buddha as approving of what we are trying (still) to learn: how to end suffering, to achieve enlightenment and goodness, and to find true happiness, if it is possible.

The good news is that for immune response, sensitivity of the virtually automatic amygdala-based emotional system, facial expression detection, and cognitive task performance guided by one-pointed meditation, there are reliable fine-grained physiological, behavioral, and, in some cases, neurological measures than can be used, even if these have not yet been used on sufficiently large populations to have really confirmed any of the hypotheses in the air. As far as measuring and locating the neural correlates for the different types of happiness, we have a long and difficult row to hoe. We need to combine very sensitive phenomenological reports about the feeling and contours that comprise the heterogeneous kinds of happiness that ordinary speech picks out. Research on "authentic happiness" holds promise for distinguishing among the multifarious kinds of happiness (as understood colloquially) by utilizing questionnaires that try to get clear and nuanced reports from subjects on their mental states (Seligman 2002, see also Easterlin 2003, 2004; Frank 2004). I like to think that my own work introducing the research program of eudaimonics (Flanagan 2007) advances the inquiry and shows that the study of happiness will get nowhere unless scholars who understand the history and philosophical texture of the multifarious wisdom traditions are involved. Indeed, without deep philosophical understanding of what various traditions promise in terms of virtue, wisdom, and happiness, including how these are alleged to interpenetrate, the neuroscientists don't know what they are looking for. This is, by and large, the case as I write.

In order for the promising program of eudaimonics, with its close mate, comparative neurophilosophy, to develop we will need thick descriptions of the multiplicity of theory- and tradition-specific conceptions that offer paths to flourishing and true happiness. We know that Aristotle, Epicurus, Buddha, Confucius, Mencius, Jesus, and Mohammed each put forward somewhat different philosophical conceptions of an excellent human life with somewhat different conceptions of what constitutes true happiness, insofar as that—happiness of any sort—is an aim. With these different conceptions well articulated, we can look at brain activity within and across advocates of different traditions to see what informative similarities and differences, if any, such examination reveals. The same strategy might work for negative emotions and destructive mental states. Get well-honed first-person reports from subjects on the negative states they experience and then look for brain correlates. With such data in hand we can then test Buddhist techniques, say, meditation on compassion, that are thought to provide antidotes for anger, hatred, and avarice. By utilizing first-person reports on experienced change in mood or emotion, we can look and see what, if anything, reconfigures itself brainwise. We can do the same for practices from other traditions. Eventually, we will want to coordinate such studies with the ever-deeper knowledge of the connections among virtue, mental health, well-being, and human flourishing, allowing science and philosophy to speak together about what practices are best suited to make for truly rich and meaningful lives. At this distant point, with an array of conceptions of excellent human lives before us, knowledge of the social ecologies in which they operate, as well as deep knowledge of how the brains of devotees of these different traditions look and work, we should be able to speak much more clearly about the nature of happiness and flourishing than we can now.

Conclusion

I have offered several reasons for a somewhat cautious, even indirect approach, to the study of happiness at the present time. For scientists: when studying a form of life or a practice that has its home in a form of life, specify very precisely what goods the life form or practice claims to offer and then explain in similarly precise detail what mental or bodily effects you predict or claim to discover among practitioners. In concert with experts on the form of life, proceed to more completely articulate what exactly it is that is being seen or revealed.[10]

The unease I have expressed about the theoretical usefulness, or lack thereof, of the colloquial concept of happiness ought to be shared by Buddhist practitioners and Buddhist studies experts. Unless the concept of happiness is being put forward in a theory-specific way, we might for now be best advised to stop talking about it, at least to stop using the everyday term *happiness* in philosophical or scientific contexts. Scientists are, of course, also entitled, indeed encouraged, if it is possible, to try to draw out and specify the ordinary understanding of the constituents of positive states of mind such as happiness. They will then have regimented, in a precise way or ways, the meaning(s) of happiness according to folk psychology.

The more theory-specific conceptions of virtue, well-being, flourishing, and happiness that we have, so much the better will our understanding be of these components of good lives. Overlapping consensus on the constituents of these things might reveal itself. Importantly, differences in conceptions of virtue, well-being, flourishing, and happiness will also reveal themselves. The overlaps and differences can be discussed and debated at the philosophical level. Comparative philosophers, psychological anthropologists, historians, and neuroscientists can chime in, wearing philosophical hats if they wish, but equally important, telling us how the brains of practitioners from different traditions light up, which neurochemicals rise and fall, and so on.

Intertheoretical conversation such as I am envisioning will put us in the exciting position of being able to have a better idea of the fine-grained states we are looking for, and to compare different theories in terms of the goods they claim to produce and hopefully do, in fact, produce.

Overall, this sort of inquiry provides a truly exciting, unique, and heretofore unimagined opportunity for mind scientists, practitioners, and philosophers from different traditions to join together in a conversation that combines time-tested noble ideals with newfangled gadgetry to understand ourselves more deeply and to live well, better than we do now. On the other hand, we need to avoid overrating brain imagery and what it shows. Some days when I think about brain imaging I am reminded of this joke: "In the beginning there was nothing and then God said 'Let there be Light.' There was still nothing, but you could see it much better."

3   Buddhist Epistemology and Science

Members of my tribe are fans of science.[1] The scientific method has shown, and keeps showing, its mettle when it comes to revealing the truth in a way no other method matches.[2] If there is room for religion, spirituality, and philosophy, in the ordinary sense, that one sees embodied in some independent bookstore sections, where philosophy books are stacked next to, sometimes with the religion books, and often include the occult and the metaphysical, it will need to be a tame kind of Buddhism, which is, at a minimum, consistent with science—"Buddhism naturalized."

The facts are that almost all of the world's major (and minor) spiritual traditions are neither tame nor consistent with science. Thomas Jefferson's *Bible*, where all the miracles and the Jesus as God stuff are removed, or Unitarian Universalism and the Ethical Culture Society favored by many urban educated types, where no traditional religious beliefs need (possibly should) be avowed, are good examples of what happens when the enlightenment epistemology of liberal, secular culture extracts what it sees as making sense in traditional Judaism and Christianity by squeezing out superstitious nonsense. What is left? Mostly ethics. What does ethics have to do with religion? We naturalists answer: Nothing. Enlightenment naturalists think that the great and pervasive mistake of most—but not all, witness Confucianism—of the world's comprehensive traditions has been in thinking that ethical and eudaimonistic theorizing need to be grounded in metaphysically deep and often untestable or incredible religious ideologies. The philosophical point is not that religion does not sometimes play the psychosocial roles attributed to it, among them "grounding" or motivating morality. Rather it is, first, that ungrounded, untestable, or false premises or ideologies fail epistemically to ground what they are said to ground; and second, insofar as religious belief motivates or produces ethical conformity, it does so by way of these same ungrounded, untestable, or false premises or ideologies. To play its metaphysical role of grounding morality or its motivational role of motivating morality, all familiar religions, witness Islam or Christianity, rely on epistemic tricks, claims about the word of God or afterlives, for example, and are thus in bad faith, philosophical bad faith. Many wise souls, like Dostoyevsky, Marx, and Nietzsche, have worked to expose these problems.

As I write, there is a cheeky and tense, but principled, modus vivendi between the Abrahamic traditions that dominate the West and the minority scientific naturalism. The respective worldviews are inconsistent, but there is an agreement not to impose the opposing views on the other. The leaders of most of the world's great religions, not just the Abrahamic ones, believe in divinities and afterlives. From the point of view of naturalism, these are epistemically unwarranted beliefs, often consoling and innocent (but not always innocent), psychologically and sociologically understandable, but not rational.

Since neither philosophy nor religion—like creative writing, poetry, music, painting, dance, baseball, cricket—is science, the question is not: Is Buddhism a science? No spiritual tradition is a science, and the only ones with *science* in their names, Christian Science and Scientology, are really not science. Nor is the question the one discussed in the previous two chapters: Can Buddhism be studied scientifically? The answer to that question is yes. Buddhism can be—in fact is already—studied by historians, sociologists, anthropologists, and lately by psychologists and neuroscientists. The question as I intend it here is about compatibility or consistency: Is the epistemology that Buddhism recommends inimical to science, does it compete with science, and when push comes to shove which trumps the other, Buddhism or science?

The interesting current situation is that the world's most visible Buddhist, the 14th Dalai Lama, is both very interested in science and claims that Buddhism should not commit itself to any beliefs that are not also scientifically credible. This is quite remarkable. It is unimaginable that the leader of any Abrahamic tradition, the Pope, the chief Rabbi in Jerusalem, or any Ayatollah—would suggest that theology should yield to science when the two conflict. A rule like this would almost certainly require abandoning beliefs in souls, afterlives, even a creator God, the last of which Buddhism already does without.

Conflict between the spaces of science and spirituality is one of the most, if not the most familiar zone of conflict among the spaces of meaning that constitute the Space of Meaning$^{\text{Early 21st century}}$. For normal citizens of developed countries the Space of Meaning$^{\text{Early 21st century}}$ consists of this set of spaces: {ethics, politics, science, technology, arts, spirituality} (Flanagan

2007). We live in, and move about, all these spaces. These spaces are part of the surround, pretty much unavoidable if you are awake. The conflict between the space of spirituality, typically in its religious forms, and the space of politics is the other contender for the zone of greatest conflict. And these conflicts ramify. So the debate about the status of the theory of evolution versus intelligent design and creationism, which can seem as a conflict between science and religion only, comes to infect debates about what ought to be taught in schools and thus demanded of educators who are paid by public tax dollars. Stem cells can be harvested to create lineages that might cure some diseases, but because some stem cells are harvested from embryos, there are fights about whether, for example, the NIH or scientists affiliated with state universities, being publicly funded, should be allowed to do such research.

The Dalai Lama and Science

Buddhism, at least in the hands of the 14th Dalai Lama, may provide the possibility proof that a great spiritual tradition and science can find peace—possibly even mutually enrich each other.[3] In several public addresses and publications, over more than two decades,[4] and most recently in his book *The Universe in a Single Atom: The Convergence of Science and Spirituality* (2005), the 14th Dalai Lama says this: "My confidence in venturing into science lies in my basic belief that as in science, so in Buddhism, understanding the nature of reality is pursued by means of critical investigation: *if scientific analysis were conclusively to demonstrate certain claims in Buddhism to be false, then we must accept the findings of science and abandon those claims*" (2005, 2–3; my italics).

This repeated statement is normally put in just this form as a sort of open epistemic welcome mat. The *Welcome Mat*: "Come sit by my side, my Western scientific and philosopher friends. Tell me what you know. I will teach you what I know. We can debate. But in the end it is our duty, on both sides, to change our previous views if we learn from the other that what we believe is unfounded or false."

But there is what Thupten Jinpa, a close collaborator and the Dalai Lama's main English interpreter, calls "the caveat." Jinpa (2003, 77) writes:

The Dalai Lama . . . offers an important caveat. He argues that it is critical to understand the scope and application of the scientific method. By invoking an important methodological principle, first developed fully as a crucial principle by Tsongkhapa (1357–1419), the Dalai Lama underlines the need to distinguish between what is negated through scientific method and what has not been observed through such a method. In other words, he reminds us not to conflate the two processes of *not find-ing* something and *finding its nonexistence.*[5]

One initial observation about the caveat: the Dalai Lama was friendly with and influenced by the philosopher Sir Karl Popper. Popper is most famous for his criterion of falsifiability: a statement (nowadays, we would say a whole theory) is scientific just in case there are (possible) tests that could test its mettle.[6] A scientific statement that is scientific sticks its neck out, and to the degree it does so, and is not undermined or falsified, it is corroborated. Popper worried about claims that appear to make assertions about the natural world, but that, through various techniques, immunize themselves from falsifiable tests. For the purposes of the present discussion, we ought to keep our eyes out for these two claims:

1. Minds are immaterial, or better, mental properties are immaterial properties.
2. Humans die, but their consciousness continues; consciousness is subject to karmic laws of rebirth.

Why should one keep one's eye out for such claims? First, Buddhists com-monly assert them. It is an interesting and important question whether either is required by or essential to Buddhist philosophy (Batchelor 2010).[7] Second, one might think that given the Dalai Lama's "welcome mat" state-ment that they are just the kinds of assertions that *might* fall to science but that, given the caveat, could never be made to yield. We'll see if this is a problem. Be thinking about it.

My purpose in this chapter is to continue the profitable recent dialog between Buddhism and science emphasizing that, by my lights, this dialog is a model for how respectful and profitable dialog between science and something in the vicinity of spirituality can proceed. I focus specifically on possible differences of opinion about (1) the neo-Darwinian theory of evolution and (2) naturalism about consciousness. Not surprisingly I use myself as the advocate of both the neo-Darwinian theory and a naturalistic view of the conscious mind because, well, that is what I am.

Since 2000, I have been fortunate to have been engaged in many dis-cussions with (mostly) Tibetan Buddhists, including the Dalai Lama, on the connection between science and Buddhism.[8] Rather than try to give a comprehensive overview of the "Mind and Life Dialogues,"[9] my strategy is to provide a critical reading of the Dalai Lama's 2005 book, treating it, as seems justified, as containing his considered view on "the convergence of science and spirituality."

Besides engaging personally in dialog with Western scientists and encouraging scientific research into Buddhist meditative practices, since 2000 the Dalai Lama has led a campaign to introduce basic science education in Tibetan Buddhist monastic colleges and academic centers, and has encouraged Tibetan scholars to engage with science as a way of revitalizing the Tibetan philosophical tradition (http://www.scienceformonks.org/). The "Science for Monks" program is itself remarkable. The consensus is that there was no internal momentum to start such a program. Achok Rinpoche, the former Director of the Library of Tibetan Works and Archives (LTWA), himself not previously learned in science, was the first Head of Science for Monks, an effort that involves one month of intensive training in elementary mathematics, cosmology, evolution, and mind science. In an interview with the Dutch scholar, Rob Hogendoorn, Achok Rinpoche explains:

If you'd go there (to the monastic institutes) yourself and say "I'm going to teach science" the abbot and senior monks would probably say: "No thank you. We're not going to listen. We don't have enough time." But when the Dalai Lama said that now is the time and that it is important to study and learn Western science, all abbots and senior *geshe's* either said Yes or kept quiet.

Not only is what the Dalai Lama doing novel, not driven internally by his own Gelug tradition, but history would suggest it is dangerous.[10] The Dalai Lama pays homage to Gendun Chöpel, one of the very first if not the first Tibetan geshe[11] to study and advocate the study of Western science. Chöpel is arguably the most important Westward-looking Tibetan Buddhist intellectual of the twentieth century. But Chöpel's life ended sadly, after being imprisoned, and in his last years in the grip of alcoholism. He is, to this day, persona non grata among most Tibetan Buddhists for his dalliance with science, communism, and modernity, and for his critiques of orthodox Buddhist epistemology (Lopez 2005).[12] On the other hand, the Dalai Lama is a wise man and it has not been lost on him that there is widespread interest among scientists and philosophers in Buddhist philosophy. Albert Einstein, most certainly an atheist by Abrahamic standards, is not the only scientist to notice that if there is to be conciliation between science and spirituality, no spiritual tradition is better positioned than Buddhism to participate in the conciliation. The Abrahamic religions, Judaism, Christianity, and Islam, are often described by Western theologians as the apotheosis of religion, finally shredding paganism, pantheism, polytheism for belief in the One True God who is the same everywhere, Yahweh, God, Allah. But modern science and theism—especially the sort that claims to be in possession of texts dictated or inspired by God—don't, as it turns out, sit together comfortably. Buddhism being intellectually deep, morally and spiritually serious but nontheistic and nondoctrinal—although often over the top, but not irretrievably so, in hocus pocus and superstition—may sit well poised to be an attractor for the spiritually inclined naturalist. Maybe.

One can imagine someone asking: Why care about conciliation or peaceful coexistence, since science now holds all the cards? One reason is that this is false. In a battle between what is epistemically sensible and what is culturally ingrained, don't bet on the former. Reason doesn't always win in battles with irrationality. If this is true, then purely as a strategic matter, it will be good if naturalist atheists were able to find some common purpose with the sensible and worthy impulses expressed in the wisdom of the ages.

The Dalai Lama believes that science and Buddhism share a common objective: to serve humanity and create a better understanding of the world. Buddhist philosophy starts *all* inquiry with the intention that it benefit *all* humanity, possibly *all* sentient beings. This is probably not the right reading of the impulse behind science. Many scientists will claim to be in search of *the* truth—regardless of consequences.[13] The aims of scientists and, what are different, technologists are multifarious. The knowledge-for-its-own-sake school of thought is common among, say astrophysics and elementary particle physicists, who often see no clear practical consequences for what they discover. On the other hand, these scientists and those who follow their work often comment on the ways such work uncovers great beauty. It serves both "the true" and "the beautiful." On the other side, there any many practically minded scientists who seek knowledge that will be, at least in the short term, useful, but then often only for individuals or countries with the financial resources to pay for what they discover. And then there are the bomb makers, some of them vicious "Chemical Ali" types, seekers of weapons of mass destruction to use against heathens and barbarians, almost always economic, political, and religious rivals. For every scientist and engineer who works in water science, agronomy, and infectious diseases, there are as many who focus on making life better with communication and technological gadgetry for those already living very advanced lives.

What is true is that science offers powerful tools for deepening human understanding of the interconnectedness of all life, although not all scientists see or avow this goal. With this much said about the actual heterogeneous motivations among scientists, it is not an idle hope that in good hands scientific knowledge can enhance wholesome, ethical goals, and lead to action that benefits all sentient beings and the environment.[14] The Dalai Lama summarized these ideas in his 1989 Nobel Peace Prize acceptance speech:

With the ever-growing impact of science on our lives, religion and spirituality have a greater role to play reminding us of our humanity. There is no contradiction between the two. Each gives us valuable insights into the other. Both science and the teachings of the Buddha tell us of the fundamental unity of all things. This understanding is crucial if we are to take positive and decisive action on the pressing global concern with the environment.

Neurophysicalism and Subjective Realism

For the remainder of this chapter, I discuss the possibilities of consilience in two areas: (1) Buddhism and the theory of evolution; (2) Buddhism and mind science. I choose these two foci, first, because the nature and origins of life and mind are hot-button issues in the West; second, because despite the polite dialog between Buddhism and science, these are two areas of controversy, sometimes not seen precisely because of the politeness of the discussions. Indeed, because of the politeness of the dialog thus far, there have been lost chances for debating Buddhists on certain matters. Buddhists, especially Tibetan Buddhists, are trained to debate, so this is unfortunate.[15]

In his *New York Times* review (September 18, 2005) of the Dalai Lama's *The Universe in a Single Atom* (2005), George Johnson suggests that there are shadows of intelligent design (ID) lurking in the text, and that there is no doubt that the Dalai Lama, despite his close collaboration with neuroscientists, thinks the issue of the immateriality of mind is hardly ruled out scientifically, in fact that he endorses dualism of some sort.

My own view is that the proponents of ID—at least in the form that aligns most nicely with Christian beliefs about an omniscient, omnipotent, and benevolent God—will find no friend in the Dalai Lama's views about evolution. One reason is that the Dalai Lama is barred, based on his own anticreationist views, which include finding no credibility in cosmological or design arguments, as well as being impressed by the problem of evil, from thinking that complexity in evolution is best explained by the occasional interventions of an intelligent designer or a team of them. Regarding mind, it is true that immaterial mental properties are not completely ruled out by mind science. But the inference to the best explanation (aka "abduction") based on everything we know, taking all the evidence and all reasonable hypotheses into account, is that there are no such things. The reason has to do with mental causation. If mental events—for example, intentions to act—are, as they seem, causally efficacious, then the best explanation is that they are neural events. This is neurophysicalism, the thesis that mental events are brain events or, at least, bodily events, and that the subjective character of experience is explained by the way nervous systems are connected to the persons that house them (Flanagan 2002). Each individual is the only individual connected to her experiences in the right neurophysical way to actually have those experiences. Realty is such that some systems are like this, systems where the first-person perspective and the third-person perspective each capture different aspects of the same real phenomenon. This view is subjective realism (Flanagan 1991a, 1992, 2002, 2007). Water is H_2O. There is only a third-person perspective on what water is. Water being fully objective itself has no perspective on the matter of its nature. Sentient beings have subjective perspectives on their own being and nature, which—their nature, that is—is part of the real, physical fabric of things, but not exhausted by the objective perspective, hence subjective realism.

Taken together, neurophysicalism, the thesis that every subjective event is realized by a neurophysical event, indeed it is that event—and subjective realism, the thesis that each person, actually each and every sentient being, is connected to herself in such a way that only she "has" her own experiences, which experiences are nonetheless all exhaustively realized neurophysically—have clear implications for how mental causation works, indeed for how it must work. Movement of body by mind, deciding to go to the movies and going, or transformation of mind by mind, resisting perseveration or worry that one feels emerging as one tries to fall asleep, is a form of system-level causation by a complex subjectively controlled, fully embodied, psychological economy that allows the mind/brain-in-the-body-in-the-world-with-a-history to adjust, modify, and change itself. One can hold onto the view that some or all mental events are disembodied, that is, immaterial, but only, as I see things, at too high a cost. One will have to either embrace that violations of physical conservation laws occur every time we act (in my case my incorporeal mind lifts 175 pounds each time I decide to go to the movies and go) or will have to embrace some form of epiphenomenalism, the view that mental states lack causal efficacy. Mental events are nonphysical, but they don't cause anything to happen. My "decision" to go to the movies is akin to a press release about what this body is about to do, but it isn't a part of any causal chain that results in my going to the movie. That results from a set of entirely physical causes. If epiphenomenalism is true, then my desire for popcorn, the taste of the popcorn, and my enjoyment of the movie are also epiphenomenal, immaterial side effects of the interesting causal action. They're cosmic oddities, nomological danglers, do nothings. In 1890, William James called epiphenomenalism an "unwarrantable impertinence" given the current state of psychology. From where I stand it still seems so. Consciousness just makes

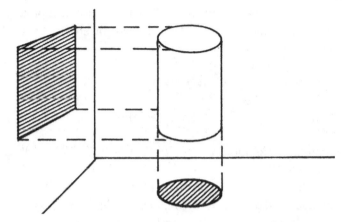

Figure 3.1
There are three epistemic positions in the actual world marked by the three kinds of pronouns—*I, you, he/she/it/they*. Picture each person as represented by a cylinder, a tall 16-ounce drink can, say. What is experienced first-personally is opaque from the point of view of the second person, from the point of view of those in various kinds of relations, which at the limit are of an I-thou sort, the kind that lovers or true Aristotelian friends have. Think of the "you's" and the "thou's" in one's life as those who stand in various external relations to the long vertical orientation of the cylinder, which represents the outside, the skin of a person—the skin, recall, is the largest bodily organ. Relations who are friends or acquaintances of utility or pleasure see the cylinder as a flat rectangle if they are far away, but start to detect dimensionality and depth as they move closer. True friends are very close and experience me, the cylinder, from all sides, but still only from the outsides—over, under, sideways, down, perhaps, but always from the outside. But no you's and thou's, no second persons in my life, no one is the history of interpersonal life in the history of the universe, has even one of my experiences, since they are not me. The third-personal perspective imagine the perspective of the neuroscientist, who gazes into my brain as I watch my children running up the driveway to greet me—has yet another, different perspective from me or my loved ones. Whereas friends, acquaintances, and the abundant anonymous souls with whom I interact, read me through my actions, by applying a commonly known theory of intentional action, by reading my self-expressions and listening to my self-representations, the neuroscientist is looking at the supervenience base, and working to link that level with my phenomenological reports and observations of my behavior.

too much noise not to be doing anything at all. Plus there is still this problem of physics: epiphenomenalism avoids the problem of energy being
introduced ex nihilo by making mind inert. But it has to explain how it is
possible for my body to produce nonphysical experiences. Ex nihilo nihil
fit: from nothing, nothing is made. Conversely, from something nothing
can be produced. Classical dualism asks for an exception to the first principle; the epiphenomenalist asks for an exception to the second.

Metaphysical Foundations of Buddhism

Buddhism originated in 500 BCE when Siddhārtha Gautama, or simply
Buddha, gave his inaugural address at Deer Park, near the outskirts of Benares, India (now called Varanasi). Depending on how one understands the
orthodox Vedic or Indic spiritual tradition of that time, Buddhism was
either a complete break with that tradition or a development of it.[16] Buddhism rejects the caste system on ethical grounds. More interesting to those
who think of religion as requiring belief in divinity, Buddhism rejects both
the idea of a creator God and an immutable, indestructible soul, atman,
on logical and empirical grounds. That said, traditional Buddhism is chock
full of ghosts, spirits, devils, deities, heaven and hell realms, and rebirths
according to karmic laws that govern the universe. Even if contemporary
secular Westerners see Buddhism as compatible with Enlightenment philosophy, many Asian Buddhists, especially the Tibetan variety, do not.

Insofar as the reigning orthodoxy conceived of Brahman as the prime
mover itself unmoved, Buddhism rejects that idea.[17] It also rejects the idea
that each individual houses an unchanging self or soul (atman). Beyond
this, many familiar Indian ideas are retained and developed in Buddhism—
although, in certain quarters, and only recently, with hesitancy. This leg-
acy includes the deep importance of the appearance-reality distinction, the
idea of reward for virtuous action (karma), the idea that suffering (dukkha)
defines the human predicament (samsara) and that liberation is possible
(nirvana) through enlightenment (panna; Sanskrit: prajna, bodhi) and virtue (sila, karuna), as well as the ideas of reincarnation or rebirth.

Let me stick with the two metaphysical beliefs that Buddhism rejects:
a creator God and a permanent self or soul. First, Buddhism sees right
through the familiar problems with cosmological and design arguments
for the existence of God. Such arguments beg the question of the origin
of the creator or designer. To say that the prime mover always was or is
self-creating and self-sustaining is to accept the infinite regress of causes
(this one a causa sui) that such arguments are designed to make evaporate,

which they reject as a possibility. If God always is and shall be, then God itself is infinitely regressive.

When the Dalai Lama listens to the story of the Big Bang occurring fourteen billion years ago, he says fine "but not, of course, the first Big Bang." This response is hardly a rejection of our theory of the Big Bang. The Dalai Lama sees the Big Bang theory as itself inadequate because it is not deeply causal enough. Some scientists themselves are now wondering if a better story doesn't involve less of a singular, original bang than an origin for this universe that involves an open wormhole from another parallel universe, with these other universes or their ancestors—possibly comrades in a vast, even infinite, multiverse—being beginningless.

Cosmologists will sometimes say one can't ask what there was before the singularity banged or how the singularity got there. What they mean is that "time," as physics understands it, begins (or becomes a useful concept) with the Big Bang. But this hardly makes the sense behind the question go away. Thus other cosmologists will admit the legitimacy of the question and say they have no clue as to how to answer it. Buddhism is comfortable with an infinite regress of natural causes. Indeed, the idea fits well with the metaphysical idea of dependent origination, according to which everything that happens depends on other things happening.[18]

The rejection of the Vedic (Indic) doctrine of atman, the idea that humans are possessors of an immutable, indestructible self or soul, comes from two lines of thought. First, there is the idea of dependent origination that I have just mentioned. Everything is in flux and all change is explained by prior change. The principle is universal and thus applies to mind. Next bring in experience or phenomenology: one will see that what one calls "the self" is like many other natural things, partaking of certain relations of continuity and connectedness. My conscious being is much more streamlike than it is like Mount Everest (which is also part of the flux, just less visibly so). Conventional speech allows us to reidentify each person by her name as if she is exactly the same over time. But in fact identity is not an all-or-nothing thing. Personhood is one kind of unfolding. The Himalayas are a very slow unfolding (one answer to how long it takes to reach final enlightenment is as long as it would take for a mountain range 84,000 times larger that the Himalayas to erode if touched once a day with a soft cloth!); humans are a faster unfolding than the ordinary Himalayas; drosophila unfold much more quickly. Each kind of thing in the cosmos is an unfolding in the cosmos, the eternal Mother of all unfoldings, and has a temporal span during which it can be said to be what it is—a mountain range, a person, a fruit fly—and after which it ceases to have enough integrity to be said to be the same thing, itself. At such a transition point, we say the thing, event, or process is gone, over, dead, that it has passed, passed on, or passed away.

This is the doctrine of anatman, no-self. Nothing is permanent, even things that seem so, aren't. If properly understood the view is not nihilistic. One of my students once asked in a very disturbed manner, "If I am not myself who the fuck am I?" I am happy to report that further therapy about the meaning of the doctrine of anatman calmed him. Indeed, in the West a very similar view is widely held from Locke to the present (Flanagan 1991b, 1996, 2002; also see chapter 4). And it fits nicely with contemporary mind science. Furthermore, the doctrine of anatman suits Buddhist ideas that persons can in fact transform themselves, become enlightened, and so on. If one's nature is, as it were, immutably fixed, it is hard to see how self-transformation is possible.

Two Empiricisms: Buddhist Epistemology and Scientific Epistemology

I've already indicated that the Dalai Lama does not enter the dialog in a completely neutral way. All inquiry ought to be undertaken so as to contribute to the alleviation of suffering. This is a proper, nonnegotiable expression of what Buddhist ethical inquiry takes as the highest aspiration.[19] With this aim and this aim alone we express our commitment to improving the universal existential predicament of sentient beings: we seek to flourish, individually and collectively, but there are features of the world and our natures or the two in interaction that present obstacles and that need to be moderated, modified, and overcome as far as is possible. Egoism, acquisitiveness, and selfishness need to be tamed or eliminated.

One reason for hopefulness about the prospects for mutual integration of Buddhism and science comes from standard Buddhist methodology that the Dalai Lama (2005, 22) describes this way: "Buddhism accords greatest authority to experience, with reason second, and scripture last." This is an auspicious starting point for the dialog. The Dalai Lama goes on to describe what he thinks is the biggest difference between science and Buddhism: the role of the scriptures. He writes: "By contrast with religion, one significant characteristic of science is the absence of an appeal to scriptural authority as a source of validating truth claims" (p. 25).

Here the Dalai Lama underestimates the role of "scriptures" in science. First, unlike the Vedic tradition of India or the Abrahamic traditions in the West, Buddhist scriptures are scriptures that are decidedly not thought to be divinely authored. They are themselves accumulations of cultural wisdom organized and authorized as authoritative because the wisdom they contain passes tests of experience and reason. Arguably, science has scriptural traditions of its own that function in pretty much the same way. When Newton spoke of "standing on the shoulders of giants," he was acknowledging his dependence on prior science. Had Newton lived when Ptolemy or Copernicus did, he might, being very smart, have come up with their theories, but he could not have come up with Newtonian physics without the antecedent work of Copernicus, Galileo, Kepler, and so on.

Both Descartes and Spinoza make much of the fact that in order to know we must trust our ancestors—trust them deeply. Spinoza points out the fact that our knowledge of parentage and the date of our birth is, in fact, what he calls "knowledge by hearsay." My students always find this a novel thought, amusing and true. Descartes's own epistemological crisis that results in his resolution to methodically doubt all his previous knowledge is motivated by the recognition that almost everything (mathematics possibly aside) he believes comes from sensory experience or from having heard about and learned what the great minds of the past discovered.

But there is one difference that makes a difference regarding the legitimacy of past wisdom. Science requires that the accumulated wisdom of its own past be intersubjectively (re-)testable, where this means that anyone with the suitable instruments can replicate the results should they come into question. Buddhism distinguishes among enlightened and unenlightened beings. This allows certain knowledge that, say, Nagarjuna, the great Buddhist philosopher, writes about to remain in place, authoritative, even if I can't confirm it by my own experience and reason. Why? Because he is more enlightened than I am. We treat Aristotle, Copernicus, Galileo, Kepler, Newton, and Einstein in similar ways.

The Dalai Lama (2005) enters the dialog with hope because of this epistemic common ground of Buddhism and science. But he also enters the dialog with concerns about what he calls "scientific materialism":

I have noticed that many people hold an assumption that the scientific view of the world should be the basis for all knowledge and is knowable. This is scientific materialism. . . . It is difficult to see how questions such as the meaning of life, or good and evil can be accommodated within such a worldview. The problem is not with the empirical data of science but with the contention that these data alone constitute the legitimate ground for developing a comprehensive worldview or an adequate means for responding to the world's problems. (pp. 12–13)

The Dalai Lama is convinced that scientific materialism is an enemy— perhaps the enemy of moral seriousness. Furthermore, like the salesperson for almost every spiritual tradition ever invented, he is skeptical that anything both truthful and uplifting can be said about the meaning and purpose of human life if materialism is true (Flanagan 2007).

The Neo-Darwinian Theory of Evolution

Assume, because it is true, that the Dalai Lama and his colleagues have been exposed to and studied the basics of the neo-Darwinian theory of evolution.[20] What, if any issues, do they have with that theory? My strategy is to claim that what can seem to be a disparate set of concerns mostly revolve around differences in views about causation, specifically, around whether there are one or two kinds of causation. Let me explain.

Darwinian theory is about the processes that govern the evolution of life. It is not a theory of everything, not even about all aspects of living things.[21] Ten billion years after the Big Bang on earth in an environment of carbon, methane, nitrogen, ammonia, water, and electricity, protein structures began to form, eventually giving rise to unicellular life. At this point the laws of evolution by natural selection began to do their thing. Over the period from four billion years ago until now many, many species formed including eventually Homo sapiens, maybe 100,000 years ago.[22]

The Dalai Lama (2005, 90) says: "My own view is that the entire process of the unfolding of a universe system is a matter of the natural law of causality." Put this way, his position is perfectly consistent with the combined story of physics, chemistry, and biology. But then immediately he claims that there is another kind of causality: *karmic causality*. Whatever karmic causality turns out to be, the idea is not crazy. After all, according to the picture of the unfolding universe I just presented there is emergence. Inorganic stuff, governed only by the laws of physics and inorganic chemistry, gives rise to organic material governed by the laws of organic chemistry. Eventually there is life, at which point the laws of biology and evolution come into play.

The first thing we need to understand is what *karma* is and means, and then what *karmic causation* means and how, if there is such a thing, it works. The Dalai Lama (2005, 109) writes:

Karma means "action" and refers to the intentional acts of sentient beings. Such acts may be physical, verbal, or mental—even just thoughts or feelings—all of which have impacts upon the psyche of an individual, no matter how minute. Intentions result in acts, which result in effects that condition the mind toward certain traits and propensities, all of which may give rise to further intentions and actions.

All this makes sense. It is nothing a philosophical naturalist will puzzle over. The actions of sentient being have all sorts of effects, some of which insofar as they involve reproduction, reproductive rates, positive and negative environmental effects, have consequences for fitness. Other effects—for example, social and political ones—may have no consequences for fitness but will affect the quality of our lives and those of future generations.

Next he says this:

> I envision karma coming into the picture at two points. When the universe has evolved to a stage where it can support the life of sentient beings, its fate becomes entangled with the karma of the beings who will inhabit it. When we use the term *karma*, we may refer both to specific and individual acts and to the whole principle of such causation. In Buddhism, this karmic causality is seen as a fundamental natural process and not as any kind of divine mechanism or working out of a preordained design. Apart from the karma of individual sentient beings, whether it is collective or personal, it is entirely erroneous to think of karma as some transcendental unitary entity that acts like a god in a theistic system of a determinist law by which a person's life is fated. From the scientific view, the theory of karma may be a metaphysical assumption—but it is no more so than the assumption that all of life is material and originated out of pure chance. (pp. 109–110)

Again, so far so good. The idea can be understood straightforwardly as follows: once sentient beings exist they think, feel, and act in ways that have effects. These effects are of two kinds: personal—both intrapersonal (on the person herself) and interpersonal (on those with whom the person interacts)—and environmental, affecting the natural and built world. To these one should add social, economic, and political effects.

Karmic causation as depicted in this way is natural. It is not due to theistic intervention at the beginning of the process, say, in creating a Big Bang with a plan, nor is there intentional (intelligent) design along the way other than the effects of the sentient beings (human and nonhuman) who eventually emerged and are creating karmic effects = effects via their actions.

Interpreted in this tame way, it is not clear why the Dalai Lama says, "From the scientific view, the theory of karma may be a metaphysical assumption—but it is no more so than the assumption that all of life is material and originated out of pure chance."

There is no reason for defensiveness. As I have interpreted the Dalai Lama's explanation, karmic causation, is a well-confirmed fact. Once there are sentient beings who can perform intentional actions up and running, they create all sorts of effects. The very idea of human sciences—*Geisteswissenschaften*—is premised on this fact. In both cases, what is being called as assumption is akin to a plausible, well-confirmed hypothesis.

Each assumption—first, that there is ordinary causation, and second, that sentient-being causation is an interesting subtype—began as an inductive generalization that was then confirmed again and again, eventually becoming regulative assumptions of *Naturwissenschaften* and *Geisteswissenschaften*, respectively. And these assumptions, which began as regulative assumptions or guiding hypotheses, keep working, keep being confirmed. So, speaking in a Kantian idiom, both assumptions now have something like constitutive status. They began as plausible inductive generalizations or inferences to the best explanation given the data, and have been corroborated again and again.

But now more puzzling ideas surface. The Dalai Lama (2005, 110) writes: "More difficult perhaps is the first intervention of karma, which is effectively the maturation of the karmic potential of the sentient beings who will occupy that universe, which sets in motion its coming into being." Let's parse the sentence into two parts. First there is the issue of when karmic causation began to operate. From a naturalistic perspective, specifically from an evolutionary and mind-science point of view, the answer is this: karmic causation began whenever sentient beings began to act and leave the effects they leave. But the Dalai Lama puts what could be the very same point, but perhaps is not, in this puzzling way: The first intervention of karma "is effectively the maturation of the karmic potential of the sentient beings who will occupy [the] universe, which sets in motion its coming into being."

This last sentence is hard to interpret. What does *its* refer to? It could refer to the time when (actually the long period during which) sentient beings evolved, became abundant, and started affecting the trajectory of the world. If we suppose that all vertebrates are sentient, then 500 million years ago is a good date to pick as the start date. Among those who accept the neo-Darwinian theory and thus who accept that sentience did evolve from insensate life (bacteria and other organisms for whom "there was nothing it is/was like to be them"), there are only stories, some more credible than others, as to why evolution favored an engineering solution that, across many distinct lineages, produced sentience. No really good view of how and why—these being different issues—it happened has been satisfactorily worked out. Although for the naturalist, any story worth entertaining must conceive things in a way that is possible according to the lights of our best evolutionary theory(ies), which, of course, is a pretty weak constraint.

That said, the Dalai Lama's statement could be interpreted as a controversial answer to question of why sentience emerged. He could mean something like this: at one point the universe harbored incipient or unactualized sentience. Still, one might say the Darwinian is committed to much the same idea: whatever did emerge, "sentience" in the case at hand, is the actualization of the potential of antecedent natural processes. So to create genuine controversy here, one needs to add: when sentience emerged it was not due to Darwinian processes. It involved instead "the *maturation* of the karmic potential of the sentient beings who *will* occupy that universe." The maturation of this potential sentience "sets in motion that universe's [the one with sentience in it] coming into being." It appears that there are two concepts of karma, one tame and one untame. Karmic causation[untame] sounds suspiciously teleological—as if the universe itself has a plan that seeds itself, that very universe, with a destination that is its future, and thus as if it involves something beyond karmic causation[tame].

We are at a good point, having come upon what seems like a difference of opinion about matters of importance, where we can understand something about how differences between the epistemology of science and Buddhist epistemology might be in play at this juncture. I just acknowledged that there exists no widely accepted story about why sentience evolved, why we, for example, didn't evolve as just very smart information processors, smart robots. Furthermore, at this time no one has a clue how to perform experiments that would show how behaviorally equivalent zombies and conscious creatures would fare against each other in a fitness challenge. That said, Darwinian theory is extraordinarily well confirmed. Work with fruit flies can let us watch Darwinian principles at work over very short periods of time, as can everyday work in agriculture science. So those who say Darwin's theory is only retrodictive, untestable, and the like are seriously misinformed. But as regards the evolution of sentience, we are pretty much, at this time, left with "just so" stories. Among us Darwinians we revert to our received wisdom: well, it happened, so it must have happened in a Darwinian way. The Dalai Lama reverts to past Buddhist wisdom. In both traditions when experience and reason lose their grip, go to received wisdom.

The Dalai Lama asks:

How do Buddhist cosmological theories envision the unfolding of the relationship between the karmic propensities of sentient beings and the evolution of a physical universe? What is the mechanism by which karma connects to the evolution of a physical system? On the whole, the Buddhist *Abhidharma* texts do not have much to say on these questions, apart from the general point that the environment where a sentient being exists is an "environmental effect" of the being's collective karma shared with myriad other beings. (p. 92)

This statement is not an unfair statement of the situation of the evolutionist when it comes to explaining the evolution of sentience. She will, as I've said, nonetheless insist that sentience evolved in a Darwinian manner.

Why? Because the theory of evolution is very, very well confirmed. It is the best—really the only—well-confirmed theory that makes the emergence of sentience in the biological world not completely mysterious. In the first instance, creatures who detected noxious and good-making/survival-enhancing stimuli by pleasant and painful experiences appeared. This turned out to be fitness enhancing. And so creatures with the capacities to have "subjective experiences" proliferated. Eventually we, Homo sapiens, came to be. Thanks to sentience and smarts we did really well. Now there are over six and a half billion of us. The increasing weight (literally, one might say) of sentient beings in the world increases the amount and complexity of the karmic effects of these beings. And this affects the way the world is, the way it is unfolding, and the prospects for all things and beings.

The point is that the Dalai Lama's wonder or worries about how ordinary and karmic causation fit together, if understood in the tame way I have recommended, are not cause for any worry from a perspective that binds neo-Darwinian theory to mind science or to the human sciences—to *Geisteswissenschaften*, conceived minus *"Geist"* more generally. Sentient creatures are part of the biological fabric of the universe, and thus whatever causal effects they produce affect the world. All the sciences taken together are in the business of explaining how the relevant causal features and factors contribute to our unfolding and that of our world.

It seems, though, that this might not satisfy the Dalai Lama since he adds: "The ability to discern exactly where karma intersects with the natural law of causation is traditionally said to lie only within the Buddha's omniscient mind" (p. 92). Here, if the Dalai Lama is seriously endorsing the idea of consulting "the Buddha's omniscient mind," is a difference that makes a difference between the epistemic rules in science and in Buddhism for how, using their respective "scriptures," we are to resolve puzzles that experience and reason don't resolve. In science even if experience and reason can't yield a definitive test for some unsolved problem, the rules require trying to gain some explanatory grip by looking to the best intersubjectively confirmed theory in the vicinity, the theory with the best potential resources for making sense of the puzzling phenomena. However, in Buddhism because some minds are more enlightened than others, they may see or know solutions that are not intersubjectively available. One might politely point out to the Buddhist that saying that the solution to the problem confronting us is only known by the "omniscient Buddha," is really just a way of saying that the issue will remain puzzling, perhaps even eternally mysterious to us nonomniscient souls. But there are two reasons for greater optimism. First, no real Buddha is omniscient, she is just very enlightened.[23] Second, the problem of reconciling a world in which no sentience exists and in which ordinary physical, chemical, and biological causation do their thing, and the world that emerges when sentience and karmic causation coemerge, is not that difficult unless one introduces either of two theses that will cause serious explanatory obstacles: (1) that the emergence of sentience was planned or metaphysically preordained, or (2) that sentient beings are not animals, specifically, that consciousness is of an ontological type that does not abide natural laws.

Invoking (1) and/or (2) is not required by the distinction between ordinary causal principles and karmic causation, nor by anything in my analysis of the Dalai Lama's views so far. Again he writes: "By invoking karma here, I am not suggesting that according to Buddhism everything is a function of karma. We must distinguish between the operation of the natural law of causality, by which once a certain set of conditions are put in motion they will have a certain set of effects, and the law of karma, by which an intentional act will reap certain fruits" (p. 90).

This can be understood simply as marking two kinds of causes: ordinary, nonintentional physical causes, and intentional physical causes. Again this seems innocuous enough. But enough is said in the Dalai Lama's book, and enough is known independently about Buddhist views on rebirth and the nature of mind, to think that the contrast between ordinary causation and *"the law of karma, by which an intentional act will reap certain fruits"* (my italics) means to say, or imply, something controversial.

What I call the tame interpretation of karmic causation involves the conjunction of three uncontroversial ideas (i) sentient beings exist; (ii) these beings engage in mentally initiated purposeful action, and (iii) all the actions of sentient beings (intentional and unintentional) have abundant effects. If (i–iii) are uncontroversial, one might wonder why it is worth distinguishing karmic causation from ordinary physical causation at all. One reason is this: even if sentient-being causation (= tame karmic causation) is not ontologically distinctive, it is epistemically and explanatorily interesting and informative to mark it off as a distinctive (sub-)type. It depicts the causal intricacies of the lives of sentient beings, especially when they act intentionally, in the right way.

According to the theory of evolution, sentience is a biologically emergent feature of nonsentient biological life. Sentient beings comprise a subset of living things. Vegetables and unicellular organisms are alive but not sentient. Sentient beings that can consciously control their own thoughts, feelings, and actions are a subset of sentient life. Some think that the relevant powers are possessed only by Homo sapiens; most others think that all mammals, quite possibly birds, amphibians, even reptiles possess the relevant capacities to some degree, at least the capacities to have experiences and to act to get what they want. Thus the idea of karmic causation makes sense, at the right level of analysis, of the operation of sentient beings. Understood in this way, it could just be called "sentient-being causation," a subtype of ordinary causation. Karmic causation so understood as sentient-being causation gives *Geisteswissenschaften* the conceptual distinction it needs to attend to the operation of the part of the world it is designed to explain. And all this can be done inside the framework of scientific materialism.

But the less tame interpretation would run like this. Karmic causation^{untame} is intended to do more work that expressing (i–iii). It names an ontologically unique kind of causation that accounts for how the psyches of future beings are determined by a set of causal processes that involve more than the environmental cum psycho-social-political-economic effects of previous occupants of the earth. What is meant by the idea of "*the law of karma, by which an intentional act will reap certain fruits*" is this: my consciousness does not die when my body does, it goes on and reaps in the next and possibly many (many) future lives what it sows in each antecedent life. This, one might say, is simply what all soteriologies (theories of salvation) or eschatologies (theories of hope for final times) say in one form or another. So in order to make clear what makes karmic causation^{untame} especially distinctive, one might add: immaterial properties of sentient beings produce causal effects in the natural world, upstream, down the road, in the future. And if one wanted to make things really wild and woolly, and violate the second law of thermodynamics to boot, one could add that the future seeds the present as much as the past constrains the present. For example, on every view the past affects who I am now. But if one thought that time was an illusion and perfectly symmetrical (violating the second law) then one could equally well think that the future affects my life now; if one also believes in future lives, then those very lives that I will live help make me who I am now. This is all perplexing and exciting, but, in an age that is post–"final causes"—causes that draw their effects to their bosom from the future— it is also incoherent.

On both the tame and untame interpretations, the world evolves as it does, in some significant measure, due to the effects of how humans live. But according to the law of karma the actual psyches of future beings are juiced by a karmic reward-and-punishment system. This is the crux, I think, of why the Dalai Lama expresses misgivings about both the randomness and lack of directionality in evolution. He writes:

From a philosophical point of view, the idea that these mutations [that seed adaptations], which have such far-reaching implications, take place naturally is unproblematic, but that they are purely random strikes me as unsatisfying. It leaves open the question of whether this randomness is best understood as an objective feature of reality or better understood as indicating some kind of hidden causality. (p. 104)

I interpret the "kind of hidden causality" referred to here as an aspect of karmic causation that gives direction to future worlds by way of the system of karmic payoffs involved in future rebirths. Something more than the efficient causation warranted by the concepts of ordinary causation and karmic causation[tame] is being introduced. And nonefficient causes are looked on with suspicion by science.[24]

If this is correct, or in the right vicinity, then the caveat mentioned at the beginning comes into play. Recall that the Dalai Lama's close collaborator and English interpreter, Thupten Jinpa (2003, 77), states the caveat this way:

The Dalai Lama . . . offers an important caveat. He argues that it is critical to understand the scope and application of the scientific method. By invoking an important methodological principle, first developed fully as a crucial principle by Tsongkhapa (1357–1419), the Dalai Lama underlines the need to distinguish between what is negated through scientific method and what has not been observed through such a method. In other words, he reminds us not to conflate the two processes of *not finding* something and *finding its nonexistence*.

The applicability of the caveat, in the present context, is straightforward: science finds no evidence for rebirth, but it has not found its "nonexistence." It follows according to the spirit of the caveat that belief in rebirth is acceptable. It is not as if it is simply acceptable because it is part of the Buddhist tradition to believe it. The Dalai Lama says that the great epistemologist "Dharmakirti clearly did not think that the theory of rebirth was purely a matter of faith. He felt that it falls within the purview of what he characterized as 'slightly hidden' phenomena, which can be verified by inference" (p. 133). Depending on how one conceives of where the burden of proof lies in this case, a comprehensive and responsible critique of the doctrine might need to look at the quality of the alleged inference, which I won't undertake here (see Willson 1987). I will say this much: the belief in rebirth is a belief with a long and robust cultural history in Tibet, India, and elsewhere in Asia. It is therefore a strong belief, resilient. But it is an excellent example of the sort of belief whose main warrant is this very social strength and whatever psychological appeal the belief has, not any features that pertain to its plausibility. Many Budd-curious and Budd-impressed Americans say politely when discussing afterlives—Abrahamic or Indic—"Well, it's possible; you can't prove there isn't any." Right, truth and proof are different concepts. One can't prove much of anything out-side mathematics. But the fact that the requirement of proof or disproof is almost always impossible to satisfy shouldn't be allowed to lead to a sort of epistemic promiscuity that lets one entertain and tolerate all sorts of beliefs that a rational person ought not to believe in. High epistemic standards matter if we are to make any headway in making political life more rational and less dangerous. Liberalism about lifestyle does not require epistemic liberalism, an anything-goes attitude about beliefs that are truth apt.

I say more about the meaning and the epistemic status of the caveat as I now bring the final (for my purposes) topic for discussion more clearly into view. This final topic involves the nature of the conscious mind, mental properties, and mental events.

The possibility that consciousness is ontologically independent of natural processes lurks in our discussion of karma, karmic causation, and the prospect that consciousness does not die when I do, or when my body dies. It is time to merge the discussion of evolution with the dialog as it pertains to the nature of mind.

Matter and Consciousness

The Dalai Lama clearly ties the two problems, karma and consciousness, together in this passage:

The problem is how to reconcile two strands of explanation—first, that any universe system and the beings within it arise from karma, and second, that there is a natural process of cause and effect, which simply unfolds. The early Buddhist texts suggest that matter on the one hand and consciousness on the other relate according to their own process of cause and effect, which gives rise to new sets of functions and properties in both cases. On the basis of understanding their nature, causal relations, and functions, one can then derive inferences—for both matter and consciousness— that give rise to knowledge. (p. 91)

It will be useful to distinguish three issues that are the big stakes concerning consciousness. First, there is the question of the role of phenomenology in the study of mind; second, there are issues of epistemic linkage between the first-personal point of view and third-personal study of mind and behavior; and third, there is the question of the ontological status of conscious mental events. I take each in turn.

Role of Phenomenology
For 2,500 years, Buddhist practitioners of mindfulness have been engaged in deep self-reflective thought. The results of their phenomenological studies

are written down, analyzed, revised, nuanced, and taxonomized beginning
with the portions of the *Abhidhamma* (*Abhidhammattha*; *Abhidharma*, Sanskrit) that were written down in the first and second centuries CE, 600–700
years after Siddārtha Gautama lived. There is nothing comparable in the
West. To be sure, we have Socrates's injunction to "know thyself" followed
profitably by the Stoics and Epicureans engaged in sustained attempts to do
so. And there is Descartes's insistence on the first-person point of view. But
for him it is the importance of the thin description of each of us as a thinking being that is key, not anything like deep thought about the contents
of mind or the interconnections among the multifarious types of mental
states, which is probably best traced in the West to Augustine's *Confessions*,
a millennium earlier. And of course in the eighteenth through the twentieth centuries, there were phenomenological movements in continental
Europe that attempted to probe introspective states but that were criticized
for doing so without epistemic constraints by behaviorism and computa-
tional cognitive science in America, especially. No matter how many sites
of good phenomenology one turns up in the West (the list will, in fact,
be long; see Guzeldere 1997), there is nothing remotely like the sustained
2,500-year research program in phenomenological psychology that comes
from the Buddhist tradition (see Thompson 2007 on the Western revival).

The Dalai Lama writes:

Buddhism and cognitive science take different approaches. Cognitive science addresses this study primarily on the basis of neurobiological structures and the biochemical functions of the brain, while Buddhist investigation of consciousness
operates primarily from what could be called a first-person perspective. A dialogue
between the two could open up a new way of investigating consciousness. The core
approach of Buddhist psychology involves a combination of meditative contemplation, which can be described as a phenomenological inquiry; empirical observation
of motivation, as manifested through emotions, thought patterns and behavior, and
critical philosophical analysis. (p. 165)

There is no longer any doubt that thick phenomenological description of
mental life is important in its own right, as well as necessary for robust
theory construction. But there are legitimate worries—one sees the concerns expressed inside Buddhism and they were pressed with a vengeance
by behaviorists—about how one knows whether one is seeing mind clearly
and describing or analyzing it accurately.[25] We can distinguish three closely
related matters of epistemic importance concerning phenomenology: (1)
Does phenomenology reveal what mind and its states are like universally?
(2) What checks phenomenology other than more phenomenology? (3)
Does phenomenology reveal anything more, any thing other, than how

mind seems first-personally? Because phenomenology is fashionable again, (1) to (3) require close attention. The good news is that we can make better progress on giving credible answers to (1) to (3) now that we have something to evaluate phenomenological reports against, namely, neural activity and behavior.

Linking the Phenomenology with the Brain and Behavior

Buddhist philosophical psychology provides a grand taxonomy of mental states. In part this is due to the effects of deep curiosity and sustained attention on mental life as such. A second reason has to do with the guiding purpose of Buddhist phenomenological inquiry: to contribute to the alleviation of suffering. The parts of the *Abidhamma* devoted to psychology draw distinctions among wholesome, unwholesome, and neutral mental states, and analyze closely the functional links among mental states—for example, what the three poisons (avarice, anger, and false view) and the twenty-four derivative mental afflictions lead to. This elaborate Buddhist psychology is of great interest in its own right, but is meant ultimately to serve Buddhist ethics.

When Buddhist phenomenology developed there was no neuroscience to tether it to. Now there is. In the twenty-first century, we are now positioned to link the first-personal descriptions of mind with third-personal descriptions of behavior and the brain. The Dalai Lama writes: "A dialogue between the two could open up a new way of investigating consciousness." This is true. Linking the phenomenological with the psychological and neural is a promising research strategy for understanding persons. It is, furthermore, the strategy now firmly in place (Churchland 1986; Flanagan 1984, 1991a, 1992, 2000b).

At times, the Dalai Lama protests too much about the lack of recognition of this point in the West. I've been saying this sort of thing for over twenty years in the company of fellow analytic philosophers and scientific naturalists, and even at the start I didn't feel remotely alone. I also know that the late Cisco Varela, champion of neurophenomenology, had the Dalai Lama's ear for a long time. One thought I have is that Alan Wallace, who has also had the Dalai Lama's ear for a long time, and who—unlike Varela and me—emphasizes issues like the comparative lack of attention to the first personal, residual suspicions about the first personal, and the relative immaturity of phenomenology in the West, has proven to be the more powerful voice in how the Dalai Lama conceives of the current state of mind science in the West. Wallace's description, and thus the Dalai Lama's description, of the situation is outdated.

There is a wonderful 1989 study by Logothestis and Schall that has been widely cited by those of us who favor this blending of the first-personal and third-personal points of view. Here I treat it as paradigmatic. The experiment is a study in binocular rivalry. When humans are shown two different stimuli—upward or downward moving lines—to each eye, most viewers see one or the other alternately rather than fusing them. Logothestis and Schall taught, via operant conditioning, rhesus macaques to report (by pressing buttons) when they experience upward or downward moving lines. By hooking up electrodes to sixty-six neurons in the areas that do motion detection in the middle temporal and medial superior temporal areas of the superior temporal sulcus (STS), the experiments show that activation in many neurons is reliably dictated by retinal stimulation (of both sets of lines), but other smaller sets are differentially and reliably linked to the monkey's phenomenological reports of seeing only upward or downward moving lines. I want to say that nowadays all good work in cognitive and affective neuroscience utilizes phenomenological reports. Work by Patricia Smith Churchland and Paul M. Churchland, Hannah and Antonio Damasio, Richie Davidson, Joseph LeDoux, Christof Koch, and frankly anyone else I can think of interested in consciousness uses the first personal and looks for brain correlates.

That said, there are legitimate residual epistemic concerns about the first personal. First, there is the *Wittgensteinian concern*: we can divide mental vocabulary in two; there are world-directed concepts and mind-directed ones. *Red* is world directed. Parents have at their disposal a good system of checks and balances to gain assurance that kids use the word *red* correctly. *Love, sad, happy*, and the like are mind directed or just plain "mental." Such states have certain world-stimulus conditions that we believe can and do produce them, but these are multifarious, as are the behavioral manifestations of these states. Parents are in an imperfect position when it comes to getting the kids to use these words in the same way they (think they) do or other kids do. We do not worry that these concepts float completely free; it is just that there is less reason to think they are semantically well behaved across speakers of the language than are world-directed concepts.

Second, there is the worry about *unconscious states*. I attribute some truth to the idea of a motivated Freudian unconscious and lots of truth to the idea of an unmotivated cognitive unconscious. Even with minimal concession to Freud, most will agree that there are self-serving tendencies to keep everything true about one's self from appearing to oneself. In addition, there are things we experience that we sensibly don't say or share.

The cognitive unconscious causes a different sort of epistemic problem, one with ontological significance. Consider the rhesus macaques that fix alternately on vertical and horizontal lines. We might be inclined to say that the activation of the neurons that are reliably, but differentially active, when they report seeing vertically or horizontally *is* the neural underpinning of the conscious percept. This is a credible inference. But whether the active set exhausts or is all there is to the conscious percept is more obscure. Phenomenology is not positioned to say much of anything useful on this matter. Several possibilities remain open. Perhaps more than the set of neurons that reliably tag "seeing vertically" constitute the percept; perhaps fewer are responsible for the phenomenology. At present no one knows even in the case in question.

Last, there is the *Rylean concern*, which has to do with making ontological inferences about the way mind is from the way mental states seem. The most worrisome inference is immaterialist: mind, res cogitans, seems unextended, immaterial, so it is. Like pretty much all phenomenology across human space and time, Buddhist phenomenology sees the way mind seems as congenial to metaphysical immaterialism.[26]

The Ontology of Mental States

Among Western philosophers and scientists there is anxiety over the continued grip of neo-Cartesian views of mind. No contemporary philosopher is a substance dualist, but property dualism charms a few heavyweights. Furthermore, according to polls, most ordinary folk believe in something like what Ryle in 1949 called "the official doctrine." Mind or at least mental properties comprise a sui generis—separate and distinct from the physical—ontological kind. What kind? Immaterial. Immaterial, but capable of making energy transfers.

Among philosophically inclined mind scientists there are a range of attitudes about how we ought to naturalize subjective experience. Why would one care about naturalizing consciousness? The reason is simple. If consciousness can be sensibly thought of as part of the natural fabric of the universe, then we are able to avoid positing ontologically queer substances or properties, and in addition the science of mind can proceed with the hope that understanding mind and mental causation is possible.

Almost every mind scientist thinks that there are neural correlates for each and every conscious mental event (and for unconscious mental events as well). For present purposes, I use Christof Koch's book, *The Quest for Consciousness: A Neurobiological Approach* (2004), as the best statement of the state of the art of consciousness studies.[27] Koch writes: "*There must be an explicit correspondence between any mental event and its neuronal correlates.* Another way of stating this is that any change in a subjective experiential state must be associated with a change in a neuronal state. Note that the converse need not necessarily be true, two different neuronal states of the brain may be mentally indistinguishable" (p. 17). The issue of relations between the two levels will be familiar to philosophers as the problem of the supervenience relation (Kim 2005, 2006).

Throughout his 2005 book the Dalai Lama seems content with the idea that there are neural correlates for every mental state. But he rightly sees that correlations do not constitute identities. There is a perfect correlation between being a living person and having a beating heart. But a living person isn't a beating heart, or vice versa.

However, even the minimalist neural correlate of consciousness view (NCC) is not always advocated by the Dalai Lama. A good example surfaces in this quote by the Dalai Lama in an article published in the *New Scientist* in May 2003. The article is called "On the luminosity of being." Under his given name, Tenzin Gyatso, he writes:

Now I'd like to say more about the fundamental nature of the mind. There is no reason to believe that the innate mind, the very essential luminous nature of awareness, has neural correlates, because it is not physical, not contingent upon the brain. So while I agree with neuroscience that gross mental events correlate with brain activity, I also feel that on a more subtle level of consciousness, brain and mind are two separate entities.

This is a rare statement, but it is important. Here the Dalai Lama reports what he "feels." One is inclined to ask or say "So what?" The question is not about what one feels or even about how things seem, it is about the nature of things. Usually the Dalai Lama accepts the NCC view, at least the minimalist version of the NCC view: every mental event has a neural correlate. But here he expresses belief in an industrial form of ontological dualism. At least for "the very essential luminous nature of awareness" there are no NCCs, because this part of mind is not physical. My interpretation for why he thinks that at least one part of the conscious mind has no neural correlates has to do with a set of ancient beliefs internal to Buddhism. The idea or the argument—if there were one—would go something like this:

i. If real purification is possible, if achieving Buddha nature is really in the cards for humans and not simply a perfectionist goal, then achieving it will require realizing a pure potential we already have.

ii. This pure potential consists in realizing the part of the mind that is not defiled in any way by the three poisons of acquisitiveness, anger, and delusion.

iii. This part cannot in principle ever have had commerce with anything material, such as the brain, otherwise it might have been defiled by the poisons and thus lack the required potential.

iv. Realizing Buddha nature is possible, and thus we necessarily possess a part of mind that is pure, that cannot in principle be defiled.

v. What part is that? "Pure luminous consciousness," a part of mind unsullied by the three poisons and also a part that will leave no traces on even the most sensitive devices that might ever be created for detecting neural correlates because it is immaterial.

One can believe this sort of thing. One can "feel" it is true. But one needs to use the caveat to do so in the face of the evidence as it now stands. Suppose (what is very controversial) that all parties accept that phenomenologically speaking there is such a thing as "pure luminous consciousness." What is the deep structure of "pure luminous consciousness"? The scientists will say that there is no evidence that "pure luminous consciousness," assuming it exists at all, is immaterial, and that it is an inference to the best explanation that it is realized in the brain. But the Buddhist armed with the caveat can truly say science has not proven in a demonstrative manner that "pure luminous consciousness" is realized in the brain. So "pure luminous consciousness" is as it seems. How's that? Immaterial and in addition lacking altogether in neural correlates.

On some other occasion I'll write more about the epistemic status of the caveat. For now I'll simply say this: the caveat permits a Buddhist or anyone else to believe pretty much whatever they want especially if the demand is that there is disproof, where disproof means something demonstrative. You, the reader, could believe right now that there are leprechauns hoisting these very letters on the page before you, but who move too fast to be caught in the act. You can't disprove it. If the caveat required concessions when there are good nondemonstrative (i.e., inductive/abductive, statistical, and probabilistic) reasons to give up a belief, then many more concessions of cherished beliefs might be required. This point, of course, does not apply uniquely to Buddhism; it is a general consequence of taking the growth of knowledge seriously and of being epistemically responsible as knowledge changes.

In any case, back to the issue of neural correlates. Most mind scientists, as I have said, believe that there are neural correlates for every mental event. Koch (2004, 10) speaks for the majority when he frames his project this way: "The working hypothesis of this book is that consciousness emerges from neuronal features of the brain. Understanding the material basis of consciousness is unlikely to require any exotic new physics, but rather a much deeper appreciation of how highly interconnected networks of a large number of heterogeneous neurons work." He explains his strategy at some length as follows:

Francis [Crick] and I are bent on discovering the *neuronal correlates of consciousness* (NCC). Whenever information is represented in the NCC you are conscious of it. The goal is to discover *the minimal set of neuronal events and mechanisms jointly sufficient for a specific conscious percept.* The NCC involve the firing activity of neurons in the forebrain . . . by firing activity I mean the sequences of pulses, about a tenth of a volt in amplitude and 0.5–1 msec in duration, that neurons emit when they are excited. These binary *spikes* or *action potentials* can be treated as the principal output of forebrain neurons. Stimulating the relevant cells with some yet-to-be-invented technology that replicates their exact spiking pattern should trigger the same percept as using natural images, sounds, or smells.

After introducing this idea that he is interested in *"the minimal set of neuronal events and mechanisms jointly sufficient for a specific conscious percept"* and indicating that many expect the relevant correlates to be found in electrical activity, Koch (2004, 16–17) suggests that the evidence so far points to roles for both electricity and biochemistry:

It is possible that the NCC are not expressed in the spiking activity of some neurons but, perhaps, in the concentration of free, intracellular calcium ions in the postsynaptic dendrites of their target cells. The proposition that the NCC are closely related to subcellular processes is not as outlandish as it may sound. Cellular biophysicists have realized over the past years that the distribution of calcium ions within neurons represents a crucial variable for processing and storing information. Calcium ions enter spines and dendrites through voltage-gated channels. This, along with their diffusion, buffering, and release from intracellular stores, leads to rapid local modulations of the calcium concentration. The concentration of calcium can, in turn, influence the membrane potential (via calcium-dependent membrane conductances) and—by binding to buffers and enzymes—turn on or off intracellular signaling pathways that initiate plasticity and form the basis of learning. The dynamics of calcium in thick dendrites and cell bodies spans the right time scale (on the order of hundreds of milliseconds) for perception. Indeed, it has been established experimentally in the cricket that the concentration of free, intracellular calcium in the omega interneuron correlates well with the degree of auditory masking, a time-dependent modulation of auditory sensitivity in these animals.

The fact that Koch—like most other wise naturalists—is hunting in these two spaces, one electrical, the other biochemical, is important. It means that we need to remember that even the best contemporary scientific work does not yet reveal how even very simple conscious percepts, seeing a red patch, seeing a particular bent paper clip, are realized.

Nonetheless, like me, Koch thinks that the weight of all the science taken together requires as an inference to the best explanation that (1) consciousness is not epiphenomenal; conscious mental events that are fully neurally realized as experiences do interesting causal work: I decide to go to the movies and I go; (2) that eventually "a theory that bridges the explanatory gap, that explains why activity in a subset of neurons is the basis of (or, perhaps, is identical to) some particular feeling, is required" (pp. 18–19). One reason to hope that the explanatory gap can be closed is that if it is not, we are left (unless science comes up with radically new laws) with no way to explain mental causation and thus to keep consciousness from, in fact, being epiphenomenal.[28]

In any case, in the most recent iterations of the dialog between Buddhism and mind science, with the one notable exception concerning "pure luminous consciousness," the Dalai Lama seems comfortable with entertaining the minimalist NCC view. But he then reports an unfortunate exchange with a Western mind scientist about mental causation:

I vividly remember a discussion I had with some eminent neuroscientists at an American medical school . . . I said to one of the scientists: "It seems very evident that due to changes in the chemical processes of the brain, many of our subjective experiences like perception and sensation occur. Can one envision the reversal of this causal process? Can one postulate that pure thought itself could effect a change in the chemical processes of the brain? I was asking whether conceptually at least, we could allow for the possibility of both upward and downward causation. ...The scientist's response was quite surprising. He said that since all mental states arise from physical states, it is not possible for downward causation to occur. Although, out of politeness, I did not respond at the time, I thought then and still think that there is as yet no scientific basis for such a categorical claim. The view that all mental processes are necessarily physical processes is a metaphysical assumption, not a scientific fact . . . .In the spirit of scientific inquiry, it is critical that we allow the question to remain open, and not conflate our assumptions with empirical fact. (2005, 127–128)

To be kind to the American scientist, his answer was okay *if* he understood the question to be the following: Can mind science make any sense of the idea that nonphysical events (i.e., events that have no matter, no energy, contain no information) can affect anything? There is nothing in any science, at this time, that allows for that kind of causation. And thus if the mind has no physical properties, it does no causal work. Consciousness is epiphenomenal.

But let's interpret the question as this: Is there any problem in contemporary mind science with the idea of transformation of mind by mind? The answer is no, but only so long as mental states have causal powers. Everyone who believes that transformative practices work ought to believe that they work because of the way some mental (sub)systems can gain control over other (sub)systems. Consider the universal experience of being tempted to do something you consider wrong, recognizing it would be wrong, and not doing it. The mental, phenomenological feel involved in such a process reveals no neural texture, but according to the ontological commitments of our best science we assume it is in fact embodied. What we now know but didn't even fifteen years ago is that higher cortical areas overrule lower ones in such cases (LeDoux 1996).

As far as doing what the Dalai Lama recommends and avoiding the deep philosophical issues for now, we need to distinguish between two questions, only one of which we should now leave open. There is the question of whether mental states might be immaterial. Then there is the question of how the embodiment of mind actually works, how exactly mental states are realized in the brain, why such and such neural activity produces blue experiences rather than red experiences, and so on. Leaving the first question open requires that we accept that we are clueless about how mental causation is possible, and, what is different, what ingredients are necessary for it. We aren't clueless about these matters. It is an inference to the best explanation that our world is a natural one, that consciousness is realized in the brain, and that mind has the causal powers it has because it is so situated.

Leaving the second question open is simply judicious since we don't know its answer. If we accept neurophysicalism and subjective realism about mind as the right way to approach answering the first question, then at least we know where to look for an answer to the second question—in the brain and body.

The Dalai Lama thinks it wise to keep both questions open. He writes this just after reporting his conversation with the American scientist:

It may well be that the question of whether consciousness can ultimately be reduced to physical processes, or whether our subjective experiences are non-material features of the world, will remain a matter of philosophical choice. The key issue here is to bracket out the metaphysical questions about mind and matter, and to explore together how to understand scientifically the various modalities of the mind. I believe it is possible for Buddhism and modern science to engage in collaborative research in the understanding of consciousness while leaving aside the philosophical question of whether consciousness is ultimately physical. (2005, 136–137)

This can be done—that is, we can "bracket out the metaphysical questions about mind and matter...leaving aside the philosophical question of whether consciousness is ultimately physical." But if we do so in the spirit of thinking that mental events might be or turn out to be nonphysical and thus possessed of no causal powers, then we are being insincere. If all we were now doing in mind science was a mapping between the first personal and the brain, then maybe we could do the bracketing in good faith. But mind science is already much more advanced than that. We are now doing this sort of mapping while at the same time trying to figure out the causal relations among various components of mind and the relations among mind, brain, behavior, and the natural and social worlds. And there is a vast amount of research now about how higher cortical regions control lower brain regions, as well as the other way around. So neutrality of the metaphysics of mind is not, as William James would say, "a live option."

A live option is this: keep an open mind about how conscious mental states are realized neurally, while assuming that they are. Once upon a time there was a view that there would be neat one-to-one mappings between the phenomenal and the physical. There is still some hope for identity theory for sensations. But almost no one believes that identity theory will work for more complex states. The judicious strategy is to wait and see how the mapping goes. It is likely to be very complex, with bridge principles that will need to be invented. And come what may, no nasty reductionist or materialist will be in any position to say that consciousness is an illusion or that you don't make choices (although he can say truthfully that you have no free will in the libertarian sense). That said, the best hypothesis is that the conscious mind is the most complicated biological phenomena ever studied. It is precious and beautiful and is part of the natural fabric of the universe. There is no longer any need for bewilderment, befuddlement, or mysterianism from Buddhism or any other great spiritual tradition in the face of the overwhelming evidence that all experience takes place in our embodied nervous systems in the world, the natural world, the only world there is.

II Buddhism as a Natural Philosophy

4 Selfless Persons

The aim of philosophy, abstractly formulated, is to understand how things in the broadest possible sense of the term hang together in the broadest possible sense of the term.
—Wilfrid Sellars, 1960

First and Second Human Nature

A philosophical psychology is to scientific psychology as theoretical physics is to experimental physics. Its job is to keep the eye on the whole, on how all the experimental data fit together into a comprehensive view of what a person, a human person, is, and what a mind is and does. A philosophical psychology ought to answer questions such as these:

- What, if anything, are humans like deep down inside beneath the clothes of culture?
- What, if any, features of mind-world interaction, and thus of the human predicament, are universal?
- Is there any end state or goal(s) that all humans seek because they are wired to seek it (or them), or what is different, ought to seek because it is—or, they are—worthy?
- If there is a common natural orientation toward some end state(s), for example, pleasure, friendship, community, truth, beauty, goodness, intellectual contemplation, are these ends mutually consistent? If not, must one choose a single dominant end? Does our nature not only provide the end(s), but also a way of ordering and prioritizing them, as well as a preferred ratio among them that produces some sort of equilibrium?
- How conducive is following our nature to actually producing what we naturally seek, or what is different, sensibly ought to seek? Could it be that not everything we seek—not even pleasant experiences or truth—is good for us?

• What is the relation between our first nature, our given human nature, and our second nature, our cultured nature?

• Does first nature continue in contemporary worlds, in new ecologies, to achieve its original ends? If so, is first nature also well suited to achieving new, culturally discovered, or what is different, created ends

• Is second nature constructed precisely for the achievement of variable, culturally discovered or created ends that first nature is ill-equipped to achieve?

• Do different societies construct/develop second nature in order to enhance first nature and/or to moderate and modify, possibly to eliminate, certain seeds in our first nature that can work against that very (first) nature and/or against our second nature and our cultured ends, which our second nature is intended to help us achieve?

Here I begin to discuss the Buddhist answers to these questions. Buddhist philosophical psychology is especially interesting to Westerners because Buddhists deny (or so it is said) that there are any such things as persons or selves (atman) while offering advice, philosophical therapy, about how best to live a good and meaningful life as a person. How a nonperson without a self lives a good human life, how a nonperson with no self lives morally and meaningfully and achieves enlightenment or awakening, is deliciously puzzling. I'll explain how nonpersons flourish, and achieve, or might achieve, the stable dynamic state I call eudaimonia^{Buddha}.

My interpretive strategy assumes this: Aristotle was right that all people at all times seek to flourish, to find fulfillment, to achieve eudaimonia, but that people disagree about what it is. People also disagree about whether flourishing is personal or impersonal, subjective or objective, whether it is something that individuals or groups that are flourishing are necessarily conscious of or not, and whether there is such a thing as actually achieving flourishing or whether flourishing is invariably a process and a matter of degree.

When Aristotle said that eudaimonia was what everyone seeks but that they disagree about what it is, he had in mind disagreements internal to the Greek situation about whether pleasure, money, reputation, contemplation, or a life of reason and virtue bring or, what is different, make up eudaimonia. And he thought that he could give an argument internal to the logic of his tradition that favored the last answer: reason and virtue. The problem repeats, however, across traditions. Thus I use—and recommend that others doing comparative work use—a superscripting strategy, eudaimonia^{Buddha}, eudaimonia^{Aristotle}, eudaimonia^{Hedonist}, to distinguish between conceptions of the good life. The superscripting strategy allows us to draw distinctions or contrasts between conceptions of eudaimonia such as this:

• Eudaimonia^{Aristotle} = an active life of reason and virtue where the major virtues are courage, justice, temperance, wisdom, generosity, wit, friendliness, truthfulness, magnificence (lavish philanthropy), and greatness of soul (believing that one is deserving of honor if one really is deserving of honor).

• Eudaimonia$^{Buddha:}$ = a stable sense of serenity and contentment (not the sort of happy-happy-joy-joy-click-your-heels feeling state that is widely sought and promoted in the West as the best kind of happiness), where this serene and contented state is caused or constituted by enlightenment (bodhi)/wisdom (prajna) and virtue (sila, karuna) and meditation or mindfulness (samadhi). Wisdom consists of deeply absorbed (intellectually and meditatively) knowledge of impermanence, the causal interconnectedness of everything, that everything (buildings, plants, animals, stars) lacks immutable essences (emptiness), and, what follows from these, that I am anatman, a passing person, a person who passes, a process or unfolding that is known by a proper name, but that changes at every moment, until it passes from the realm of being altogether. The major virtues are these four conventional ones: right resolve (aiming to accomplish what is good without lust, avarice, and ill will), right livelihood (work that does not harm sentient beings, directly or indirectly), right speech (truth telling and not gossiping), right action (no killing, no sexual misconduct, no intoxicants), as well as these four exceptional virtues: compassion, lovingkindness, sympathetic joy, and equanimity.

Atman and Anatman

I should explain what a person^{Buddha} is and is not, and how a person^{Buddha} is possible given that there are no selves. Although Buddhists are said to deny that there are persons and selves or persons with selves, this is not really so. Or better, it is so, but the devil is in the details. When properly interpreted, Buddhists believe that there are persons, and that talk of persons and selves is harmless so long as we recognize that *person* and *self* refer to something, a pattern that is conventionally useful but that does not name anything "ultimate" or "really real." Some kinds of persons, eternal persons, and some kinds of selves, indestructible transcendental egos or immortal souls, do not exist at all, but Heraclitean selves do exist. Heraclitean selves are like Heraclitean rivers where both subsist in a Heraclitean universe. We are

Heraclitean selves (or, as I will soon say, Lockean selves) living in a Heraclitean universe. Heraclitus said you cannot step into the same river twice. Both you and the river will have changed between t1 and t2, whatever the interval. Does this mean there is no river and no you? Of course not. I have stepped into the Eno River numerous times. The water in the Eno, the cells on the surface of my skin, my age, and my state of mind were different each and every time I stepped into the river, which was also different in numerous hard-to-notice ways. But it is Owen who has stepped into the river each time. I, like the river, have changed some since the last time. One day there will be no more Owen and eventually no more Eno River. At that point both will have changed a lot. When the properties that make persons and rivers the things they are evaporate, those things cease to exist. That is the nature of things in a Heraclitean universe.

In trying to explain what personal identity is, what makes a self, philosophers look for what conditions are required (necessary) to account for personal sameness, and what conditions are enough (sufficient) to account for personal sameness. Sometimes these come apart: decapitation is enough for death but not required; a good heart is necessary for good health but not enough, and so on.

Locke is the canonical source in analytic philosophy for what is called the consciousness criterion of personal identity. For Lockeans, conscious memory is both necessary (required) and sufficient (enough) for personal identity. If someday I am in a permanent coma, I will be the same man (same body more or less), but not the same person, since my consciousness is missing or seriously degraded.

Locke (Book II, Section 9, Chapter 27) writes this:

Personal identity. This being premised, to find wherein personal identity consists, we must consider what person stands for;—which, I think, is a thinking intelligent being, that has reason and reflection, and can consider itself as itself, the same thinking thing, in different times and places; which it does only by that consciousness which is inseparable from thinking, and, as it seems to me, essential to it: it being impossible for any one to perceive without perceiving that he does perceive. When we see, hear, smell, taste, feel, meditate, or will anything, we know that we do so. Thus it is always as to our present sensations and perceptions: and by this every one is to himself that which he calls self:—it not being considered, in this case, whether the same self be continued in the same or divers substances. For, since consciousness always accompanies thinking, and it is that which makes every one to be what he calls self, and thereby distinguishes himself from all other thinking things, in this alone consists personal identity, i.e. the sameness of a rational being: and as far as this consciousness can be extended backwards to any past action or thought, so far reaches the identity of that person; it is the same self now it was then; and it is by the same self with this present one that now reflects on it, that that action was done.

Person[Buddha] (pudgala) is close to person[Locke] and far from person[Reid] or person[Butler], which for ease of expression I'll call person[Soul] since Thomas Reid and Joseph Butler, both of whom did battle with Locke, insisted that only an immutable soul could account for personal identity, how I am the same person over time. The dialectic in contemporary post-Lockean philosophy is between two conceptions of personal identity. Person[Locke] is not stable or rigid, although it might seem so phenomenologically. Person[Soul] is the view that my possession of an immutable soul is necessary and sufficient for personhood; consciousness detects this soul, which is what makes me who I am. But consciousness, which is changeable, doesn't constitute me as the same, it detects the underlying sameness I already possess or am. Each person is an individual who has an unchanging essence that makes him or her who they are, an indestructible diamond at the core of other ephemeral, contingent characteristics. To be sure, conscious continuity is evidence of identity, but it is not identity itself. Consciousness changes over time, identity doesn't. Strict identity, assuming there is such a thing, consists in each individual's possession of a self-same soul. A self-same soul, an indestructible core, the diamond-in-the-rough-that-is-me, holds together all that is fleeting and superficial about me, including consciousness. This is myself, atman.

One reply is this: they say that diamonds are forever. But this is false. Diamonds come from compressed coal. And diamonds dissolve, ashes to ashes, dust to dust. Diamonds just dissolve very, very slowly.

If personal identity isn't strict, if I am not self-same over time, if instead my selfhood is a matter of degree, then it is only my psychological connectedness and continuity that need explaining. A psychologically connected and continuous self is anatman.

Buddhist metaphysics privileges processes and events. Perhaps it does more even than privilege processes and events: what there is, and all there is, is an unfolding (the overarching process, the Mother of all processes, which is itself an unfolding) in which we participate. What we call and conceive as "things" are relatively stable processes or events inside the Mother of all unfoldings. The picture here is familiar from contemporary physics (which is why A. N. Whitehead at the dawn of elementary particle physics endorsed "process philosophy"). Person[Soul] is the view that what makes an individual the same person over time is each individual's possession of an immutable, indestructible essence (= atman). Person[Locke] is the view that a person is an unfolding that has stability in virtue of possessing certain kinds of psychological continuity and connectedness—for example, first-personal memory connectedness (= anatman).

Buddhism is sometimes said to be incoherent because it gives advice on how to live a good life as a good person, while denying that there are persons. But Buddhism does not deny that there are persons[Buddha] who live lives. It denies that a person—any person—is an eternal self-same thing, or possesses an immutable, indestructible essence, which is its self (atman). If you think you are or possess some such thing—a Self or a Soul or Atman—you are mistaken. If you don't think this, then you are not making a common and morally consequential metaphysical mistake. The consequential moral problem is that selfishness or egoism, despite being a commonly adopted strategy for living, does not bring eudaimonia[Buddha]. If I don't conceive of myself as a metaphysically permanent ego, as atman (which is a mistake since I am anatman), I am better positioned to adjust how I live—specifically less egoistically—so that I have a chance to achieve eudaimonia[Buddha]. But who or what is the "I," such that it—"I"—can sensibly desire to achieve anything, to be anything, over the course of a human life?

Human Nature and the Human Predicament

Setting nirvana as a postmortem state aside, eudaimonia[Buddha] is the highest good, the summum bonum for sentient human beings-in-time.[1] We are not there yet. What route or path (dharma) should we take to get from here to there? To answer, we need to know our starting point. What is our nature, what is our predicament?

The Buddhist answer is this: humans are beings-in-time who are thrust into a world in which the first universal feature of being-in-time-in-the-world is that you are an unfolding, not a thing in an unfolding, but an unfolding that is part of a greater unfolding, the Mother of all unfoldings. At each moment that you are unfolding or becoming in the greater unfolding, which is the sum of all unfoldings, you considered as a series of connected and continuous events—as anatman—have desires that you want satisfied. But your desires cannot be satisfied. There are several reasons: sometimes (actually often) one's wanting nature overreaches and asks for more than the world can give. Other times, one changes enough so that if and when one gets what one wants, one (actually one's successor self) no longer wants it. Still other times, one makes mistakes about what one wants and about what getting what one thinks one wants will do for oneself—for instance, make one happy. Then there is the fact that even when one gets what one wants one doesn't get to keep it for very long or, what is different, there isn't enough of it.

The first of the "four noble truths" of Buddhism says that there is dukkha. Some say dukkha means that always and everywhere all there is for humans (and other sentient beings) is suffering. But this interpretation of the first truth as saying that what there is, and all there is, is suffering is hyperbolic. Steven Collins (1998, 140) writes: "The translation of dukkha as suffering is in non-philosophical contexts often best, but it is misleading conceptually. It is patently false for Buddhists as for everyone else except the pathologically depressed, that everything in life is suffering." A more plausible (charitable) interpretation is this: the world in which we are thrust, and in which we live, is one in which the supply of things that can satisfy our desires is outstripped by our desiring nature. This interpretation is reinforced by the Second and Third Noble Truths, which spell out the causes of suffering as follows: sometimes there is not enough objectively as in the case of shortages or scarcity of material resources. Other times, we want more than is sensible or sufficient, as in the case of having a satisfactory car but wanting the finest there is, or in cases where there is love and one wishes never for the bloom to fade or even more unrealistically for the beloved (or oneself) never ever to change or die. And then there is the fact that we are prone to making mistakes and repeating them. Most people, even those with lots of experience on the hedonic treadmill, and who know that accumulating more wealth or stuff never brings stability and serenity, nonetheless keep seeking more and more. This is not, as they say, a merely philosophical observation or position. There are lots of data from psychology and behavioral economics that secure the point (Flanagan 2007). Dan Kahnemann, the Nobel Prize winner in economics, tells us that the biggest flat line in the history of economics is the one that measures happiness increases about 60,000 USD in income (http://www.ted.com/talks/daniel_kahneman_the_riddle_of_experience vs memory.html). Money, above 60K, does not bring happiness.

The First Noble Truth of dukkha says, then, that humans are desiring beings who want their desires satisfied. Our desires are sometimes satisfied short term. But long term, no one gets everything she wants (the picture is familiar from Freud and Mick Jagger). Things are unsatisfactory in a literal sense: desires are unsatisfied.

What to do? We can't do much about the features of the world that don't deliver what we want (at least not individually and not immediately), but we can do a lot about the features of ourselves that grasp egomaniacally, that continually overreach, that cause us to think (mistakenly) that we need what in fact we don't need, and that cause us to become angry and frustrated when our consumptive ego doesn't get what it wants.

To overcome our consumptive ego, insofar as it engenders its own dissatisfaction, it makes sense to follow the Noble Eightfold Path. The Noble Eightfold Path (see Rahula 1954/1974) is the solution, insofar as one is possible, to the problem of dukkha. The Eightfold Path contains the sort of information that one could carry on a card in one's wallet, but its bulleted form is misleading. The Eightfold Path is actually the entry ticket to an elaborate and complex form of life, to a long and winding road or path (dharma) that one will need to follow if one has any hope of attaining eudaimonia[Buddha].

To review, the project as laid out by the Noble Eightfold Path is to practice the four conventional virtues (sila) in the schema for eudaimonia[Buddha]: right resolve (aiming to accomplish what is good without lust, avarice, and ill will), right livelihood (work should not harm sentient beings, directly or indirectly), right speech (truth telling and not gossiping), and right action (no killing, no sexual misconduct, no intoxicants).

The Noble Eightfold Path contains the blueprint, a framework of tried-and-true practical wisdom for the project of moderating desires, tuning desires to be less acquisitive, less avaricious, and less insatiably consumptive, so that the inevitable shortage of satisfactions causes as little pain and suffering as possible.

The four conventional virtues are not sufficient to tune down destructive desires and to achieve eudaimonia[Buddha]. Additional precepts are required; these are usually five or six added to the original four, totaling for list keepers ten commandments.

1. Do not kill sentient beings.
2. Do not steal.
3. Do not have illicit sexual relations.
4. Do not lie.
5. Do not use drugs or alcohol.
6. Do not overeat or overdrink (i.e., eat or drink more than necessary for sustenance).
7. Do not gamble.
8. Avoid the use of immodest perfumes or clothing designed to attract others.
9. Do not sleep on high, luxurious beds.
10. Do not handle, process, or possess gold or silver.

In addition to these ten conventional virtues, one needs to attain wisdom (prajna) about such matters as the fact that everything is impermanent and that the self is one of the impermanent things (anatman). Gaining metaphysical wisdom supports the worthy aim of seeing reality as it is, as well as the aim of developing strategies and techniques for moderating and modifying, possibly eliminating, destructive states of mind that interfere with the project of achieving eudaimonia[Buddha] (Flanagan 2000a; Goleman 2003a, 2003b).

Buddhist ethics is metaphysically rich and is in that sense cognitivist, or, to put it another way, being morally excellent, as conceived by Buddhism, requires seeing things truthfully without delusion or wishful thinking.[2] A morally good person does not achieve eudaimonia[Buddha] unless she also knows a fair amount of Buddhist metaphysics, prajna.

In addition to practicing the conventional virtues listed and gaining the requisite metaphysical insight into the ubiquity of impermanent processes, including understanding oneself as an impermanent process, the Eightfold Path also requires the practice of mindfulness and concentration.[3] Mindfulness and concentration are most familiar to Westerners as meditation.

Three Poisons

Original sin, Buddhist style, consists of the three poisons of delusion (moha), avaricious, greedy desire (lobha), and hatred (dosa). The poisons obstruct gaining eudaimonia[Buddha], and they come with being a human.[4] It would be good to learn to moderate, modify, or eliminate the poisons. Luckily the universe unfolds (some Buddhists are fine with there being no overarching reason for things unfolding as they do; others posit karma to explain how and why things unfold as they do), so that we are positioned to see that our desiring nature overreaches and in particular that it contains the three poisons of delusion (moha), avaricious, greedy desire (lobha), and hatred (dosa).[5] Delusion (moha) causes us to think we need things we don't need (things that will not make us happy but that will make us suffer instead). Avaricious desire, thirsty egoism (lobha), causes us to throw caution to the winds as we seek to acquire and hoard the stuff we think (incorrectly) we want, as quickly as possible. Anger, resentment, jealousy (dosa) makes us hate, despise, and wish to crush whatever and whoever gets in the way of our acquiring what we (mistakenly) think we need in order to be happy.

Think of the three poisons as deadly weeds or as the seeds for poisonous weeds, for kudzu, which, if it grows, sucks the life out of everything in its way. The project is to keep these poisonous weeds from overtaking the garden, from sucking the life out of the good seeds or beautiful plants, or from pulling all the nutrients from the soil. If we can do this, stop or control the poisons, then we have a chance (1) to not suffer, and (2) to achieve a modicum of happiness (sukkha), or if not sukkha, then something better: happiness[Buddha]. How is this possible? By living a life that is eudaimonia[Buddha].

Wisdom (prajna) and virtue (sila) go some distance toward keeping the poisons under control and thus increase our chances of achieving eudaimonia[Buddha]. But there are other tools required, specifically concentration, mindfulness, meditation. We can understand what meditation is supposed to do if we look closely at the intricate analysis of mental life provided by the first great psychology text in any tradition, the Buddhist *Abhidhamma* (Pali) or *Abhidharma* (Sanskrit) (Bodhi 1993).

Abhidhamma, the First Moral Psychology

Abhidhamma is part of the original three baskets of the Pali canon (compiled between 100 BCE and CE 400, one-half to three-quarters of a millennium after the Buddha lived) and contains the earliest compendiums of Buddhist metaphysics. Understanding the nature of things—space, time, causation, impermanence, dependent origination, no-self (anatman), possibly emptiness (sunyata) and the like—is the basis of wisdom (prajna), which, along with virtue (sila), is a necessary condition for eudaimonia[Buddha]. But wisdom and virtue are not sufficient to produce eudaimonia[Buddha]. In addition to wisdom and virtue, a third element is required: concentration and mindfulness. Concentration and mindfulness are techniques for mental and moral discipline. Socrates says that "the unexamined life is not worth living." "A good life is a mindful life" are words that the Buddha did not say, but that capture nonetheless the spirit of Buddhism. Here is a rough compare and contrast between the meaning and spirit of the Socratic maxim and the Buddha's emphasis on mindfulness. Both aim at improving the moral quality of life. For Socrates, examination or attentiveness is directed at action-guiding beliefs. Euthyphro comes to court to prosecute his father for allowing a servant to die of exposure in a ditch, where he was being detained for the murder of another servant. Socrates asks Euthyphro why he is charging his own father with manslaughter. Euthyphro answers that it the pious thing to do. Socrates asks what the nature of piety is and the dialog unfolds in the attempt to define the terms *pious* and *piety* in such a way that could provide warrant and justification for believing that he, Euthyphro, was doing what was right, just, pious in prosecuting his father. Normally, when Socrates plays gadfly, his interlocutor is exposed as someone who believes things that are unwarranted.

Buddhist mindfulness is less dialogical in process than Socratic self-knowledge, less concerned with epistemic justification of belief, and more concerned with the intrapersonal regulation and attunement of psychic factors that motivate one's Dasein, one's being-in-the-world, to produce the effects, both intra- and interpersonal, that it produces. Imagine a Euthyphro who could explain what piety is and thereby provide epistemic justification for prosecuting his own father, but who was too invested in personally bringing his father down, with whom he had issues, as we say. Such a Euthyphro has justified beliefs but there is something weird, unwholesome about his motivation. A mindful Buddhist Euthyphro would sense this, possibly see this, and perhaps be able to say what is wrong and why, possibly change himself, adjusting his psyche.

If this makes classical Buddhism sound like a form of depth psychology, this is because—like the psychology of the Greek tragedians and the later Hellenistic philosophers (chapter 6), but probably not the classical Greek rationalism of Socrates, Plato, and Aristotle, it is a depth psychology.

A brief tour of the *Abhidhamma* reveals why "concentration," understood as acute sensitivity to the patterns that mental states abide as they unfold, and "mindfulness," understood as what Foucault calls *technique de soi*, are necessary if eudaimonia[Buddha] is to be attained. It is commonplace across varieties of Buddhism to distinguish between meditation that hones attentional skills (and is "one-pointed") and meditation that is not one-pointed but serves, say, to improve one's character or improve behavior or both (Dreyfus 2003).

The first thing that will strike the Western reader who has taken Psychology 101 (thus everyone) is that the *Abhidhamma* taxonomizes mental states into wholesome and unwholesome and, to a lesser extent, neutral kinds. This can generate the observation (really it's almost always intended as an objection) that "this is ethics, not psychology." And indeed it is. Or better: it is both psychology and ethics. The 14th Dalai Lama (2005, 165–166) writes: "The principal aim of Buddhist psychology is not to catalog the mind's makeup or even to describe how the mind functions; rather its fundamental concern is to overcome suffering, especially psychological and emotional afflictions, and to clear those afflictions."

So Buddhist psychology is overtly normative or, to put it more precisely, ethics and psychology interpenetrate. But if this is right as regards the ultimate concern of Buddhist psychology—and it is—then positivist reactions will surface and we will hear not only that this isn't psychology but also that it is shockingly irresponsible to mix scientific psychology with ethics.

There is a principled reply that can work to deflate the objection: think of psychiatry and abnormal psychology texts, or of anatomy and physiology texts, or of surgical manuals. All these bleed normativity. Concepts of health, well-being, and proper functioning are required or assumed by these fields and they are normative, possibly taken-for-granted normative concepts, but normative concepts nonetheless. Is that an objection to these texts and the fields they represent? Even engineering is normative. The principles of structural engineering enable us to build bridges and skyscrapers that last. That is what structural engineering is for. The fact that engineering is normative is not an objection to its status as science. Indeed, we like it that engineers operate with good design ends in mind. Thus the fact that the mental and moral sciences are normative, as is engineering, is not an objection in and of itself. One can, of course, criticize a physiology, psychiatry, or engineering text if it gets the facts wrong or if it imports controversial or unwarranted norms without marking this; otherwise not. The fact that the *Abhidhamma* combines descriptive as well as normative insights gathered from the Buddha's teachings is not an objection of any sort, so long as the norms can be supported by evidence that embracing them captures worthy aims, and that abiding them increases the chances of achieving whatever good it is that the norms aim at, namely, eudaimonia[Buddha].

The *Abhidhamma* is a masterpiece of phenomenology, an early exercise in analytic existentialism, which is, I think, one reason it appeals both to analytic philosophers and to phenomenologists and existentialists, although the latter is nowadays a misleading divide. And despite what the 14th Dalai Lama says about not being concerned with taxonomy, the *Abhidhamma* remains arguably the best taxonomy of conscious-mental-state types ever produced. In that sense it is analytic with a vengeance.

The book begins with a decomposition of consciousness (Citta) into conscious-mental-state types. These number 89 initially, and reach 121 after some adjustments. Each type is characterized in terms of the sort of object it takes in (so visual and auditory consciousness differ in an obvious way: vision decodes light as sight or as "seeings," and the ears decode sound waves and hear sounds); its phenomenal feel (e.g., sad, happy, indifferent); its proximate cause or root (e.g., there is greed-rooted and hatred-rooted consciousness—I have your money and I am happy; this might be so because I hate you, or I might like you but nonetheless want your money); and its function or purpose (scientific consciousness may seek to uncover the nature of things by decomposing them into elements, possibly ad infinitum, whereas musical consciousness functions to reveal or create patterns or relations among sounds).[6]

Everyday Mindfulness and Special Rx for Poisons and Other Acute Conditions

Buddhism is both analytic and deep, analytic in the way I have just been discussing, deep in the sense that depth psychology is said to be deep, when it posits motives in human nature, in persons, that are causally highly consequential but that are not always visible to the people themselves, the very people motivated by these motives. This is revealed in the elaborate analysis of the hidden, deep nested structure of the three poisons contained in the *Abhidhamma*. The three motives of thirst and acquisitiveness (basic egoism), anger and resentment, and delusion, especially about what I really need or should sensibly want—for example, if I want to be eudaimon[Buddha], which is a necessary condition for being happy[Buddha]—are first elaborated as giving rise to "the Six Main Mental Afflictions," attachment or craving, anger (including hostility and hatred), pridefulness, ignorance and delusion, afflictive doubt, and afflictive views. These in turn are roots for the "Twenty Derivative Mental Afflictions": anger, which comes in five types (wrath, resentment, spite, envy/jealousy, cruelty); attachment, which also comes in five types (avarice, inflated self-esteem, excitation, concealment of one's own vices, dullness); and four kinds of ignorance (blind faith, spiritual sloth, forgetfulness, and lack of introspective attentiveness). Finally, there are six types caused by ignorance + attachment: pretension, deception, shamelessness, inconsideration of others, unconscientiousness, and distraction.[7]

The decomposition reveals how the poisons ramify, how they mutate into, and germinate and generate, new poisonous offspring, which create ever-new obstacles to eudaimonia[Buddha]. How does all this taxonomizing and decomposition relate to concentration and mindfulness, to what we call meditation? The answer, I hope, is obvious. If you know how the mind works you are positioned to control it. This would be good, because we know (thanks to the Four Noble Truths) that you can't (normally) control the suffering that the world summons up on your behalf (the tsunami hits), but that you can control the contribution you (as anatman) make to your own dukkha and to the dukkha of those with whom you interact.

When we follow the trail of the three poisons, we see that there are many, many psychological ways by which we undermine our quest for eudaimonia[Buddha] and the possibility of true happiness, happiness[Buddha], that living as a eudaimon[Buddha] might, given certain additional favorable conditions—good luck, good innate temperament—also help produce. We will need multifarious mind control techniques suited for different kinds of mistakes and missteps. This is the work of mindfulness and meditation.

Although I won't fuss over the distinction between mindfulness and meditation here, a caveat is in order: I have been insisting throughout that the Western emphasis on meditation, especially sitting meditation, is simply not nearly that big a thing across Asian Buddhisms. That said, mindfulness, as a form of attention to the purity of one's motivational states, is emphasized across the Buddhisms. Everyday mindfulness, conceived as mental attentiveness, is often equated with meditation. Sometimes mindfulness techniques are taught initially meditatively, sometimes not. But most Buddhist people in countries as diverse as Thailand, Tibet, and Japan do not sit. Nonetheless, they will all say they practice mindfulness. Being mindful, at least trying to be mindful, is part of what it means to be a Buddhist. Compare: most Christians are taught to pray, say they pray, believe in the power of prayer, and so on. It is highly variable when, where, how, and why they pray, and whether their prayers are in the spirit of the tradition, and thus for the good of others, or selfish, "foxhole" prayers. Same situation among the Buddhisms.

Some meditation techniques are suited for everyday problems, so one famous antidote for lust involves imaging the object of lust old and decrepit or, as necessary, dead and decomposing (Sāntideva). This will not appeal much to modern sensibilities. Nonjudgmental detached thought acknowledges that normal folk might have thoughts about having sex with strangers on the subway or occasional homicidal thoughts about other drivers or rude telephone solicitors and recommends that one notice such thoughts, but allow them to pass through one's mind without judgment (and of course without action).

There are many kinds of mental discipline or meditation. The familiar practice of concentrating on the breath (for hours) is for what? A very Buddhist idea is that such attention will teach impermanence. Every breath yields to the next, every sensation I attend to changes, sometimes quickly, sometimes slowly. But always each sensation yields to another. Some forms of concentration involve trancelike techniques (dhyana) whose explicit function is practice in learning about impermanence or emptiness by analyzing and decomposing some thing or experience in thought. In this way concentration meditation yields a piece of Buddhist metaphysical wisdom (prajna), possibly two, impermanence and emptiness.

Another idea (about 50 percent certified Buddhist) is that attention meditation is for training in attention itself, which will come in very handy when one needs to figure out what state one is in and why, this being necessary if one is to effectively control negative states of heart and mind. A common view in the West is that concentration meditation is good for helping people focus at work, in relationships, and so on—part of good mental hygiene, possibly an antidote for the ubiquitous ADD, which all young males were diagnosed with starting in the 1980s, and that has now become a glib equal opportunity—young, old, male, female—moniker, and for which ironically "speed" is one answer.

Then there is specifically moral meditation. Metta meditation (metta = lovingkindness), for example, involves guided thought experimentation, pitting one's selfish side against one's compassionate, loving side. One might visualize oneself in an open field with moderate resources (money, food), with other people or a group in need of those resources. One then imagines—to one's left and right respectively—a more and less selfish version of one's actual self, one who wants to horde all the resources and another who wishes to help those in need by great acts of altruism. Normally, when metta meditation goes as planned, one will find oneself identifying with one's loving self and not with one's inner selfish creep. And this will help strengthen that positive and (now) reflectively endorsed identification.

Overall the Buddhist *techniques de soi* are similar to some techniques of cognitive-behavioral therapy, but with a depth-psychological twist, since the three poisons create mischief in multifarious, often sneaky ways. Whether meditation be focused on the breath, or whether it involves relaxation exercises, or the antidotes for lust and anger, or physical techniques such as yogic exercises, the aim of meditation is to amplify wholesome ways of feeling, thinking, and being and to reduce, ideally to eliminate, the afflictions of the mind.

The Bodhisattva's Psyche

To deepen our understanding of eudaimonia[Buddha] it will be useful to speak about the four exceptional virtues required for eudaimonia[Buddha] that the bodhisattva works to develop and exemplify:

Compassion (karuna)
Lovingkindness (metta; maitri)
Appreciative joy (mudita)
Equanimity (upekkha; upeksa).

Any person who cultivates these four exceptional virtues is a *bodhisattva*, a Buddhist saint, or better perhaps, she has entered the bodhisattva path. These four virtues are the Four Divine Abodes (brahmaviharas): "illimitables" or "immeasurables" (appamanna).

A philosophical psychology must answer the question of how it is possible for persons to get from first nature to the normatively endorsed second nature, in the present case from a first nature partly constituted by the poisons to a second nature where these are quieted, quelled, or eliminated and the expansive virtues of the bodhisattva are embodied. The answer, similar to Mencius (the great Chinese philosopher), Aristotle, Hume, and Darwin, is that, in addition to the bad or destructive seeds or sprouts in our nature, there are also the seeds of fellow feeling, empathy, and compassion. An attentive moral community works to suppress, weed, and eliminate the bad seeds and to cultivate and grow the good seeds.

The divine abodes are states of mind of the individual who has them, or better perhaps, they engage the heart-mind of the person who enacts them, and they have a unique first-personal phenomenological feel for that person. Each abode also necessarily involves a distinctive and wholesome state of mind toward others, which normally involves dispositions to act in certain wholesome ways toward these others.

The aim of compassion (karuna) is [to end the suffering of others]. The aim of lovingkindness (metta) is [to bring happiness to others in the place of suffering].[8] Sympathetic joy (mudita) is [joy at the success of, or, what is different, the good fortune of others]. Sympathetic joy is appropriate even in zero-sum games, where the one who I am happy for has just beaten me fair and square.[9] Even equanimity (upekkha) has the good of another as its object, which shows that the translation of upekkha as equanimity is not perfect. In English, equanimity can refer to a narrow state of my heart-mind that has nothing to do with anyone else's welfare, and that is not directed at, for, or toward anything outside me. My being calm and serene might make me more pleasant to be around, or more caring toward others, but it is not constitutive of equanimity, as we English speakers understand the state, that it has this aim or quality.

This is not how Buddhists understand equanimity. Equanimity (upekkha) means more than personal serenity. It is constitutive of upekkha that I feel impartially about the well-being of others. If I am in the state of equanimity, interpreted as upekkha, I am in a state that involves, as an essential component, equal care and concern for all sentient beings, minimally, sentient human beings. We might translate upekkha as "equanimity-in-community," if it helps avoid confusion with our understanding of equanimity as a purely self-regarding state of mind.

The four divine virtues complete the picture of eudaimonia[Buddha]. Perhaps with the description in place we can feel our way into what it would be like to achieve eudaimonia[Buddha], as opposed to what it would be like to achieve eudaimonia[Aristotle], or even some more familiar conception such as eudaimonia[North Atlantic Liberal Early 21st Century]. Each conception of the good life both presupposes and requires a certain psychological configuration, a neuro-biological configuration. Buddhism is better than most other traditions in spelling out the psychology and explaining how to attain it. That said, a Westerner might wonder this: What "reasoning" could lead a tradition to develop a theory of eudaimonia that entails that the best life for a human is a life of maximal service to others?

One Buddhist answer, which might not seem incredible to a natural-ist, is this: our epistemology values experience first and foremost. When experience is not transparently conclusive about some matter of impor-tance, we try to reason our way to a conclusion. Our wisdom literature is a compendium of past observation and reasoning. It is not the word of any god (we don't have a God),[10] so we do not normally go to that literature for the truth. Instead we send truths we discover by observation and reason to that literature. Our wisdom literature contains the (fallible) conclusions we have reached based on past experience. It does not tell us what is true a priori. The answer, therefore, as to why eudaimonia[Buddha] has the character it has, and why, in particular, it claims that a life of maximal devotion to others is the only kind of life that has meaning and significance, and that might bring happiness (sukkha) or, its ideal relation, happiness[Buddha] to the person who lives this way, is because it is true. And it is true because we have watched many experiments in living, many different strategies for flourishing, and eudaimonia[Buddha] is a form, possibly the only form of life, the only a way of being and living discovered so far that consistently yields true happiness, happiness[Buddha]. Among the various good ideas for how to transform first nature into one of the many possible second natures that humans are capable of becoming, eudaimon[Buddha] is a good ideal, a great ideal, a worthwhile way of making ourselves if we want to flourish and be happy. The reason eudaimonia[Buddha] is a way, possibly the way, is alleged to have to do with this fact: recognizing that I am a selfless person metaphysi-cally, anatman, helps me see that I have reason to be less selfish morally.

Experiments in Eudaimonics

The claim—that among all known experiments in living, only eudaimoni-a[Buddha] produces "true happiness," happiness[Buddha]—appears to be empirical. It would be nice know if it is true. Earlier in part I, I introduced the idea of eudaimonics, the scientific study of eudaimonia (Flanagan 2007). Studying eudaimonia empirically has proven exceedingly difficult. One reason is that a certain circularity worry looms over evidence in favor of a particular conception of eudaimonia. I do not think the reason has to do with the fact that eudaimonia is an inherently mysterious phenomena. The worry is that the confirmation bias—seeing confirmation everywhere—is almost guaranteed to do mischief when one is looking for evidence of happiness and flourishing among people who antecedently advocate and endorse living according to the lights of that conception and in addition claim (or hypothesize) that that way of living will produce happiness and flourishing, as they, the in-group, conceive such things. So that is one big problem for eudaimonics, what I call the "internalist predicament" (Flanagan 2007, chap. 4). A related problem is due to the fact that there is a multiplicity of conceptions of flourishing and happiness. The semantics of the concepts involved in eudaimonics, flourishing and happiness, are hardly unequivocal and require considerably more delicacy in interpretation than investigators have thus far shown. Indeed, I became convinced of the merits of the superscripting strategy—eudaimonia/happy^{Buddha}, eudaimonia/happy^{Aristotle}—because of a large amount of loose talk on the alleged connection between happiness and other good states of the mind, body, and world and Buddhism. Let me explain from the perspective of the internalist predicament a further reason to worry about the flurry of activity discussed in chapters 1 and 2, which is dedicated to establishing that Buddhists are especially happy people

Recall that at the beginning of the twenty-first century, and thanks largely to the 14th Dalai Lama's collaboration with Western philosophers and scientists, research exploring, and also often claiming, a link between Buddhism and happiness began to appear (Davidson 2000, 2003, 2005; Davidson and Irwin 1999; Davidson et al. 2003 Flanagan 2000a, 2002, 2003a; Goleman 2003a, 2003b; Gyatso 2003a, 2003b).

Much of this work stands in a lineage of credible work from the 1970s that claimed that certain kinds of meditation are useful in relaxing high-strung folk, and in that way leading to better cardiovascular health. But the turn-of-the-century work was overtly eudaimonistic—it claimed that there was an unusual link between Buddhism and happiness. The hypothesis that Buddhism leads to happiness, or that Buddhists are very happy, is thought to have been confirmed (at least this is so among people I speak with who have any opinion at all on the matter) and not merely advertised by Buddhists to have this effect. But that is not so. And what I have said so far explains, at least to a point, why it has not been confirmed. But there is more. In part 1, I raised various logical and methodological concerns about the claim that Buddhism has a statistically significant connection to happiness. Now we are in a position to raise further worries about this scientific research, given our deeper understanding of Buddhist philosophical psychology and recognition of the internalist predicament.

First, the research on happiness depended on prior findings that show leftward activity in prefrontal cortex (LPFC) among (mostly) American students who report being in a good mood.[11] But we do not know whether and, if so, how, being-in-a-good-mood[American] is related to, for instance, being-in-a-good-mood[Tanzanian] or how being in a good mood relates to such concepts as happiness, fulfillment, and eudaimonia. These terms are used differently in different theories.

Second, suppose (incredibly) that (1) being in a good mood = eudaimonia across all countries, cultures, theories, traditions, and that (2) being in a good mood = eudaimonia lines up perfectly with LPFC activity. If (1) and (2) were true, then we would have learned that LPFC isn't all that illuminating, since we know in advance that different conceptions of eudaimonia are different in their causes and constituents, in how they feel and how they are characterized phenomenologically. There is, for example, eudaimonia[Buddha] and eudaimonia[Aristotle], and these ought not to reveal themselves in exactly the same way in the folk who realize these differing conceptions of eudaimonia. The reason is simple: the cognitive content and the virtues involved are different. An Aristotelian has the virtue of military courage, the Buddhist (perhaps) not. Comparative neurophilosophy teaches: different forms of life, different brains, dispositions, and behavior. It would be extremely odd if theories that offer such different psychological and phenomenological economies looked or measured the same objectively in the brain. It makes no sense.

Third, the research on Buddhism and happiness is almost always on whether Buddhist-inspired meditation, but not, for instance, Buddhist robes or Buddhist haircuts or even Buddhist ethics, produces good effects. But there is no control for these other variables. Further, the good effects of meditation that are studied are often about things that are broader or narrower than anything that could be described as eudaimonia/happiness[Standard American] let alone as eudaimonia/happiness[Buddha]. As we have seen, there is research on ADD, on the number of influenza antibodies after flu shots with and without meditation, on arthritis pain, and much else. It is a truism about comprehensive forms of life that their advocates claim many good results, virtue, health, happiness. If the claim is that they produce these good results at a higher rate of return than competitors, it is, as we say, an empirical question, not settled by self-advertisement.

Fourth, much of the neurojournalism that claims to be reporting what good effects of Buddhist practice have been *confirmed*, actually reports what studies (often pilot studies) are being undertaken or, again—and even worse—what Buddhists say about what Buddhism delivers (see Stroud 2008 for an egregious example of both the latter tricks). But the latter only involves announcing once again what Buddhism promises or claims is on offer, not what it has been shown to deliver in ecologically valid settings.

Fifth, the only meta-analysis that has been done so far on the good effects of Buddhist-inspired meditation on mental and physical health over the last fifty years (through 2002)—by Ospina et al. (2007) for the U.S. Department of Health and Human Services—claims that the results are inconclusive.

Finally, we have seen how we might proceed: (1) get clear on what conception of eudaimonia is being studied (i.e., eudaimonia^{Buddha}, eudaimonia^{Aristotle}, eudaimonia^{Hedonist}); (2) because each kind of eudaimonia is said to differ in terms of the mental states that cause and constitute it, expect these differences to show up when you look at the brains of those who (are thought to) embody the relevant kind of eudaimonia (e.g., serenity and equanimity are part of eudaimonia^{Buddha} but not part of eudaimonia^{Aristotle}, and if eudaimonia^{Buddha} and eudaimonia^{Aristotle} are realized in actual people, in the advocates of each form of life, then the brains of practitioners should light up in different ways, not in the same way, as most of the research so far assumes); and (3) if the researchers are assuming that there is a state of the mind-brain that is the essence, or kernel, of "true happiness"—where "true happiness" is a normal accompaniment of all the different kinds of eudaimonia/happiness^{Superscripted}—then they need to explain what this essence is, and why we should believe there is such a thing.

Eudaimonics can and should proceed, but only if there is a clear understanding that the question of what eudaimonia is, where (if anywhere) it is located, how it is realized, and which conception of eudaimonia is the best, the real deal, is not a question that falls within the domain of brain science. It is a wide normative question about mind-world-norms-ends fit. Eudaimonia^{Buddha} and eudaimonia^{Aristotle} are only two from among several credible conceptions of the good life and both are defined as syndromes, ways of being and living with distinctive causes and components. Whatever it means to be eudaimon^{Buddha} or eudaimon^{Aristotle}, it involves a great deal more than what goes on between the ears.

This is a good way to end. It leaves the philosopher with this delicious question: Is eudaimonia^{Buddha} a good way to live and be only for Buddhist persons, or does it depict a way of living that is *the* best, or at least better than other contender conceptions of eudaimonia for all human persons? Is the kind of happiness Buddhism offers, happiness^{Buddha} and what comes from eudaimonia[Buddha], *the* most desirable kind of happiness for all persons or just for Buddhist persons? As the teacher says, Why? Why not? What would Plato, Aristotle, Confucius, Jesus, Mohammed, Hobbes, Kant, and Mill say about the picture of eudaimonia[Buddha] and the defense of it? Likewise for happiness[Buddha]. Explain and defend your answer.

Conclusion: First and Second Nature Scorecard

While you work on the exam questions, I'll give answers to the questions with which I began:

• What, if anything, are humans like deep down inside beneath the clothes of culture? ANSWER: First nature contains the three poisons of acquisitive desire, anger/resentment/jealousy, and delusion; it also contains seeds of fellow feeling.

• What, if any, features of mind-world interaction, and thus of the human predicament, are universal? ANSWER: The untamed desires of first nature cannot be satisfied. Either we get what we want, and we then discover that we have changed and no longer want it (so much) or it has changed and is not so desirable; or there is scarcity so that what we want is what others also want and thus there isn't enough for all of us. Dukkha, unsatisfactoriness, samsara are universal features of the human predicament.

• Is there any end state or goal(s) that all humans seek because they are wired to seek it (or them), or what is different, ought to seek because it is— or, they are—worthy? ANSWER: Yes. The goals of first nature, my personal flourishing and happiness, are not inherently bad. It is just that we are all over ourselves in the sloppy pursuit of these goals, and we are confused and deluded about the shape, texture, and quality of what will bring true flourishing and true happiness. We think that getting what first nature impels us toward will bring these goods. It won't. What we really want and should want (if we could see clearly, without delusion) is to flourish as selfless persons, to absorb the impermanence of all things, including oneself, and to seek to eliminate suffering now, wherever it occurs in my vicinity, where you are now and where I am now. This is eudaimonia[Buddha]. Eudaimonia[Buddha] is a condition for the possibility of happiness, not the happiness that first nature impelled us to think we want and need, but rather happiness[Buddha].

• If there is a common natural orientation toward some an end state(s)— for example, pleasure, friendship, community, truth, beauty, goodness, intellectual contemplation are these ends mutually consistent? If not, must one choose a single dominant end? Does our nature not only provide the end(s), but also a way of ordering and prioritizing them, as well as a preferred ratio among them that produces some sort of equilibrium? ANSWER: Humans seek all these things. They come in wholesome forms and unwholesome forms. Some are specified by first nature, for example, pleasure. Others such as the ways and means of being an excellent friend or making and appreciating wholesome forms of beauty involve discovery and creation. Buddhism is a comprehensive philosophy that provides insight into which forms of these goods are worthy and which not. The life of a bodhisattva or any other type of eudaimon[Buddha] exemplifies the varieties of (mostly) worthy forms of attachments to these ends. But there is no exact ratio among the wholesome or worthy ends that is the right ratio. Eudaimonia[Buddha] involves skillful means to find a satisfactory equilibrium among all the wholesome ends available to successful Buddhist persons.

• How conducive is following our nature to actually producing what we naturally seek, or what is different, sensibly ought to seek? Could it be that not everything we seek—not even pleasant experiences or truth—is good for us? ANSWER: The problem with desire is either we desire things that are not really good, either in themselves or for us, or our desire or attachment is excessive, occluding the value of other goods, becoming addictive. Practice in mindfulness is an antidote.

• What is the relation between our first nature, our given human nature, and our second nature, our cultured nature? ANSWER: First nature contains the poisons, which cause trouble if they are not watched, moderated, modified, possibly eliminated. First nature also contains seeds of fellow feeling, empathy, and compassion. The project is to grow the latter and tame the former.

• Does first nature continue in contemporary worlds, in new ecologies, to achieve its original ends? If so, is first nature also well suited to achieving new, culturally discovered, or what is different, created ends. ANSWER: Unlike Darwinism, Buddhists don't say much about what first nature is good for (reproductive success, perhaps). But like pretty much every theory of human flourishing, Buddhists see that first nature, at least certain aspects of first nature, obstruct achieving eudaimonia[Buddha].

• Is second nature constructed precisely for the achievement of variable, culturally discovered or created ends that first nature is ill-equipped to achieve? ANSWER: Yes.

• Do different societies construct/develop second nature in order to enhance first nature and/or to moderate and modify, possibly to eliminate, certain seeds in our first nature that can work against that very (first) nature and/or against our second nature and our cultured ends, which our second nature is intended to help us achieve? ANSWER: Yes.

5   Being No-Self and Being Nice

The Buddhist Metaphysics of Morals

How is Buddhist metaphysics, Buddhist wisdom (prajna; Pali, panna), Buddhist views about ultimate matters, the nature of things as they really are, connected to the ethic of compassion and lovingkindness that Buddhism endorses? Does the metaphysics logically entail the ethics? Or does the wisdom component of Buddhism give some reason, but not a decisive reason, to be a virtuous Buddhist? Or are they, the metaphysics and the ethics, epistemically completely independent but nonetheless compatible, like a black top and a white bottom, but not plaids and stripes, and this because we connect the two in imagination for utterly contingent linguistic or historical reasons? Does Buddhist wisdom require truth or can it allow noble lies or consoling fantasies?

Every tradition has to answer for itself two questions: (1) What is morality (as it conceives it)? (2) Why be moral (as it conceives it)? If there are answers to these two questions, they would come in the form of reasons, reasons that explain what morality consists in, what morality asks of us, what it demands and requires of us, as well as reasons that explain why I should give a hoot about what it requests, recommends, requires, or demands. Reasons express thoughts. So if there were reasons that provide good answers to these two questions, they would count as (part of) wisdom.

There are similarities and differences in answers to the first question across traditions, in terms of the content of morality—polygamy is morally permitted (most world cultures), polygamy is not morally acceptable (North Atlantic cultures); polygamy is acceptable, but only polyandry (Islam), not polygyny (which is acceptable in Nepal); euthanasia is morally acceptable (Holland), is not (America), and so on. The second question is almost always answered in transcendental metaphysical terms or theologically, not always in terms of a personal God who is omniscient and rewards and punishes as in the Abrahamic traditions, but by something out of this world. Something nonnatural, outside the practical world of human moral interaction, is what grounds morality: Heaven's mandate, God, laws of karma. It would be good if there were a naturalized Buddhism that was capable of answering questions about the nature, function, and reason for morality inside the natural world, not outside it.

Here I focus on the Buddhist answer to both questions. On the nature of morality, these questions provide focus: How does Buddhism recommend that moral personality/character be structured? What virtues does Buddhism endorse? What vices does it recoil from? How is a good Buddhist person supposed to behave? Regarding the reasons (if any) to be moral, one wishes to know: What reason is there to abide what Buddhist morality requires? Why should I care? What's in it for me? Why shouldn't I simply seek to maximize pleasure? What does my being compassionate and loving-kind have to do with my individual flourishing or happiness?

The answer to the reason-to-be-moral question, what I'll call the motivational question,[1] is alleged, inside Buddhism, to have something to do with seeing things as they really are, which is wisdom. The project of this chapter is to see if we can make sense of this claim.

Wisdom (prajna; Pali, panna) consists of these three theses:

• Impermanence (anicca)
• Dependent origination (pratītyasamutpāda)
• No-self (anatman)

In Mahayana Buddhism, this thesis is added:[2]

• Emptiness (sunyata)

If there was a Buddhist Credo, a proclamation statement of what Buddhists believe, it would say this: "I believe that everything is impermanent, that everything (including my state of mind) is subject to the principles of cause and effect, and that given that I am among the things-that-there-are, I am impermanent and subject to the laws of cause and effect."

Buddhists claim a connection between understanding one's own self, paradoxically as anatman—as no-self—and an ethic of compassion and lovingkindness. Both developmentally, and if and when Buddha nature, bodhisattvahood, or something in the vicinity, is achieved, diminishing the grip of the illusion of metaphysical egoism is causally connected to being good. What sort of connection is there—might there be? That's the main question.

To get a feel for how the connection between a metaphysical claim and an ethic might work, consider a sort of standard-brand Christian view, which claims that there is an omnipotent God who, for eternity, rewards and punishes conformity to the moral law. This metaphysical thesis, if believed, is highly motivating. Less obviously motivating would be a view such as Kant's that says that persons are ends in themselves and that allegedly warrants conformity to abiding the categorical imperative(s) that requires treating others as ends. Unlike the robust Christian conception from which Kant's philosophy derives, one wants to ask this question: What exactly is it about the belief that others are ends in themselves—without the belief in a rewarding or punishing God—that would or ought to motivate me to treat them as such? Since Buddhism lacks a punitive God, the question for a defender of naturalistic Buddhism is why and how believing that I am no-self, a selfless person, anatman, should motivate me to care about you, let alone to show great compassion for you, or for that matter for my future selves, which are very remote. One might suspect that the motivation to be moral does not really require or benefit from any understanding of metaphysical selflessness, because Buddhism has something more or less equivalent to a punitive God, namely, a karmic system that rewards and punishes. Knowing this will motivate a prudent person to be moral. True. But what I am curious about is the claim that the better way, the better reason to be motivated to abide morality, is via the wisdom route, specifically from understanding oneself as anatman.

Buddhism, insofar as it is discussed by Western philosophers, is usually depicted as an arcane, superstitious, and metaphysically muddled religion or philosophy, in the pejorative sense, despite the fact that Buddhist practitioners seem to be kind, gentle, compassionate folk. On this view, Buddhists have queer ideas but are nonetheless, in spite of this, morally admirable—confused but compassionate.

I claim the queer-ideas charge—especially as it regards the Buddhist metaphysic of the self—can't be made to stick. Indeed, both the central tenets of the Buddhist metaphysic of the self and the associated ethics might, even ought, if understood properly, to have real appeal to twenty-first-century analytic philosophers and scientific naturalists. This is because the metaphysic of the self is similar to the now-dominant view of the self within analytic philosophy and cognitive science, and thus it aligns nicely with scientific naturalism. Furthermore, the moral perspective is compelling in its own right. There are arguments, as we philosophers say, for the view that love is a great good, perhaps the highest good, for the view that we flourish only if we are compassionate and lovingkind. Living this way is not good because the Son of God reported that his Father said so. Love is the greatest good for finite human beings because only in love can creatures such as us flourish and find happiness. Or perhaps, if not "only in love" do we flourish; love is a tried-and-true, fairly reliable route to flourishing.

Plato and the Bodhisattva

In the "Allegory of the Cave" in the *Republic*, Plato raises this motivational problem: Why would anyone who escapes the cave of ordinary habita-tion—the dark and dank world of shadow and illusion—and who sees THE GOOD—represented famously by the (initially) blinding light of the Sun—ever go back to help less fortunate souls out and into the light? Plato never offers a satisfactory answer. We are left with the impression that some phi-losopher kings will choose to go back (actually, "the necks" of those who reenter "are turned"—but let's assume this increases their motivation rather than forces them totally against their will). One possibility is that some-thing they see, when they see THE GOOD—some feature of THE GOOD they detect—motivates them to return to help others escape from the world of shadow and illusion. But it is hard to understand what it is about seeing or recognizing THE GOOD that would be motivating (it is the same prob-lem as thinking that everyone is an end deserving of respect, on the one hand, and wanting to treat them as such, on the other hand). In the *Sympo-sium* and the *Phaedrus*, Plato provides a way of explaining enhanced moral motivation, without requiring any "neck turning." When the wise person sights THE BEAUTIFUL, as well as THE GOOD, deep love (Eros) is activated. Since love, especially erotic love, is inherently conative, the source of moral motivation is easier to understand and explain.

Early Buddhists pose exactly the same problem. Buddha means "one who is enlightened or awakened." Among enlightened or awakened souls some, the arahant—people we might call saints or holy persons—stay in the light once they find their soul illuminated and work at their own spiritual perfection. Others, the bodhisattvas—now "awake"—dedicate themselves to lovingly waking others from the illusory and nightmarish dreamworld of ordinary existence.

Whether one admires the arahant or bodhisattva more is one way of marking the distinction between some varieties of Theravada and Mahay-ana Buddhism. Both ideal characters are wise and compassionate and mind-ful, these being constitutive of a person who flourishes Buddhist style. The difference is that the arahant is filled with and feels deep compassion, but he doesn't necessarily act on his compassion. The bodhisattva does.[3]

Just as Plato doesn't explain satisfactorily why some philosopher kings go back into the cave while others do not, Buddhist texts are not particularly helpful in explaining why some enlightened souls are arahants and others bodhisattvas. But we are left with this much: the bodhisattva, more than the arahant, is powerfully motivated to act compassionately, or perhaps we should just say that he acts that way to a higher degree or more often, leaving matters of feeling and motivation aside. Whether we should say that the bodhisattva is more compassionate than the arahant depends on one's criteria for saying that.

Remember that the Mahayana bodhisattva takes these vows:

Sentient beings are numberless; I vow to liberate them.
Delusions are inexhaustible; I vow to transcend them.
Dharma teachings are boundless; I vow to master them.
The Buddha's enlightened way is unsurpassable; I vow to embody it.

In the abundant trash talking that occurs between Mahayana and Theravada Buddhists (often called Hinayana = small vehicle, rather than the Great = Maha vehicle by Mahayana), Mahayanans claim that the bodhisattva sees a truth about herself more clearly and deeply than the arahant, and seeing this truth motivates her to be more deeply compassionate.[4] Her insight about the nature of her self leads her to flourish, or to see prospects for flourishing in a way that makes her want others to flourish as well. This requires her to assist others by helping them on the dharma path—THE WAY—from darkness into the light, from the crazy dreamworld to wakefulness.[5] Often, not surprisingly, the first steps need to involve material sustenance, enough water and food to give me the energy to move and pay attention to who I am, where I am, and with whom I am.

The first point is this. In separate places between the fourth and sixth centuries BCE, Plato and the Buddha describe the human predicament as involving living in darkness or in dreamland—amid shadows and illusions. The aim is to gain wisdom, to see things truthfully, and this is depicted by both as involving finding the place where things are properly illuminated and thus seen as they really are. In addition, both Plato and the Buddha think that not every enlightened or awakened soul will be motivated to help others move from darkness to light, from dreamy sleep to wakefulness.

The second point, the one I focus on here, is a different but related coincidence, which I discussed some in the previous chapter: the Buddha advances a view of the self that will most likely be familiar to analytic philosophers who have read John Locke, David Hume, William James, and Derek Parfit.[6] Parfit explicitly states that for him, seeing himself as (what

I'll call, following Collins 1988) a SELFLESS PERSON makes him see that he has less reason than he thought to be selfish. And this motivates him to want to be less selfish. It isn't that accepting the view that persons are self-less logically necessitates unselfishness—and thus motivates unselfishness as logical necessity might. There seems room in the space of reasons simply to take in and absorb the insight about being a selfless person, and to have thereby made a gain in wisdom, a gain in seeing oneself truthfully, but not to have one's personal or interpersonal attitudes change at all.

Suppose I know the best way to drive from New York to Boston. This is just a piece of knowledge. It is motivationally irrelevant unless I want to drive to Boston, which is a totally independent fact from whether I know how to get there. Why isn't no-self just a piece of information, motivation-ally irrelevant unless I want to be compassionate, which it seems could arise as a desire independently of any belief whatsoever? A seizure after all might produce such a desire.

Here is one credible idea for how the wisdom component might relate to the compassion component in some actual human cases: whether the rel-evant motivation kicks in depends not so much on seeing a strict logical rela-tion between a certain metaphysical view of the person and a certain moral posture, since there is no such strict logical relation. Rather, being motivated to adopt the virtues of compassion and lovingkindness depends on the clar-ity and depth of one's understanding of the metaphysical thesis that I am a selfless person. One doesn't just have to think the right thought, but has to think it with feeling, or, what is different, to think it in the right way. That is, to the degree that one sees that one is a selfless person one will see that one has reason to be less selfish. But this will motivate only to the degree that one is motivated in advance to think/feel that selfishness is a vice—that is, only if one has a positive attitude toward being unselfish.

This is all, I admit, very complex. Assuming one thinks that one is anat-man and cares about that fact, then there is the possibility that one is moved to reenter the cave and help others out—to go to the bedside of the dreaming souls and awaken them. If this much is true or in the vicinity of the truth, then in order to understand Buddhism we need to get clearer on the meta-physical thesis that persons are selfless and then to understand what relation this thesis has to the moral claim that we have reason to be less selfish.[7]

Well-Being for No-Selves

Many have thought, and not without warrant, that a theory that decon-structs the self into a series of self-stages, and then into self-moments, and these into instantaneous, extensionless, and empty space-time points, ought to lead straightforwardly to extreme hedonism. Why not simply work to maximize pleasure in the vicinity of where I am now? If I really am "jumpin' jack flash," if, as far as my Dasein, my there-being, goes, there is no "there" there, why not be all over myself in the present moment maxing out "my" hedonic score now, in this very instant, in this me-moment? Hedonism of the present moment seems rational if I am anatman.

But almost all varieties of Buddhism say otherwise. Despite the insistence that there is only anatman where other Indic traditions say there is atman, that there is no-self where everyone posited self, this radical metaphysical position encourages even greater altruism than the mother tradition called for. To understand the relation of no-self to compassion, it will help to explain how Buddhism sees the distinction between the metaphysics of self, as seen from the ultimate perspective, and the self as practically understood, from the conventional perspective.

Buddhism advances a unique but not totally novel (Hinduism and Jainism share many components) picture of the flourishing person that involves paradigmatically attaining wisdom (prajna) about the true nature of the self (that there is no-self), which positions one to be less egotistical and, at a minimum, to feel great compassion (mahakaruna). How is this supposed to work? Does it really work?

To speak in Aristotelian terms, all Buddhist sects agree that achieving wisdom and (at a minimum, feeling) compassion are necessary conditions for flourishing, for achieving eudaimonia[Buddha]. Indeed, if we are wise and compassionate and mindful we achieve our proper function as sentient human beings. Furthermore, the person who is wise and compassionate and mindful has strong prospects for being happy[Buddha]. How does one go about being compassionate? Is there a set of virtues or a rule, akin to the Golden Rule or Kant's categorical imperative, which one ought to enact or follow in order to be compassionate? Here scholars divide.

In his fine book, *The Nature of Buddhist Ethics*, Damien Keown (1992/2001, 23) writes that "Buddhist ethics is altruistic, a form of qualified absolutism, objectivist, naturalist, and teleological (but not consequentialist)." Meanwhile, in his equally fine book, *Consequences of Compassion* (2009), Charles Goodman claims that Theravada Buddhism is best read as a kind of rule consequentialism and that in Mahayana, especially by the eighth century in Sāntideva, we see the emergence of a full-blown other-regarding, tactical, and situationally sensitive act utilitarianism, according to which a good Buddhist is an aficionado of "skillful means."

It is true that the focus of all Buddhisms is on alleviating suffering, and that the idea that suffering is intrinsically bad, is a commonality with every variety of Buddhism. That said, I mean to be neutral on this argument internal to the interpretation of historical Buddhism. But following the anachronistic and ethnocentric methodology I advocated in the introduction, I take this much from both wise men: a secular Buddhism attractive to twenty-first-century naturalists will need to have elements of both an Aristotelian virtue theory and an altruistic consequentialist theory because these theories, as well as naturalized rights-based deontological ethical theories, are blended in and favored by contemporary naturalists.[8]

That said, I do recommend the following interpretive tactic. The concern with individual well-being makes Buddhism easily understandable as eudaimonistic, where really all I mean by this is that Buddhism can be understood as a theory that gives an answer to this question: What are the causes and constituents of human flourishing?[9] Buddhism in both its classical and contemporary forms is first and foremost a theory of personal flourishing. The contemporary Thai analytic philosopher Somparn Promta (2008, 111) writes, "Buddhism seems to originate as a personal way of life." And he goes on to explain the weakness of contemporary East and South Asian Buddhism as a social and political philosophy in terms of its origins: "The picture of Buddhism as a personal way of life makes it very hard to expect political or social views concerning right, liberty, justice, freedom, etc. from Buddhism."[10]

That said, the philosopher kings who do not reenter Plato's cave, and even more so the arahant who focuses mainly on deepening his own enlightenment, on perfecting his personal holiness, should make it clear that eudaimonistic theories in virtue of being agent-centered can vary in how much interpersonal virtue is emphasized or whether is it universally required. Although the arahant can be accused—perhaps legitimately— of some form of spiritual self-indulgence, it is telling that to be counted among the enlightened souls even he must feel great compassion for all sentient beings. What doesn't seem required is that the arahant act on this feeling. But again one must give reasons for why the bodhisattva's life is better—better for whom? — than the arahant's life. The fact that every person is no-self doesn't obviously decide the matter.

So far I have said that flourishing Buddhist style involves wisdom and virtue/compassion and meditation. Understanding what is meant by wisdom is difficult and idiosyncratic. It involves seeing things truthfully, which first and foremost means seeing truthfully how the world is (impermanent) and what a person is (no-self). This, not surprisingly, can sound preposterous to our ears, so I need to explain further, and still more deeply, how I can be a person who is, nonetheless, no-self.

Two No-Self Views

All manner of confusion can be avoided if we distinguish between the metaphysical and moral theses associated with the no-self view. The metaphysical thesis is the thesis that there is no permanent, immutable, abiding self (atman) that either stands behind or, what is different, stands behind, contains, absorbs, and directs all of an individual person's thoughts, emotions, actions, and experiences. The moral thesis says that people are typically too selfish and that things would be better—indeed, we would have better prospects for flourishing and happiness—if we were less so, in particular if we were more compassionate and consistently expressed the virtue of lovingkindness.

Carefully distinguishing the two—normally conflated—theses has two welcome results:

1. Buddhist philosophy is saved from charges of logical incoherence in virtue of promoting, for example, self-knowledge and self-control while denying that there is any self to know or control.
2. A conception of personal happiness—happiness^{Buddha} that accrues to individuals, relatively stable beings of a sort familiar to Western philosophers from the eudaimonistic ethical tradition is revealed as a central aim of the good life as conceived by Buddhism.

To explain how the view of no-self might sensibly support Buddhist ethics, it is most helpful to ask about the Buddhist metaphysic of morals. Independently of its Kantian resonance, it may seem odd to speak of a Buddhist metaphysic of morals since in many quarters Buddhism is understood as providing a practical ethical system independent of any background metaphysic. This is partly due to the fact that Siddhārtha Gautama claimed to be offering practical advice on how best to live while at the same time eschewing metaphysics. But this, I think, is a serious misrepresentation. To be sure, there is some ethical wisdom contained in the Four Noble Truths, the Noble Eightfold Path (right conduct, right speech, right livelihood), and so on, that any sensible person might find useful. But Buddhists claim that you can't really get or wish to abide the view on offer—the ethical form of life—unless you get your head around a fairly, possibly very, controversial view of the self.

Buddhist ethics, as I understand it, both then and now has many commonalties with other Indian ethical theories—in terms, for example, of the virtues (doing no harm, self-restraint, and self-control) espoused. But where it broke ethically with its mother traditions in 500 BCE—for example, in greater emphasis on the virtue of universal compassion and on the vices associated with acquisitiveness—the source lies to a significant degree in a difference in philosophical psychology, in the metaphysics of persons. The Brahmanic tradition that Buddhism is both connected to and a reaction against was, according to almost every scholar, over the top as regards atman. So, not only were individuals possessed of an immutable, indestructible atman. Some, perhaps many Brahmins were asserting that they were ATMAN. What exactly this means or meant is a tricky question. But by almost all accounts it was a form of irreverent narcissistic boasting—claiming that my individual soul (atman) was one with the indestructible soul (ATMAN) of the universe (BRAHMAN).

The Buddhist break with the mother tradition that grounded personhood in an immutable, indestructible atman was not revisionist. It was radical. Indeed, it was eliminativist. Atman, the self, the soul, is a fiction. Remove it from the ontological table of elements. There are still persons who live lives in community with other persons and sentient beings, and they have personalities, characters, traits, and virtues. All that is denied is that persons possess selves, or that they are run by selves, even by their own selves, and this because of dependent origination that says nothing is self-originating.

Some say that there is no explicit mention, let alone explicit rejection of the orthodox belief that the essence of each individual comes from her possession of an indestructible soul or atman in the early Pali canon—that the explicit rejection of the atman doctrine comes later. But one does not need to be a logical wizard to see that the atman doctrine is incompatible with the view of the person articulated by the Buddha in his inaugural speech at Deer Park in Benares. The metaphysical doctrine of no-self (anatman) is at the core of the Four Noble Truths enunciated in that speech. The therapy for suffering involves overcoming the poisons in one's nature that lead one to behave as if one thinks one is a permanent selfsame being (atman) who can appropriate, possess, and keep what one egoistically wishes to own. The therapy of desire prescribed in the Noble Truths links the deconstruction of the metaphysical ego (atman) with the diminishment of moral egoism.

Anatman

Understanding and absorbing the fact that I am anatman takes one a certain distance down the road to flourishing because one sees one's nature truthfully, without illusion. The wise person sees herself as a somewhat stable, enduring part of the perpetual cosmic flux. Despite possessing a continuous and connected conscious stream, autobiographical memories, certain enduring personality traits, interests, projects, and relations, the wise person sees herself as no-self, as atman-less. Being therapeutic, Buddhism doesn't simply advocate recognition that there is no-self. One needs to absorb and eventually live this truth. And that takes time, practice, meditation, probably living in a community where the beliefs in impermanence and no-self are shared, get into one's blood and bones, and the like.

How does seeing one's self as no-self (anatman), as impermanent (annica) and empty (sunyata), as neither diachronically nor synchronically possessed of an immutable essence, help alleviate personal suffering? The answer is complicated. Suffering has many sources. Suppose I have a great meal or a great sexual experience. It is over. I have good memories of the experience but I am disappointed that it is over. Why be disappointed? It was a good experience and now it is over. All good things come to an end. Things change, I change. That's the nature of things. If I understand and accept this, my attitude to passing good experiences becomes more accepting. It is in the nature of the universe that all things myself included change. But I, this continuous being, had the experience. If it was good, I can revisit it in memory as often as I wish. That's fine so long as I don't make the mistake of wanting it again now, that exact same experience. Wanting in this way would involve a cognitive error, wishing for what is impossible: to possess what is in the past now, exactly as it was.

Or suppose I feel angry or guilty because I have been wronged or done wrong. In either case what is done is done, the bad act is in the past. I can clutch to its memory and remain furious or guilt-ridden. But why do that? Let it go with the aim of avoiding similar situations down the road. Remembering what went wrong so as to avoid similar mistakes is fine, but getting stuck in deep resentment or regret involves trying to hold to the now something that is in the then. It is a familiar fact that we can get a fair distance in screwing ourselves up trying to do this. But insofar as we succeed at undermining our own peace of mind, it is because we work to use our powerful memories to make what was then seem as if it is now, demanding that what is past now be just as it was then. This is what resentment is, grasping anger in order to feel it again. We are working to get memory to defeat time. Memory can't in fact defeat time. But if we pull out the plugs it can seem to do so, and in seeming to do so it can, indeed it will, undermine the serenity and tranquility we sensibly seek. Letting go, not clutching to my self what is in the past, is made easier—in a therapeutic sort of way—if I possess two components of wisdom: first, there is understanding that I cannot defeat time because nothing can; second, there is understanding that the self that so tirelessly clings and clutches to what is over, despite seeming to be the selfsame self, isn't. To think otherwise, and especially to hold what has disquieted my soul to my breast now is to try to work myself into something that I cannot be, a selfsame ego that can continue to hold in place now what is no longer there. What is it that is no longer there? Two things: the experience that I clutch and the self that had the experience.

One might think that one could follow the sort of advice just recommended, whether you believe that you are constituted by an immutable and indestructible atman or not, and whether one has any interest in or commitment to Buddhism. In fact, I think this is true. As I indicated earlier, traditional Indian ethics cited compassion as a virtue and acquisitiveness as a vice long before the Buddha came along, and during a period when everyone believed in atman.[11] What the Buddha claimed was that seeing oneself in the right way, as anatman, would make craving and acquisitiveness easier to overcome and in this way make compassion and lovingkindness to oneself and others easier to experience and act on.

The Emptiness Move

It was Nāgārjuna who, in the second century CE, explicitly generalized the no-self doctrine from persons to all natural things by way of the thesis of emptiness (sunyata).[12] The doctrine of dependent origination of all things (pratityasamutpada) is the doctrine that all things are related, impermanent, part of the flux, and thus in that sense lack intrinsic (nonrelational) being. Nothing possesses a self—that is, nothing is itself intrinsically, not persons, not trees, not continents, not the starry heavens, nothing. In this sense, everything is empty. The Madhyamaka (Middle Path) tradition in Mahayana Buddhism originates in philosophical commentaries that take various important sutras as their point of departure. The spirit of these commentaries is to press readers' philosophical grasp of doctrines such as anatman, dependent arising, and emptiness in such a way that they will lead to seeing that so grasping these doctrines gives one reason for unselfishness in the moral sense. Or to put it another way: Nāgārjuna presses for philosophical clarity with the aim of having this clarity gain moral motivational bearing and force.

All forms of Buddhism think there is a connection between egoism and craving and that the connection can be (at least partly) undermined by seeing that I am anatman. Mahayana Buddhism, however, criticizes Theravada Buddhism for not taking the critique of atman far enough. This happens, especially, in the Madyamika critique of the Theravadan view of anatman as not radical or deconstructive enough. The critique utilizes the logic of the original argument for anatman. We start off with what we think to be a unitary substance: the self (atman). As we examine this "substance" more closely we find that it is neither unitary nor substantial after all. What we call "the self" conventionally is in fact an aggregate of consciousness, matter, perceptions, mental formations, and sensations. Thus there is really (in the ultimate sense) no-self. Minimally "the self" is an aggregate; it is divisible, not indivisible as Descartes insisted in *Meditation* VI. This is where (allegedly) the Theravadan Buddhist stops with his critique of atman, allowing that what seems to be atman dissolves into the substantial reality of the five aggregates. But the five aggregates have self-being; they are miniatmans. That is, decomposition or deconstruction bottoms out in the aggregates. A person, a self is a conglomeration of these five elements. But according to the Madyamika critique if nothing has self-being, then even the aggregates must be aggregates of other items; even they can be broken down into further parts from which they derive their being. And so on down the line, ad infinitum.[13] To stop at any point in our deconstruction of absolute being into derivative being would be to admit that something has absolute self-being (compare to Greek atomist arguments to the effect that bodies are reducible, but only to the base level of indestructible atoms). Thus the preliminary conception of anatman with regard to the self is judged half-hearted because it only dissolves the substantial self (atman) into lower-level substantial things or selves. The logic that allows deconstruction of atman to anatman eventually yields the doctrine of the emptiness of everything (sunyata).

The doctrine of emptiness makes even more sense when we set the original critique in the context of the escape from dukkha or samsara, from suffering and the cycle of suffering. Suffering comes from attachment, attachment to those things that the mind thinks it can hold onto, rely on. The aggregate "my consciousness" remains a prime candidate for such attachment. If there were anything that had absolute being, then it would not be irrational to be attached to that thing as a metaphysical ground for living and being. My consciousness (atman) might seem to fit the bill of such an immutable, permanent thing. But it doesn't because every consciousness is part of the flux and empty. Thus attachment, excessive attachment to my consciousness, at any rate, is irrational.

One interesting feature of Nāgārjuna's argument is that he thinks he cannot stop with the negation of all being, for if he did, then emptiness itself would have self-being and thus not be subject to dependent origination. But everything is subject to dependent origination, which means that everything, even emptiness, changes. Hence emptiness has no ultimate reality either.

But here we can get help from something like Bertrand Russell's theory of types. When I assert that "All things are empty," I seem to need to assert next that emptiness is empty. But not if emptiness is not a thing. That is, if emptiness just means that no thing has intrinsic existence, is self-originating, and so on, then I've said all I need to say by asserting that "All things are empty," because lacking intrinsic existence, not being self-originating, is just what the state of being empty is or, better, means. The state of being empty is not a new thing that itself has to be accommodated by the doctrine of emptiness. Alfred North Whitehead, Russell's pal, the Anglophone "process philosopher" par excellence, warned of "the fallacy of misplaced concreteness" in his attack on substantialist metaphysics. Nagarjuna's mistake is taking emptiness to be a thing. It is not. Emptiness is just the predicate that says things don't have thingness in any deep sense. So emptiness itself, being of a different type than "things," does not itself fall to the same deconstructive logic that all things do.

I can put the point in somewhat different terms. All "things," souls, trees, houses, and so on, and all phenomena, such as even formerly stable or relatively stable processes like my continuous consciousness, are, by the logic involved, empty. But emptiness just means that these things are not stable, indestructible, immutable, and so forth. And the main reason that all things and phenomena lack these properties, and thus are empty, is because of dependent arising. One might think that in asserting that everything is empty I am claiming that there exists some new relational property (emptiness) among things and processes, which property I use to undermine the sensibility of thinking of things and processes as things and processes. And, if I think this way, I might well think that I am required to assert that even dependent arising, dependently arises, and in the same way and for the same reason that emptiness is empty. But this would be to say more than needs to be/should be said. To be sure, the doctrine of dependent arising—the idea that everything participates in the flux—undermines a substantialist metaphysic of the relata in the flux. They are not themselves things or processes with intrinsic (read "nonrelational") essences or natures either diachronic or synchronic. They can't be (never were) sui generis substances, things, or processes.

There are no such things or processes. This much saves me from one set of illusions. So far, so good. Next question: What, if any difference, should seeing that things and processes are empty make in how I think and speak? One possibility is that I can still think and speak as I did before, minus the "substantialist illusion." This is allowed so long as phenomena are still possessed of various kinds of relative stability and permanence. So now that I no longer (if I did) treat things as substantial (i.e., as nonempty), I can still point to many of the same regularities as I did before—for example, fire, itself fluxable, causes equally fluxable water to boil, which produces steam; persons are born, develop, die. Indeed, the Madyimaka critique normally allows that conventional/nominal essences remain even after more robust, metaphysically excessive essences are deconstructed. In certain Zen circles, there is relishing the return of the ordinary, the phenomenal world of people, rivers, and trees once emptiness is well understood. Emptiness undermines substantialist metaphysics; it does not entail metaphysical nihilism. The relationality among now reconceived stuff remains. It is this relationality of everything that emptiness names. But if that were true, then claiming the relationality (i.e., emptiness) of relationality would be either a sort of *façon de parler* that simply emphasizes that I really mean that everything is in flux, or an uninformative analytic truth/slogan. One reason I don't need to assert that EMPTINESS IS EMPTY as if it is cognitively significant/ meaningful is because "emptiness" is not introduced as a property anything has; it is introduced as a term that allows us to deny that things possess a property (or set of properties)—intrinsic existence—that everything, in fact, lacks. It would only be necessary to say something like, emptiness is empty, if someone really thought that the logic involved worked by surreptitiously introducing a new relational property—emptiness—that names a property itself possessed of intrinsic being. But no one who was really following the argument could think that emptiness named any such property. Since no such property is introduced in the argument, there is no logical reason to say that emptiness is empty.

One further thought: one could imagine a way the doctrine that everything is empty (without, so far, the claim that emptiness is empty) could be taken up in a way that involved "emptiness grooving" or "emptiness tripping" (1960s or 1970s, respectively). Imagine an individual who is absorbed by the facts that everything is in flux, that nothing is stable, and that deconstruction is a never-ending process, and who seeks a state of immobilizing awe at these features of reality. Here, it seems, we have some sort of a problem yet again with craving. As a matter of therapy, we might wish to say to such an individual: "Everything is empty, even emptiness." But in this case, we would not be making the unwarranted metaphysical claim, but intending to say something like this: "Look it, it is guaranteed that you are in flux and get to live amidst the flux. And it is good that you are now able to live in and appreciate the moment. But there is something wrong with your attitude. Your craving/attachment is too strong. This is probably caused by the fact that you still hold on to the illusion that you are a permanent thing that can somehow possess or appropriate the flux. You aren't, so you can't. Enjoy the flux, but stop trying to possess it."

The overall claim is that seeing your nature without illusion as anatman produces the best psychological environment to let go of unhealthy craving. Egoism that takes the form of acquisitiveness of multifarious sorts is the main cause of suffering. I get what I want—money, power, fame—and yet these don't bring lasting happiness. Why is that? Because the I, the self, who wanted and acquired these things has changed from then to now. If I recognize this in advance I will change perhaps what I want now in the expectation that it will make me happy later.

So too with destructive emotions, such as anger and guilt: I was harmed then or I did wrong then. The feelings may have been appropriate then. But holding resolutely to them now usually causes only suffering and harm. Learn and move on. You or I then did wrong, but the self now who insists on gripping the anger or guilt is a different self, the closest continuer of that self, but a later self or self-stage. I have changed. The anger and guilt then don't need to be held to my bosom now. If I think that I am at all times in my earthy career the selfsame self, then I am gripped by an illusion that makes it psychologically sensible to powerfully attach all things, pleasant and unpleasant, to MY SELF. If I can loosen the grip of this illusion about the self and thus gain wisdom, I will find it easier not to try to appropriate the world to myself, to hold and lock experience in me-ness. Egoism wanes and fellow-feeling gains a firmer grip as I see that my relation to my past and future self differs in degree but not in kind from my relations with others. The world is in flux and so am I. So are you. So are we all together. Be compassionate and lovingkind to yourself and to others. The Buddha says "Everything is impermanent, strive on with awareness." If you do things right, if you pay attention to the flux and the patterns it embodies mindfully (remember you are part of the flux), you will be wise and see reason to be compassionate, and to live a good human life as eudaimon[Buddha].

Comprehension of the doctrine of anatman and its suite—impermanence, dependent origination, and emptiness—is the sine qua non for true success in living as a eudaimon[Buddha]. Despite the Buddha's resistance to answering certain metaphysical questions (ten or twelve depending on how you count) that his disciple Malunkyaputta puts to him, his moral conception depends on the momentous metaphysical maneuver of revealing atman, the soul, the self to be a fiction. Siddārtha refused to answer questions about the origins of the universe, space, and time and also about his own fate after death. He was not asked directly, at least not early in his teaching career when these other deep questions were posed, whether he was atman or anatman. However, the overall message of the Pali canon is clear: enlightenment depends in some significant way on seeing oneself as anatman, as no-self. This is one reason I insist on speaking of the Buddha's metaphysic of morals. Insight into anatman provides some reason, although not sufficient reason perhaps, to be a less selfish person.

Was the Buddha like Nietzsche's peacock, who hid his true colors but called them his pride? Probably not. But he was a teacher who often held back in order to teach, to get certain points across. His initial resistance to discussing certain metaphysical questions posed by disciples has caused some to claim that Buddhist ethics is metaphysically disengaged or neutral across the board, and just consists of a set of practical ethical suggestions that are to stand on their own. It is not. Not at all. The consistent claim across almost all Buddhisms is that if we absorb or internalize a certain metaphysic of the self, that I am no-self, anatman, then we will be motivated or see reason to be compassionate and lovingkind.

Nirvana and Afterlives for No-Selves

Selfless persons are something we naturalists can believe in. Selfless persons whose consciousnesses continue after they die are not something we can believe in. The problem is that orthodox Buddhism is all about rebirth, sometimes gazillions of rebirths. One rebirth is too many for the naturalist and more is not merrier.

There is some consolation perhaps in the fact that virtually every description of nirvana, the ideal state achieved only by truly enlightened souls, Buddhas—when they depart the earth—makes it seem identical to what we would think of as the state of "just being dead," a state totally unaccompanied by the presence of any deity or communing with some heavenly host of (other) saved souls. Personal consciousness ends, and one's body and spirit are taken to—absorbed into—Nature's bosom. Gone altogether is me.

But it would be misleading to take this as what the Buddhist view about what happens after death really is or comes to, although I think it is what the Buddhist view ought to be if it is to make sense for us now. So something needs to be said about reincarnation or rebirth, as most Buddhists prefer to call it. Despite pressure from the anatman doctrine not to think this way, most East Asian and Southeast Asian Buddhists I have asked believe in literal reincarnation where one's soul, one's atman, or a Buddhist facsimile of atman, enters different living bodies depending on how one's previous life has gone. If your karma was bad you might be reincarnated as a sewer rat. If you live a worthy sewer-rat life, you might be reborn as a cow, ascending once again in the great chain of being. A long-term succession of good lives might result eventually in making it back to human form. Should you, in one of your human lives, become enlightened in the sense of achieving eudaimonia[Buddha], then when you die, nirvana—the state of complete nonbeing—awaits.

The Dalai Lama has told me in a private audience that he doesn't believe in reincarnation in this literal sense. This is good because the view is impossible to make sense of. The details of how reincarnation could even begin to work for a being that has no-self presents serious logical problems. Prior Indic religions as well as the Abrahamic traditions in the West have the resources, in virtue of believing that each person possesses an individual atman or soul, to make sense of reincarnation; Buddhism does not—at least not if the view involves *me* going on after I die.

There is still the problem, I admit, of charitably explaining what some Buddhists are talking about when they speak of rebirth, which they do, since I've insisted that the classical Indic conception of reincarnation is incompatible with all forms of Buddhism. Here is my best explanation. Take seriously the doctrine of the flux, dependent arising, and the like: when my body dies, supposing I am buried, it provides nutrients to the ground in the vicinity. So I (my bodily part) contribute rather directly to the lives of the plants that grow above me. Similarly, suppose, as is inevitable, that new sentient beings arise in my (former) world. Perhaps, in an analogous way, my consciousness seeds certain aspects of the lives of these sentient beings. I consciously built this house. I am dead and gone. The new owners live in the space designed and built by me. They partake, in some perfectly understandable way, of my former consciousness. Collectively, each generation seems to participate in the world as prior persons left it. There is nothing metaphysically spooky about how that happens.

It is sometimes said by Buddhists that a person's consciousness is especially likely to reappear, and in fact reappear as a troublemaker, if one dies before one eliminates the thirst to acquire stuff and to exist forever as an acquisitive being. This unquenched, possibly unquenchable thirst (tanha), becomes the condition or spark that gives rise to a new set of volitions and a new consciousness somehow continuous with the old. The standard analogy is to a row of candles: rebirth is like the wind blowing out the candle at the head of the row and causing—by its sparks—the ignition of the next candle and so on.

This simile suggests that I, conceived as no-self, as anatman, continue over the years as the original flame continues, or can be said to continue, over the row of candles. But the question is not to explain how my personhood continues over the years or how a flame persists across the row of candles, but to explain how my consciousness or the flame could continue over the years or across a row of candles once it has been clearly extinguished for a time, specifically at the time of my (last) death or during the time between my (last) death and my (next) rebirth. And the simile is of no help whatsoever with that problem.

My consciousness, as it dissolves, seeds new sentience perhaps, but it doesn't constitute or substantially survive in a new sentient being. Naturalistically, we can understand how each of us is the closest continuer of a person who existed a year ago, namely, the person we were then. We cannot understand how a new biological being is the closest continuer of the person I am after I die. We might say a clone would be such a being. But this is a mistake. A clone will not be psychologically continuous with me, and so will not be related to me as stages of a person are normally related to earlier stages, and thus will not be my closest continuer, except in a thin biological sense. In situations where a person is dead, has passed away, there are no close continuers of that person. I am gone, that person who was me is over and done with. My effects, of course, remain for a while. And that matters. Quite possibly, the effects of my life matter a lot to how things go in the world near where I once was, especially in the short term, and also for similar reasons to how the quality of my life is assessed by others. But such evaluations of the effects (and aftereffects) of persons and of the goodness of past lives require nothing metaphysically complex, certainly nothing about rebirth, reincarnation, nirvana, and the like.

Actually the Pali canon contains three different conceptions of nirvana. Call them N1, N2, and N3. N1 is the state in which you have achieved peace and tranquility because your consciousness is gone, your career as a person is over, and you are as dead as the proverbial doornail. N2 is the sort of nirvana a person who is still alive can achieve if she achieves a state of enlightenment and is no longer controlled by the poisons of egoism and avarice, anger and resentment, and delusion. She lives a life of eudaimonia[Buddha]. What is N2 like? Well, since you are not dead when and if you achieve N2, there is something it is like for you to be in N2—whereas there is nothing it is like to be in N1. In N2 you feel extreme tranquility, serenity, equanimity in virtue of having overcome or eliminated the poisons in your nature and because you live a life of eudaimonia[Buddha]. Perhaps you are also happy[Buddha].

N3 is like N1 except that in N3 you gain peace and tranquility because you reached N2 while alive. N3 is phenomenologically equivalent to N1, it feels the same (like nothing at all), but it is normatively and etiologically distinct. N3 is the reward for achieving N2 while alive, and it comes after achieving N2, whereas N1 is just what ordinary death is or brings: nothingness.

Buddhism naturalized can allow for N1 and N2, even N3, if we think of N3 as a description of how certain lives unfold, and don't add that the enlightenment that comes from living as eudaimon[Buddha] is what produces or causes the postmortem peace. That is produced in all cases by death itself. N3, on a tame interpretation, is simply a normative proposal that the best kind of life is one where one is eudaimon[Buddha] and happy[Buddha] and then dies good and happy. On this interpretation the *because* in the sentence "N3 is like N1 except that in N3 you gain the peace and tranquility because you reached N2 while alive" is not a causal *because* but a you-deserve-it *because*, as in "she is valedictorian because she had the highest grades in the class." Getting the highest grades did not cause her to be valedictorian, but she is the valedictorian and deserves to be the valedictorian because she worked so hard, got the highest grades, and so on. Likewise, a eudaimon[Buddha] deserves to die with a peaceful heart and mind because he has lived well. But, on this reinterpretation, this demythologization, the concept of nirvana interpreted as N1, N2, or N3 is completely tamed. From the naturalist's perspective this is a good result; for the traditional Buddhist it may seem disenchanting.

Fluxing in the East

Buddhism offers a path to personal flourishing, eudaimonia[Buddha], and happiness, happiness[Buddha]. Even if there is no atman backing you up. You—the person you are—are still there. Furthermore, you have a certain constancy, a personality—a character even. Indeed you must be something rather than nothing, you must have an abiding presence—not, of course, one of self-identicality over time but of personal continuity and connectedness—for the recommendations to live wisely and virtuously to make any sense.

The no-self view in Buddhism is a response to Brahmanic and Vedantic views that posit an immutable self. The Buddha's view is that there is no such thing as that self. Like Hume, he never finds such a self in experience. What he finds is something like the Jamesean or Joycean stream of consciousness. The phenomenology of a continuous stream is backed up by the doctrine of dependent origination according to which everything is in flux, everything is causally connected to other things, and thus nothing has independent existence such that it could be said to possess an intrinsic, nonrelational existence or essence. The doctrine of emptiness is the thesis that no intrinsic, nonrelational, essences exist. So when a Buddhist says that the self is empty or that a tree is empty, she is just asserting that it is part of the flux. She is not saying anything particularly weird or mysterious.

Buddhist views on the metaphysics of causation, as they consist of the doctrine of dependent causation and the doctrine of emptiness, are at the root of three related theses: (1) First-cause arguments for a deity fail, thus leading Buddhism to be nontheistic in one familiar sense. (2) Everything, including each plant, each animal, each person is in flux. (3) Things that seem permanent and that seem to possess intrinsic and nonrelational essences possess only relative, nominal, or pragmatic permanence.

Notice that the view is compatible with their being certain natural kinds. Gold is the substance with atomic number 79 and water is H_2O. There is no problem with it being necessarily true that certain types of identities obtain. But gold and water themselves are part of the flux; they come and go. Perhaps someday there will be no water. We can still say that if there were any water around it would have to be H_2O. But there isn't any of that stuff around any more. And so it is with the self, it changes over time, and someday each one simply evaporates, passes away, and is gone. Perhaps some day they all will. At that point there will be no persons, but much else may still be happening, as it did for the first ten billion years after the Big Bang, before there was any life on earth. To make human consciousness a necessary condition for the existence of things, as idealisms East and West have done, is one of many forms of egoism, a type of epistemic hubris.

One is naturally inclined to ask: Okay, if my indestructible self does not ground or constitute my personal identity, what does? Nothing does. Atman is a fiction. And personal identity is too. There is no such thing as personal identity except in the unexciting sense that at each moment in time each of us is who she is. Persons exist, persist, and endure. Who I am now is powerfully connected, via memory and my conscious stream, to who I was before. The plausibility of the metaphysical claim that there is no-self, if properly understood, is—as I've indicated—one that contemporary analytic philosophers and philosophers of mind should find attractive. This is because the view is credible. Indeed I think it is true. Still, we have not yet seen what it is about metaphysical selfishness that warrants, or gives reason for, moral compassion.

It makes matters more interesting that several analytic philosophers and cognitive scientists, including Derek Parfit, Francisco Varela, Evan

Thompson, and Eleanor Rosch, have also suggested that accepting a very similar metaphysical thesis provides reason(s) for being less selfish. And Varela, Thomson, and Rosch claim, speaking for science, that the conception of the deconstructed self advanced by cognitive science is straightforwardly Buddhist and thus gives support to Buddhist ethics. Parfit, on the other hand, claims that the ethical implications of his metaphysic support a consequentialist ethical theory independently of any prior commitment to consequentialism. Whether this is true or not, Parfit's meaning is that persons who see themselves selflessly have reason to be less egotistical, to care about the weal and woe of others, and to give more resources to others. Let's take a closer look at how these ideas are developed in Western philosophy.

Fluxing in the West

Plato indicates the source of the doctrine that everything is in flux: "Heraclitus, I believe, says that all things go and nothing stays, and comparing existents to the flow of a river, he says you could not step twice into the same river" (*Cratylus* 402a).

Heraclitus did proclaim that everything is in flux, but he did not say what Plato says he did. Heraclitus said that when you step into the same river, you do not step into the same water. Now, he would in fact have agreed that you don't even step into the same river if you require strict identity, since some properties of the river will have changed between even brief steppings. But even on the Heraclitean view, where everything is in flux, there are certain similarity and continuity relations that obtain that make it sensible to say "This is the same river I stepped into yesterday." We have strategies for picking things out on the basis of criteria other than strict identity that allow us to call them "the same." Aristotle, long before John Locke, argued that the criteria by which we reidentify plants, animals, and persons involve similarity, not exact sameness. A plant is the same plant now as it was last month just in case its biological being is continuous with the seedling it was, and so on.

Fast forward: by the seventeenth century some version of the "All is flux" doctrine was widely accepted. But still three and only three things were unfluxable:

- God
- Individual souls
- The Laws of Nature

Philosophers start to hit God (= Brahman) and the Self (= Atman) hard in the modern period, and because the unfluxability of God and of souls are logically connected in Western metaphysics, they unravel together. That said, over 90 percent of Americans still believe in God and immortal souls. Furthermore, many nonbelievers in God or the soul are very selfish. And some orthodox religious types—"true believers"—are very compassionate. This is why I suggested earlier that the relation between giving up the belief in immutable stuff (Self, God, the World) at most might create favorable psychological conditions—but not logically necessary conditions—for certain new and improved attitudes.

The assault on the self that is soul-like begins with Locke and on my preferred version wends its way through Hume, James and eventually to Parfit. Locke says *person* refers to an "intelligent Being, that has reason and reflection, and can *consider* itself as itself, the same thinking thing in different times and places" (my italics) (Locke 1690, Essay Bk. II, Ch. 27, section 9).

Locke suggests an alternative, person^{Locke}, to the theory of the self/soul that one sees in Judeo-Christian theology, and that is philosophically defended by René Descartes and later by Thomas Reid and Joseph Butler among others, what I call person^{Soul}. Locke argues that it is memory continuity and conscious connectedness that make a person the same over time, whereas the alternative view, person^{Soul}, claims that memory or consciousness is evidence of identity but not constitutive of it. What makes for my identity is my immutable self (or soul).

Even if one is impressed by Locke's view, there is still for some the gnawing feeling that there must be something that makes me the same person over time, not just at each moment in time, which is trivial, and thus that satisfies Leibniz's law . Leibniz's law spells out the necessary and sufficient conditions of the identity relation. It states that for identity to be accurately attributed to, or predicated of, any two (seemingly distinct) things, they must share all the same properties. It can be expressed formally as follows:

For any two things 'x' and 'y', x is identical to y if and only if, for any given property 'F', x has F if and only if y has F.

Someone might try to stake out a moderate position between person^{Soul} and person^{Locke} in this way: start again with the question, what (if anything) makes me now, the same person I was at fifteen or twenty-five or thirty-five? For soulophiles or soulophiliacs, it is my possession of the selfsame immutable soul. For some—maybe a former soulophile working his way beyond his soulophilia—it is a conscious state and/or recollection of a very special sort. Who I am as a person now—call this my "personality"—is different from who I was then because decades of new experiences and memories have been added, and some, possibly many of these, help constitute who I am, what I am like. But it, my personality, we might say is "pretty similar," "more or less" well preserved despite some obvious changes. According to the view I am thinking about, there is one special thought or memory that keeps reappearing, the experience of the same reflexive consciousness. At fifteen, twenty-five, and thirty-five I had a certain experience of my own phenomenological unity, call it my phi-experience. And now several decades later, I have the experience of my phenomenological unity and it is exactly the same experience as my earlier phi-experience. Each one of us has recurring phi-experiences subscripted for each of us uniquely. From some list of properties $P1 \ldots Pn$, all of them will fail to satisfy Leibniz's law, except for the recurring phi-experience of my me-ness, of my own self-identicality. On this view, it is the recurring phi-experience that makes me the same person—Leibniz-identical now to myself at all earlier ages. Interpreted this way, the view, a sort of half-hearted Lockean view, could be agnostic (as Locke himself was) about what causes the reappearance of the phi-experience, or better, what it supervenes on—it might be a nonphysical experience or be some repetitive neural event. But he is convinced (according to the view on offer) that over time I keep having phi-experiences that are the exact same experience at $t1$, $t2$, $\ldots$, tn, even if the time intervals are on the long side—for example, a decade each.

The trouble is that this moderate view—sort of between atman and anatman—is open to a deadly objection. The only evidence for the exact sameness of phi-experiences over time is that they *seem* to be the exact same experience. But the only possible justification for the view that each token phi-experience *is* the exact same experience (where phi-experience is the type consisting of identical token phi-experiences) each time it occurs is that (1) it *seems* as if it is the exact same experience, conjoined with (2) an incorrigibility thesis that is implausibly strong and transparently begs the question by simply warranting the inference from *seems* to *is*.

Consider a test of my bodily continuity that I'll call the Mirror Test. Every day when I wake up and look in the mirror I look like myself from the day before. But if I were to look at mirror snapshots from my birthday at fifteen, twenty-five, thirty-five, and so on, I would see big changes. Yes, I am the same person housed in the same body, but the body as seen in the face has changed a lot. We naturalists say the situation is the same with your psychobiological self—it changes a lot over the course of your life; you experience the changes incrementally because of your epistemic position.

You are with yourself all the time, everyday you meet, indeed you have become your own closest continuer.

We can understand the battle Locke began and that is now won, this way: there is a distinction between personal integrity or sameness and strict identity, and only personal integrity and sameness—but not identity—can be ascribed to us—except in the unexciting sense where each of us is self-identical at each moment in time. Think of the integrity of my personality over the last thirty years as being like the integrity the Charles River possesses over the same thirty-year interval. For many purposes, we say both Owen and the Charles are the same. For me it is my personality, my core beliefs, my temperament, my overall appearance that remain more or less the same, and for the Charles it is its source, its course, the whereabouts of its banks, and so on. Of course, I am a conscious persisting being and the Charles is a nonconscious persisting entity. There is "something it is like" to be me but nothing it is like for the Charles to be itself. This is a difference that makes a difference. In virtue of being a creature possessed of conscious continuity and memory I possess a personality, a narrative identity, and lots of "know-how." Natural selection endowed our kind of animal—but not rivers—with fancy reflexive capacities, some of which route through consciousness. Who I am now, what I see, learn, and know, affect judgments I make now about what I should do next, including making plans about how I ought to be and to live. Rivers, like persons, are self-adjusting dynamic systems. What rivers do without consciousness, we do with consciousness. Rivers can't be happy. We can—solely in virtue of being conscious. But neither rivers nor persons, nor their effects, last forever.

If Locke's philosophical importance is that he claimed agnosticism about the basis or source or ground of personhood—it could be brain-based or based on something immaterial—while maintaining that there is, nonetheless, something that accounts for personhood over time, later naturalistic thinkers made the next brave move. All the evidence points to the hypothesis that personal identity in the sense that matters, namely as psychological continuity and connectedness, comes from the way we are embodied, from our possession of brains and bodies of a certain evolved kind. There is nothing, no property, not even phi-experience that subserves personal identity in the strict sense. Many of us think that there is no such thing as personal identity in the strict sense, except in the unexciting sense that each and every thing is self-identical at each moment in time. There are continuity and connectedness relations that are matters of degree and make a person more or less the same over time, but never exactly the same. The Buddha worked his mind around this idea in 500 BCE.

Buddhist Eudaimonia, Encore

I've been insisting that Buddhist ethics is eudaimonistic because it is dedicated to the task of providing a theory of individual human flourishing, eudaimonia^{Buddha}, and individual happiness, happiness^{Buddha}. Eudaimonia^{Buddha} and happiness^{Buddha} require meticulous attention to the structure and content of the psychology of persons because wisdom, virtue, and mindfulness work in the first instance through the heart-minds of individuals. A moral theory that informed people how they ought to behave to maintain order, or to do their duty or meet their obligations, might not have much of anything to say about individual flourishing or happiness. Some say that utilitarianism or Kantianism are like this, insofar as well-being or duty impersonally construed are in primary focus.

There might be eudaimonistic theories that are not virtue theories; classical hedonism is a plausible candidate: do whatever will give you pleasure. Following this imperative—a categorical one—requires no complex structure to moral personality, perhaps no structure at all. But Buddhism is a eudaimonistic virtue theory. A good Buddhist person is one who possesses and displays the conventional virtues of honesty, modesty, reliability, and patience, as well as the greater virtues of compassion, lovingkindness, sympathetic joy, and equanimity-in-community.

It is a necessary but not a sufficient condition for being a eudaimonistic theory that individual human flourishing and happiness are taken to be great goods and thus central and worthy aims. I will not insist that to qualify as a eudaimonistic theory, happiness of any sort must be identified as the summum bonum, the highest good. Indeed, I think the best way to read Buddhism—and the same can be said for most other eudaimonistic theories—is in a way that makes a wise and virtuous and mindful life the highest form of life, with happiness a normal accompaniment of such a life. Flourishing, as we are asked to understand it by contemporary philosophers who work on the ancients, is a superordinate theoretical concept rooted in Aristotle's biology. Each kind of thing has its proper function (ergon); a thing is a good or exemplary member of its kind if it satisfies its proper function, if it actualizes its proper potential. A nonconscious plant flourishes if it grows in nutritious soil, in a favorable climate, with whatever amounts of sun and rain it needs, resists the vicissitudes of weather and pests by luck or its own strength, and grows and survives as a hearty, well-formed member of its kind. The conditions of being a healthy oak or cactus or orchid are objective in the sense that there isn't anything it is like subjectively for the plant to flourish, since there is nothing it is like to be a plant for the plant. This is the reason it makes sense to speak of plants as flourishing, but is odd to speak of a happy oak or cactus or orchid. Aristotle, in fact, explicitly states that one cannot properly speak of a plant in eudaimonistic terms, as eudaimon. This might seem confusing since the view on offer is that eudaimonia is best translated as "flourishing," and Aristotle thinks, as do we, that it makes perfect sense to speak of plants flourishing.

Here is the best explanation of the muddle I have come up with. Only sentient beings can find their good in, or as, eudaimon because prototypically—or normally—a sentient being's proper function is achieved by achieving a condition that includes feeling a certain way, a way best characterized as involving feeling happy or better, being happy, as this is conceived internal to a particular tradition. For Aristotle the proper function of the human psyche is achieved in the first instance by living a life of reason and virtue. The concept of flourishing is applied in the first instance in human cases when the proper function of a person, rather than an orchid or a toad, is achieved or satisfied. Our proper function is satisfied when we live rationally and virtuously. Living rationally and virtuously is what I'll call an objective feature of a person. Happiness, contentment, serenity, and the like normally accompany living this way. But there is no necessary connection. Indeed, some people seriously deficient in reason or virtue, irrational souls and morally negligent types, seem to feel happy (but see chapter 6). Unless we stipulate that happiness only comes with rationality and goodness, which seems psychologically implausible, and perhaps for this very reason simply stipulative, then we might say such folks—irrational types and those seriously deficient in virtue who feel happy—are happy. I want to allow that both a lunatic and morally evil person—even both at once—could be happy, according to some conception or other. Then there is the converse prospect: a rational and virtuous person who is unhappy. Such persons, it seems to me, are not rare. Early wounds to self esteem and/or self-respect, as well as unfavorable weather within—depression and anxiety—can cause difficulties in being happy. There are hints that the Greeks might respond in the low self-esteem/self-respect case(s) that there is a deficiency in rationality: the person who feels unworthy, but is in fact worthy, is not fully rational. Okay. But who is fully rational? And that aside, I don't see how this sort of response—the imperfect rationality response—works against cases where an individual suffers from unfavorable internal weather. Sad or anxious temperament seems neither rational nor irrational—more suited to judgments of bad luck than judgments of deficient rationality.

To reiterate: there are intricacies about the relationship between the highest good (summum bonum), our proper function (ergon), and our final end (telos). If our proper function (ergon) is a life of reason and virtue, then reason and virtue could be conceived as the highest good. But eudaimonia looks like the final end. If so, achieving our proper function is a necessary condition, or partly constitutive, of happiness. But bad luck can thwart happiness even for a fully rational and virtuous soul. On this way of thinking, we could achieve the highest good by satisfying our proper function but not have achieved our final end. Then again if we identify the summum bonum with our telos rather than our ergon, things line up a bit more sensibly.

I am inclined to say that there are two necessary, and jointly sufficient, conditions for being a eudaimonistic theory. The first is that the theory describes what social and wider ecological conditions are necessary for individual flourishing or happiness. The second is that a eudaimonistic theory commits itself to describing how the psyche ought to be structured so that an individual with the right abiding traits or dispositions and/or convictions can flourish or be happy (in the relevant senses of flourishing and happiness, in the present case, eudaimonia^{Buddha} and happy^{Buddha}) in that ecology.

It is worth highlighting that an ethical theory can claim that the aim of the good life is well-being, or what is different, happiness, and can aim to promote such well-being and happiness without qualifying as eudaimonistic. There are three main ways a theory can claim that well-being and happiness are the main ends but not be a eudaimonistic theory. First, it can so badly misconceive flourishing and happiness, true happiness, at any rate, that it doesn't deserve the name. Hedonistic theories aim at happiness, but it is the wrong kind of happiness—too low, too ephemeral, too tumultuous (see Callicles in Plato's *Gorgias*). Second, a theory can fail to be a eudaimonistic theory not because it aims at kinds of happiness that are base, fleeting, or tumultuous, but because it aims at happiness in too impersonal a way. Standard-brand consequentialism is an example. How is it possible that consequentialism could fail to count as eudaimonistic given that it explicitly tells us to maximize welfare or happiness? The main reason is that it is a necessary condition for being a eudaimonistic theory that it provide an account of what makes for individual happiness, a good and contented individual life, and classical consequentialism typically fails to do so.[14] Third, an ethical theory might claim the right kind of happiness is the aim, but think that abiding by a certain rule alone—say, the principle of utility—could make for a happy and good life. Such a theory would meet the first necessary condition but might fail to meet the second: it would not require moral personality to be structured by abiding personality features, other than whatever it takes to abide by the general-purpose moral rule it advocates.

This sentence is intentionally cagey. I am saying that more than simple rule following is required by eudaimonistic theories. "Abiding personality features" is a placeholder for what else, what more, is required than adherence to a rule. It is most natural to speak of abiding virtues and character traits. But if one says that one might be met with this objection: belief in character traits and in virtues and vices is sweet but so old fashioned. Psychology and philosophy have discovered that there are no such things.

A reply is necessary. Here's why: even if we can, as I say is easy, save Buddhism from the objection that there are no selves in the strong eliminativist sense that would require that we (who aren't either) cease and desist from offering any advice to such selves about how to flourish and be happy, the second objection that there simply are no character traits, no such things as virtues and vices, would seriously undermine Buddhism naturalized because Buddhism naturalized, as I conceive it, is a eudaimonistic virtue theory. One might think that some Buddhists might relish the joint deconstruction of the self and what it is alleged to hold, character traits, virtues, and vices, and so on. Yes, some would like this sort of eliminativist deconstruction. But it is unwarranted. There are character traits and there are virtues and vices. Buddhism requires that there be such things as virtues even if from the ultimate perspective they, like everything else, are empty. Let me explain.

The Nonexistence of Characters and Character Traits

What basic entities and basic events or processes are theories of moral personality committed to? Persons? Persons with personalities? Personalities constituted by character traits—for example, virtues, like compassion and lovingkindness, and vices, like dishonesty and intemperance? Assuming that there are character traits, are these traits causally efficacious and in persons, like area V1, which is part of the visual system and is housed in the brain? Or are character traits dispositions, tendencies to express reliably certain patterns of perception, feeling, thinking, and behavior, similar perhaps to my know-how for bike riding, which is not in me as an area of my brain is in me, but is a disposition in me that is activated by my bike and desire to ride to work on it, and that is not possessed by my friends who don't know how to ride bikes? Or, more skeptically, could character-trait ascriptions have predictive or some sort of instrumental value, but name nothing real, nothing that ought to be part of a philosophically respectable metaphysic of mind and morals? Consider: One can reliably orchestrate one's days around sunrises and sunsets, even though since Copernicus we know there are no such things (the earth moves, not the sun). Or consider: Is the part of physics committed to studying solids committed to their really being solids, as opposed to providing an analysis for how things that are mostly empty space might seem solid? Along these lines, one might wonder: What do the experts, in this case psychologists, say about the commitments of every moral philosophy ever invented—yes, every single one—to the reality of some such apparatus as reliable traits of persons, commonly designated in the moral sphere of life as "virtues"? Has psychology revealed that there are no such things? A couple of mischief-makers in philosophy say yes. But they are mistaken. I'll explain.

This sort of skeptical question is perfect for the Buddhist. After all, Buddhists say there are no selves. And if there are no selves, then there can't be any traits that such selves have or possess because there are none. But the question and the answer require delicacy since, as we have seen, there are Buddhist persons who live lives, and who possess character traits, personalities, and so on conventionally, even it they don't ultimately possess such traits, even if all these attributions are empty. The distinction between the conventional and ultimate levels helps us understand how despite commitment to anatman, Buddhism requires that there be persons who flourish—if they do—and are happy —if they are—because they possess, among other things, certain virtues. Buddhism requires that there be virtues—the bodhisattva is compassionate and lovingkind—so it matters to the Buddhist as much as to Western virtue theories that there be such things as virtues, that virtues are not fictions.

It may surprise psychologists that the debate that occurred within psychology in the 1970s and early 1980s about the ontology of traits, despite having reached a resolution in psychology—Walter Mischel, for example, is a defender of a hybrid "social-cognitive" view—and that retains a place for judiciously depicted personality traits, survives in philosophy.[15] "The Nonexistence of Character Traits" is the title of a twenty-first-century paper by an important philosopher, Gilbert Harman (2000). I take some responsibility for the fact that philosophers are carrying on this way, since I was the first philosopher to call attention to the debate among psychologists about these matters, and to claim that the debates about persons and situations had important implications for ethics, especially virtue theories (Flanagan 1991b). It did and it does. But this point—which was intended to be a complex one calling on moral theorists to speak more precisely about the nature and structure of the variety of components that comprise moral competence—opened the door to a playground where a small band of mischievous hyperbolists, really just two, have had their fun for too long making ontological mischief. Here I try to quiet the cheerleaders within philosophy (Doris 1998, 2002; Harman 1999, 2000), who say that character traits are like phlogiston or unicorns, and thus that moral theories that depend on trait posits, virtue theories first and foremost (in fact, the criticism if it were apt would apply to all moral theories West and East) are nonstarters.

In an encyclopedia piece on "Moral Psychology: Empirical Approaches," Doris and Stich (2008) write: "Initially, philosophers interested in the empirical literature advanced views that were, in varying degrees, skeptical of the conceptions of character current in virtue ethics but this skepticism subsequently drew spirited replies from defenders of virtue ethics and character psychology." In the endnote attached, they write: "The issues were first broached in Flanagan's (1991) important discussion, but Flanagan did not advance the aggressive skepticism of later writers." This is true. I "did not advance the aggressive skepticism" that exactly two "initial" writers in the text, now (exactly two) "later" writers in the endnote, namely Doris and Harman, advanced aggressively, incredibly, and with much fanfare. The reason I did not claim there were no character traits is because there are character traits. This was obvious when I wrote *Varieties* in 1991, and it is obvious now, two decades later. At that time, after examining the trait research as well as the situationist challenge to a trait ontology, I advocated a modest conclusion that both philosophers and psychologists ought to exercise care when speaking of virtues, and more generally when speaking about the nature and structure of the multifarious components of human moral psychology, precisely so that concerns of both ontological legitimacy and psychological realizability can be satisfied.

So when the "aggressively skeptical" conclusion was pressed with no important new psychological research or new philosophical arguments backing it, I expected the noise to abate amid the variety of wise responses to the hyperbole—which included some "spirited replies from defenders of virtue ethics and character psychology" to the no-character-traits claim (e.g., Annas, forthcoming; Kamtekar 2004; Merritt 2000; Miller 2003; Sabini and Silver 2005; Vranas 2005; Sreenivasan 2002, 2008). But it hasn't. The claim that there are no character traits and that psychology has shown this to be so, continues to be made despite my initial arguments (Flanagan 1991b), and despite the latter able responses from defenders of various philosophical virtue theories on behalf of the specific conception of virtue advocated by different virtue theoretical traditions.

Since I opened the door to the playground where its defenders play, I'll cut to the chase and try to make quick work of putting to rest the idea that there are no traits of character. Reference to virtues and vices, and to the aim of trying to equip agents with a good character comprised of virtues is psychologically, sociologically, and politically wise, as well as ontologically respectable. This is good news since if there were no virtues ontologically, Buddhism (like all other virtue theories) would be a nonstarter as an ethical theory.

Several claims must be distinguished: Are there any character traits at all? Are there virtues—"habits of the hearts and mind" that pertain to moral life—among the character traits that there are (like Dewey, I think that using a language of moral habits instead of virtues and vices is best, but I won't fuss over the linguistic matter here)? Are character-trait attributions, specifically virtue attributions, just instrumental devices that third parties and first persons use to predict or, what is different, sum up or describe and type heterogeneous behaviors? So that, for example, saying "I am shy" or "She is shy" is a way of telling you that you can expect from me or her some of the behaviors that we folk around here call "shy," but that doesn't name anything more than that, doesn't refer to anything psychological or inner about either one of us—the way, for example, "bad weather" names a practically informative heterogeneous kind, but not a meteorological kind. Or, finally, are virtues psychologically real and thus respectable members of the ontological table of elements? The answers are yes, yes, no, yes.

In philosophy, and in Britain, just as Lawrence Kohlberg's moral psychology program was being launched in Chicago, Elizabeth Anscombe (1958) argued that the enlightenment ideal of rule-abiding principled reasoners was distant from the way(s) good people, even the principled reasoners, normally operate, and she recommended a revival of ancient virtue theory, which was still, she thought, being deployed by moral teachers, even if not philosophically defended. Anscombe said that normative ethics might as well cease until we philosophers had a better and more credible idea of the equipment real people deploy in moral life. My overall aim in *Varieties* (Flanagan 1991b) could be read (it wasn't consciously so) as an attempt to advance Anscombe's program by making the case for ethical theorizing that is psychologically realistic. I tried to reveal how much fertile underexplored common ground there is between philosophers and psychologists, including on such issues as what good character is, what it consists in, and how predictively reliable it is. I was not aggressively skeptical of virtue talk because whether or not virtue talk was problematic depended on what was being assumed by such talk. What I did say was this: if, or insofar as, virtues or moral character traits are reified as *things inside persons* or, what is different, are conceived to be *situationally insensitive*, there are problems. If you don't commit what Whitehead memorably called "the fallacy of misplaced concreteness" with respect to virtues, and if you don't think virtues make one's character immune to deficiency in the domain that the virtue is set up to cover, then you are off to a good start in proposing a psychologically and philosophically viable normative conception. I argued that philosophers, my main audience, who work in moral psychology ought to speak carefully about the psychological equipment involved in various types of moral competence in accordance with what a judicious interpretation of the psychological evidence requires.

Simplistically we can divide communities who speak about traits, moral habits, and virtues and vices into three: philosophers, psychologists, and ordinary people. I have no firm opinion about what ordinary people think about the metaphysics of traits or how they work psychologically, nor does it matter very much whether and how nonspecialists think so long as they can acquire a morality and teach it to their charges. I understood the question of whether moral character traits exist to be a question about what the experts say are legitimate posits, not in the first instance what ordinary people assert or assume or imply by their talk of virtues and vices.

We had better hope that morality can be taught without knowing what it is (just as we assume that kids can learn that night follows day and day follows night without knowing what night and day really are or why they follow each other), or why exactly one should be moral, and certainly (because no one knows) how the multifarious components of moral competence are configured in the mind-brain-world. In any case, what ordinary people think or are ontologically committed to is not really any of my business as a philosopher. I only want to know what kinds of ontological commitments talk of traits commits philosophers to and how such talk fares in terms of what psychologists who pay attention to such matters say traits are or might be. It is these disciplines that have to make the world safe for character traits, and then only if there really are any. Naturalism 101.

So, what is a moral trait? In particular, what would a virtue (or a vice) be if there were any? On a first pass, and in the spirit of Aristotle, but also Confucius and Buddha, we can provide this schema:

A virtue is a disposition {to perceive, to feel, to think, to judge, to act} in a way that is appropriate to the situation.

Philosophers who know the history of ethics (not even all ethicists do) know that not all these components are thought necessary for every virtue. How many of these five components are required or thought ideal is variable. It may depend on the particular person, the virtue, and the demands of the social world. On almost every view, one at least needs to *perceive* that a situation is of a certain kind and then to think, although perhaps not declaratively, that something ought to be done (not always by me). I see the old lady on the bus, judge that she could use my seat, and give her my seat (as I ought to do). But some virtues, especially in an expert, may require little or no thought. I see the old lady and give her my seat. So we can imagine the schema written this way, where &v = and/or:

A virtue is a disposition {to perceive &v to feel &v to think &v to judge &v to act} in a way that is appropriate to the situation.

A moral habit or virtue so defined or characterized by this schema could be mainly, possibly purely, *behavioral*. A person sees a person in need and reliably helps (traits like being agreeable, or assertive, or being a hard worker might be better examples of traits that in some people are best described behaviorally). Such an individual gives helping no thought nor does she get emotional about the situation. Another individual sees a person in need and reliably helps, but always *feels* for the person in need, perhaps before she helps, perhaps as she is helping, possibly after she helps. A third person is (or is thought to be) an extremely sensitive detector of neediness, and *perceives* more, or different, people as needy than the first two. A bodhisattva might be like this.

The familiar but different ways that various philosophical traditions conceive of virtue track alleged differences among persons, and can be represented by the schema. Socrates and the Stoics do not think "feeling" is desirable in the activation of the virtues, whereas Plato and Aristotle think it is essential. Confucius and Mencius think we just need to grow the good seeds that are already inside us in order to become virtuous, whereas Mozi, who comes between the two, is said to think the mind is a moral tabula rasa and thus that virtues like compassion and honesty will need to be built from scratch in the way my ability to play a musical instrument is (but see Flanagan 2008). Hindus, Buddhists, and Jains all think that there are poisonous dispositions in our natures, which require elimination in order for positive dispositions, the virtues, to take hold. Iris Murdoch and Simone Weil emphasize acute, particularistic perceptual sensitivity more than most ancients, in part because of the more complex requirements of modern social worlds. The virtues of the Buddhist arahant or the Christian ascetic don't require much in the action department, but the virtues of the bodhi-sattva, as well as Confucian virtues, do. And so on.

All this disagreement is possible and perfectly legitimate because ethical life requires decisions about how best to teach the youth, to maintain virtue and order, and to live satisfying, meaningful lives in different kinds of social worlds.

Everyone has a virtue theory. Even philosophers like Kant and Mill, who are thought to have alternatives to virtue theory, have elaborate theories of virtue. But, as expected, these rule theorists think that one crucial virtue will be a cognitive metavirtue, which (possibly orchestrated by an on-guard attentional mechanism) will kick some moral problem cases upstairs for cognitive testing by the categorical imperative or principle of utility, respectively. The main point for now is that there is lots of disagreement among philosophers who advocate the virtues, about which, and how, among the above aspects of virtues—perceiving, feeling, thinking, judging, and acting—ought normatively to be tuned up or down (Homiak 1997, 2008; Sherman 1989; Swanton 2003). Furthermore, every moral tradition that works with and through virtues thinks that such tuning up or down, even building from scratch, if necessary, is possible (you learn bike riding from scratch; why not the same, if necessary, for being honest?), and thus that the virtues are psychologically realizable. One might ask: Okay, suppose I accept that honest people exist. Is their honesty behavioral or psychological? The answer is that it depends on the form of life and how it constructs virtues in its charges. Both kinds of virtues are possible and real; they are actualized in different kinds of communities.

On the schema for virtue provided above, and on the assumption that the perception of the situation as calling for moral attention (component 1) must occur with at least one other ingredient from the list, there are fifteen combinations—disposition kinds—for a minimal virtue ascription. If we imagine adding "aptness conditions" on the degree to which other components can and should be expressed, so that turning off one aspect, say feeling for the Stoics, means 0 activation, and that we can turn each aspect (of the four remaining) up by 1s to a maximum setting of 5 (say, feelings of sympathy or empathy in theories that favor such feelings), then the possible general ways of doing or activating each virtue would on the order of 1,250.

Still, what kind of thing is a virtue? The answer is that virtues, if there are any, are dispositions. But they are different kinds of dispositions. Virtues comprise a multiplicity of kinds: a virtue might involve all five of the elements or components in the schema above or it might only involve two, say, perceiving and doing. (In America it is common to emphasize these two elements as the most important.)

Much silliness can be avoided if we to remind ourselves of this: if virtues exist at all they exist as dispositions. Solubility and flammability are dispositions and dispositions are cashed out in terms of subjunctive conditionals. Saying that sugar is soluble means if sugar were put in water it would dissolve. Where is the solubility when the sugar in not in the water? In might seem natural to say it is *in* the sugar. But that is not quite the right answer. And the problem is that asking *where* for dispositions is to ask a bad question. If virtues and vices exist, and they do, they are instantiated in neural networks. A virtue, if it is accurately ascribed, names a real and reliable pattern among relata (normally consisting of states or processes in a person and the world). A virtue is not itself a thing. Nor are virtues ontologically spooky. Sugar will reliably dissolve in water, and we can explain why in terms of the chemical process that ensues when water and sugar come into contact. Sugar and water causally interact to cause sugary, nongranular, water. Likewise I have the ability to add numbers. If you ask me to add 57 and 34, I can do it. No one knows where and how this ability is housed when it is not being activated by arithmetic questions, but no one would be driven to skepticism about the reality of the ability to do addition and subtraction, and to think that this ability—because it is nowhere in particular—is nothing at all when it is not active. We are pretty certain the ability is real and is housed in neural networks in my brain.

Now one can start to see how a mistake might be made. We might think that a virtue is a causally efficacious thing inside a person when it isn't such a thing or literally such a thing. A virtue does play a causal role, and it is mostly inside the person. But it is not totally inside a person and it is not a thing. Instead a virtue, like all other character traits (if there any), is a reliable habit of the heart-mind. It has characteristic activating conditions, so that tokens of a situation type (old people on buses and subways) activate a neural network, which has been trained to be activated by situations of that kind. In robust cases (according to the schema above), a situation that deserves moral attention activates a {perception—feeling—thought—judgment—action} sequence. The full sequence goes from a situation in the world to an action in the world, and thus there are at least two components that are not literally "in" the person—although both the perceiving and the action are done by the person with the virtue (or vice). Eventually I give the old person my seat. Whether there is feeling, thought, or judgment along the way depends on whether I am a novice or an expert and on whether my form of life built me to just do the right thing, or to feel and do good, or to feel, think, and do good, and so on.

So, the ascription of a virtue or a vice is normally an ascription of a disposition that reliably activates the desired sequence. Although it is not quite right to say that the solubility is in the sugar or the honesty is in the person, it is acceptable to speak this way so long as one is careful. We say that the sugar *is* soluble or the person *is* honest or that the sugar cube or the person *has* such and such property because the disposition moves with the person (or sugar) across situations of a certain kind, and that is because the disposition is instantiated in the sugar chemically and in the person neurophysiologically; it is activated only when the sugar or person come into contact with the right activating conditions. The activation of the virtue requires that the person with (who possesses the disposition for) the virtue be in a token (instance) of the type of situation that the virtue is (was designed to be) responsive to.

So virtue as defined, or better, as characterized above is a disposition, not a thing. There is no reason for metaphysical anxiety. Reality is filled with many real "things" that are not really things. Days occur. They go by. But the days aren't things. Perhaps they are events. Love and friendship are among the most important things in life despite not really being things. Tables and chairs and rocks are things unless you are Heraclitean—as I have suggested Buddhists are—in which case they are just slow-moving unfoldings, processes. In a world conceived along event or process lines, dispositions might seem less queer. But even if you think that most things are real substantial things, you'll still need to allow dispositions, causes, space, time, and the like, to explain what happens among the things, and none of these are themselves things.

Dispositions, like solubility and flammability and honesty, have instantiations all over the place in things and in events in the world, and some things are prone to showing the disposition in active form and others not—gas is flammable, water is not, people but not rocks and turtles can be honest, and so on. A virtue does not qua virtue have location, although it, or better, its components are activated in space and time. If the virtue involves activation of a feeling (e.g., an empathic state), then this occurs at a place—in my body/brain at a time. If a virtue involves an action, this requires place and time—but the action is hardly in me, although my actions are mine. My actions involve me-doing-things-in-the-world. Finally, virtues, according to the schema, are defined in terms of the characteristic situations that activate them, so they cannot be thought of as situationally insensitive. They are defined as dispositions that are active only in certain situations. The essence of a virtue is to be a disposition designed to be situationally sensitive.

The Phenomenology of Virtue and Vice

In my work in the philosophy of mind (Flanagan 1992, 1996, 2000b, 2002, 2007), I have recommended using what I call "the natural method." In making decisions about the nature and function of conscious mental states, or states with conscious components, consult the phenomenology as well as the psychological and neuroscientific research. This is helpful in the case of virtues, because one of the many reasons to think that there are character traits and that they are psychological—unlike the disposition of my digestive system to digest food, which is a nonpsychological disposition—is because they possess phenomenal aspects. Indeed, the claim that some dispositions are more than behavioral is ancient. Before Socrates, Plato, and Aristotle made arguments for the psychological reality of virtuous dispositions, Confucius and Mencius in China and Buddha on the Indian subcontinent, provided phenomenological evidence for their reality. Mencius claims that everyone (even Hitler, we might say) will feel himself moved (emotionally and physically) to want to rescue a child falling into a well (*Mencius*, 2A6). This is a protomoral disposition that is recognizable as psychologically real. If we wished, we could measure what is going on in the body and the brain of people who have the Mencian (pre-)disposition. To explain how or why this disposition to save the child is activated without training (assuming it is), we would need to go to evolutionary biology. The reason the phenomenology matters is that it adds credence to all the other evidence that character traits are real: it feels like something to have that child-saving urge that may be felt recognizably by simply hearing about it, just as it feels like something to be shy or to experience lust. President Jimmy Carter once told a *Playboy* interviewer that he experienced "lust in his heart" and not just for his wife Rosalyn. Most normal people are familiar with the feel and the activation conditions of sexy thoughts and feelings. It does not require expertise in rocket science to explain why humans are reliably disposed to feel, think, and wish to act on these desires. Whether one's sexual disposition becomes a virtue or a vice depends on how the person and her moral community manage to structure the natural psychological economy of the underlying disposition. In any case, the possibility that character-trait descriptions are simply descriptively and/or predictively useful summary statements of behavioral tendencies is belied in many cases by the phenomenology. One doesn't just act honestly or compassionately or sexually. Activation of these dispositions normally—especially in moral ecologies that pull for the feeling to accompany the behavior—involves a robust and distinctive phenomenology.

So, the character-trait skeptics cannot win on the metaphysics or the phenomenology. They sometimes act as if they can win based on the empirical evidence. But this is not so. Walter Mischel (1968) challenged the ability of personality psychology to reliably predict and, what is different, to explain behavior on the basis of trait ascriptions, citing a low *correlation coefficient*. A correlation coefficient is the statistic that describes the degree to which traits and behavior are correlated (and ranges from -1 and +1). The correlation coefficient is a measure of actual effect size, which is a different and stronger measure than statistical significance, which is a measure of how unlikely relative to chance a result is. Mischel claimed that the average value for the correlation coefficient between traits and behavior using personality tests was 0.30. Nisbett and Ross (1980) put the number at 0.40. The idea is that both numbers are pathetically low. But they aren't. They are quite high.

Suppose chance would yield 50 percent accuracy in guessing what person P will do in S, where S is a high-stakes situation where dishonesty will pay. A prediction of what P will do in S based on information about a trait—for example, honest or dishonest—with a correlation coefficient of 0.40 will improve one's accuracy by 20 percent. That is, using the trait information gathered by valid and reliable testing (not just any old person's opinion) will increase accuracy in prediction to the level of accuracy 70 percent of the time (Funder 2001, 81; Hemphill 2003).

A standard move is to say this: "Well, that still leaves 30 percent of the time that you won't predict correctly using trait ascriptions, and this missing 30 percent must be explained by the situation." But there is a misstep here. First, one cannot determine the power of situations, or whatever the main cause(s) is or might be, by subtraction. Second, it is incorrect to frame the debate so that it seems to be about the degree to which the situation or the trait (or set of traits)—in our case, a virtue or vice—does more of the explaining. Although it is commonplace to take the lesson of famous social psychological experiments to show that the situation overpowers the person and her traits, it is entirely possible that the so-called missing variance can just as easily be explained by other personality traits as by features of the situations. Third, no reasonable person would deny that situations might in fact overpower a disposition. There are abundant examples: sugar is soluble means sugar dissolves in water, but sugar in ice (= water) doesn't display its solubility. Why not? Slow down the motion of the water molecules and the dissolution doesn't happen normally. Fourth, when classic experiments (obedience to authority, bystander effects) are reanalyzed algebraically, converting the social psychological statistics to a correlation coefficient, which measures the relation between features such as degree of isolation in Milgram-type experiments or the number of bystanders in Samaritan-type experiments, these features have a correlation coefficient of 0.40. So knowing about these aspects of the situations will yield the same sort of increase in predictive power as knowing about traits. That is, the predictive value of these specific features (isolation; number of bystanders) of these unusual situations, which social psychologists know antecedently produce odd effects, is about the same as the average predictive value of trait attributions. I have heard no philosopher make these points. I do, because they matter. Both situations and traits are real—they must be to get these real effects. And no one would be led to be a situation skeptic based on the fact that very refined analysis of the kinds of situations or the aspects of situations (like the water that is ice) that produce unexpected results yields predictive accuracy with 30 percent misses. That is, no one (happily) is led to be a situation skeptic based on a 0.40 correlation coefficient in cases where our intuitions are strong that the situation must be doing the mother lode of causal work.

Debates about the relative causal efficacy of traits versus situations involve a comparison of the relative causal power of two kinds of causes, where both exist. There are traits and there are situations. They interact. End of story. Any questions about the phenomenology, robustness, globality, and causal efficacy of character traits are empirical questions that ought to be discussed and evaluated on a case-by-case basis. Such questions are not questions about which philosophers' opinions carry any weight. The upshot is this: the argument about the nonexistence of character traits is much ado about nothing. It fills a niche that (still) deserves to remain empty.

In *Varieties* I asked, what lessons should a defender of psychological realism draw from this research? I said this: "Traits are real and predictive, but no credible moral psychology can focus solely on traits, dispositions, and character. Good lives cannot be properly envisaged, nor can they be created and sustained, without paying attention to what goes on outside the agent—to the multifarious interactive relations between individual and the natural and social environments" (Flanagan 1991b, 312). I (still) agree with myself. The good news for the present project is that it is a strength, not a weakness, of Buddhism that it conceives of flourishing and happy Buddhist persons as flourishing and happy precisely because they are possessed of stable character traits that we call virtues.

Ethical Ecologies and Eudaimonism

Aristotle, who offers one of the first virtue-based eudaimonistic theories in the West, develops his version by asking questions such as these: What is the proper function (ergon) of a person? What is the final end (telos) of a human life? We can, in fact, interrogate Buddhism with this conceptual apparatus, but it is not the most natural way to get a feel for Buddhism. The concepts of proper function (ergon) and final end (telos) are distinctively Greek concepts rooted in Aristotle's metaphysical biology and cosmology. If Buddhism is eudaimonistic, as I claim, it is not because it in fact uses this very same conceptual apparatus in hoisting its conception of the good life. But it can, I have insisted, be helpfully understood in terms of such concepts, especially the concepts of flourishing and happiness as they require a certain kind of good character.

On one standard, but, as I've said, somewhat misleading, reading of the origins of Buddhism, it is based on Siddhārtha Gautama's practical solution to the problem of living with suffering, and not in anything like systematic philosophical reflection, at least not systematic reflection with Greek concepts. Nonetheless, the Aristotelian apparatus is useful in understanding what Buddhism is about, or to put it differently, the Buddhist solution to the problem of how best to live can be profitably understood in terms of such concepts as the proper function of humankind, virtue, happiness, and flourishing. All these things are real even if I am anatman and ultimately everything is empty.

According to the Buddhists, we succeed at realizing our proper function if we live a life of wisdom and compassion and mindfulness—the New York pretzel. To the degree that we realize our proper function we are living truthfully and well. Wisdom and virtue/compassion map exactly onto the place of reason and virtue for the Aristotelian. This structural isomorphism aside, they—both reason and wisdom and virtue and compassion—are substantively very different between the two theories. The wise and compassionate Buddhist is a different sort of person than the rational and virtuous Aristotelian.

Reason in Aristotle is a modification of the Platonic view, according to which the properly structured psyche is one where rationality is analogized to the charioteer who controls the wild horses of appetite and temperament. For Aristotle, probably as for Plato, the need to continuously reckon with the wild horses inside each person diminishes as moral development takes place. One who is properly morally educated has a calm disposition and thus rarely do the untamed forces of appetite and temperament gain control of the chariot and its driver. The person whose rational side is well developed possesses the virtue of *phronesis* (practical intelligence). The irrational, troublemaking parts of the psyche have been tamed, quieted. And thus she sizes up situations as they are, and when action is called for, she chooses according to the doctrine of the mean, producing the right action, no more and no less.

One sees similar concern for rational self-governance and actions that accord with the mean in Buddhism. But the wisdom that holds the place that reason holds in Aristotle's ethics is not the same as Aristotelian reason. Insofar as that sort of reason is there and is recommended (as it often is as "skillful means"), it is doing its work, gaining its momentum, from somewhere else within the overall framework of a wider Buddhist moral psychology.

Wisdom refers specifically to seeing things truthfully and aligns in that way with Aristotle's practical reason (phronesis). But, as I have argued throughout, it refers first and foremost to these three or four theses: impermanence, dependent origination, no-self, and often emptiness. Question: Which of these three or four beliefs is most important? Answer: They are equally important and logically interpenetrate. Even if the belief in anatman gets the mother lode of attention, and is claimed to be true on phenomenological grounds or on mindful self-inspection, it is maximally secured metaphysically as a consequence of impermanence and dependent origination, with emptiness being a further implication of these three. One might wonder whether, given his substantialist metaphysic, Aristotle could agree with the relevant view. I think he could. But even if he could, there is no place where he asserts, defends, or emphasizes anything like the no-self view.

What about the relation between Aristotelian virtue and the Buddhist virtues? Virtue, for Aristotle, includes a host of intellectual and moral particulars, a list of virtues that the virtuous person possesses: phronesis, justice, courage, magnanimity, generosity, and so on. It might look as if the Buddha thinks that there is just one virtue: compassion. But that isn't so. Like Aristotle's, his list is long. Remember that there is conventional virtue, sila, which consists of no killing, truthfulness, noble labor, no sexual misconduct, and so on. And then there are the excellences of the bodhisattva—compassion, lovingkindness, sympathetic joy, and equanimity—which function as a moral ideal for everyone.

The lists differ, and what this shows, among other things, is that ethical conceptions are best viewed as having evolved to suit the needs of particular ecological niches. Ethics is human ecology (Flanagan 2002). Ethical conceptions catch on in their original environments if they are perceived as doing a good job relative to those needs. Sometimes, when things go well, an ethics is a functional adaptation in an ecology that serves the interest of a wide swath of members of that ecology, and results in an equilibrium that is good for all, or more likely, most. At other times, the ethics is a functional adaptation to the interests of the most powerful in the ecology, which results in an equilibrium for only some.

Whereas Aristotle is strong on justice and courage, he is not strong on compassion and lovingkindness. The magnanimity or generosity that the great-souled person displays doesn't involve much in the way of fellow-feeling and, on some takes, smells strongly paternalistic and self-ennobling. Justice, meanwhile, gets little explicit attention in Buddhist texts. To be sure, one sees considerations of fairness (or unfairness) in Buddhist egalitarianism and, in particular, in the rejection of the Indic caste system. But the conception of justice is not nearly as well developed as it is in Aristotle, whose own conception, we might note, wasn't so well developed that he himself saw anything wrong with slavery (usually of POWs). This is, of course, a different point than whether there is, in fact, anything wrong with slavery from the point of view of his ethical system. If there is, even Aristotle didn't see it.

This much establishes the fact that despite the structural isomorphism of reason and virtue and wisdom and compassion in, respectively, Aristotle's and the Buddha's conception of a properly functioning person, these concepts are substantively different in precisely the ways one would expect they would need to be in order to explain the differences in the conceptions of human flourishing each theory offers.

There is, from our current position, no obstacle to enriching our own conception of human flourishing by borrowing and mixing from each. After all, it would be odd to think that eudaimonistic conceptions that arose 2,500 years ago in ancient Greece, or, in what is now Nepal, could simply and straightforwardly suit our purposes. There is that flux, remember. Different times and places, different problems, different needs.

For both Aristotle and Buddha, and for us now, realizing our proper function (assuming we buy into the idea that there is something to the idea that there is a human proper function) succeeds fully only if we are rational and virtuous or wise and virtuous, as these are understood internally within each tradition.[16] For the Buddhist, living truthfully and well, if done with mindfulness and right concentration, puts true happiness of a calm, serene sort within reach. There is joy and delight in the vicinity. A similar, but not exactly the same sort of happiness, reliably comes to Aristotle's rational and virtuous person. Within Buddhism the pivotal move is to claim that seeing the self truthfully, as anatman, and structuring one's psyche in accordance with this insight, can help—in a therapeutic sort of way—to break the grip of selfishness.

Buddhism and Modern Moral Philosophy

One reason eudaimonism is sexy, and flourishing and happiness are in, is because there is a perceived lack in what Alasdair MacIntyre (1981) calls the "project of the enlightenment"—exemplified by consequentialist and Kantian moral theories—to pay adequate attention to personal flourishing or (what is related, but different) to the structure of human personality that would reliably lead people to do what is good and right as well as to flourishing and happiness.

It is the impoverished picture of the moral agent, a lack of emphasis on moral personality, that Elizabeth Anscombe bemoans in her famous 1958 paper, "Modern Moral Philosophy." In *After Virtue*, MacIntyre uses Anscombe's critique as part of his argument for the failure of the "project of the enlightenment." The claim that the Enlightenment project has failed is provocative but on the preposterous side. Enlightenment values are now in our blood and bones, and these values—justice, fairness, dignity, respect, and maximizing welfare—are worthy ones.

A better diagnosis—consistent with Anscombe's original complaint—is that Enlightenment moral theories are conspicuously weak when it comes to providing a theory of individual human flourishing. Is the problem irreparable? I think not. Furthermore, I don't think it is helpful, let alone correct, to treat ancient and modern ethical theories as rivals. There are rivals within each group—Stoicism, Aristotelian, Epicureanism, and Buddhism are rivals, as are consequentialism and Kantianism. What there is not is rivalry between agent-centered eudaimonism and the impersonal project of the Enlightenment, or at least between agent-centered theories, on the one side, and theories of interpersonal good and right, social coordination, on the other side.

Philosophers will legitimately wonder, in hoisting an ethical theory, which among three choices—a certain conception of a flourishing person, a theory of right, or a theory of good—has logical or justificatory priority. And which one is chosen will make a difference in the logical structure of the theory that emerges, as well as in certain trump calls. But there is, of course, always the antifoundationalist or pragmatist strategy of working to build a theory that adequately attends to personality, as well as to the demands of rightness and goodness in a manner that suits our needs, all things considered. In any case, I don't see that there is any conceptual reason why one cannot end up advocating, for example (pardon the unwieldy name), a eudaimonistic consequentialism with deontological constraints no matter where one starts.[17]

That said, the strength of Buddhism is in providing a theory of the flourishing person who is typically engaged in communal relations where her compassion shows, and it shows because she does not take herself too seriously and is not more attached to her future selves than to the selves of others. This allegedly has something to do with understanding the metaphysics of anatman. How Buddhism, or any other eudaimonistic theory, for that matter, might be worked into—or coordinated with—theories that concern themselves with the right and/or good is a worthy project, and one that I remain optimistic can and should be developed.

Despite the fact that Buddhism is a rich eudaimonistic theory, it does not contain an equally well developed theory of how the right and good, impersonally construed, are to be attained (at least it is not in the league of consequentialism or Kantianism in doing so). However, a person who flourishes Buddhist style typically concerns herself with the flourishing of others. So there is in this eudaimonistic theory an explicit recognition that interpersonal good will flow from the existence of flourishing Buddhist individuals—that interpersonal good is connected to intrapersonal good. Indeed, on certain readings of the texts, being wise, being good, and doing well are trebly co-constitutive of flourishing. This is the reading I prefer. But again I must acknowledge that there is a strain, particularly in the Theravada tradition, where the key is to flourish individually by gaining wisdom and enlightenment. Feeling compassion will ensue to some high degree. But whether this feeling will do any work beyond making the enlightened person feel happy and holy is unclear.

Conclusion: Resisting Anatman Extremism

I close with a question, well, really two related questions. One might legitimately wonder whether rejection of the atman doctrine automatically takes you to the anatman view. In one sense it must, since if you don't have an atman, you are anatman. But this glib response sidesteps the concern I mean to raise. I have tried resolutely to state and defend the doctrine of anatman in a way that will make it maximally palatable to analytic philosophers and cognitive scientists. According to my rational reconstruction, anatman is the view one gets when one reads Locke, then Hume, then William James,

Minsky, Dennett, Parfit, and Varela et al. This, I must admit, is not the way the doctrine is articulated within Buddhism, because there are different sources. But suppose it was for a moment. Assuming one accepts the view that the two views, person^Locke and anatman, are roughly the same, the first question one might ask is for further clarification as to why the view of no-self engenders compassion and lovingkindness. Parfit himself does entertain the prospect that recognition of my mutability and finitude, the fact that I am a selfless person, or something in the vicinity of a selfless person, might make me feel depressed, more indifferent to myself and to others than I was when I was under the illusion that I was more than that.[18]

And one is left to puzzle over how and why it is that the anatman view is normally seen as providing greater motivation for appropriate self-love, as well as for greater compassion and lovingkindness than for pessimistic resignation, a sort of indifferent "going-with-the-flow" or a maximal hedonism of the present me (this would be a "love the one you're with" philosophy, where the one each of us is always with is our present self!). In fact, it does result in the resigned attitude for some Buddhists, which is why one sometimes hears the complaint that Buddhism is pessimistic or nihilistic or that it engenders passivity. But it is not supposed to work this way. Again, one wishes to know why. One idea is that the only attitude one can take to being anatman that allows prospects for flourishing and happiness is the nonindifferent attitude, the one that involves feeling, possibly living with great compassion.

This reply is not totally lame. The lesson of this chapter—for its author, at any rate—is that it remains unclear whether and how the anatman view logically entails the canonical Buddhist ethical view. And we are left wondering about the question with which we began this chapter: How does one get from the metaphysical insight that I am a selfless person to the ethic of compassion and lovingkindness? The latter response suggests that the motivation to live compassionately comes from choosing to take the only attitude available toward being a selfless person that holds prospects for flourishing, for as much happiness and goodness as a selfless person has prospects of achieving. For myself, I am strongly inclined to accept this answer to the puzzling motivational question with which we began, namely, it is just a contingent empirical fact about the way we gregarious social mammals have evolved that first fitness and then flourishing come from extending ourselves to others (see Churchland, 2011, for neurophilosophical support for this view).

A related but different worry comes from the way Buddhists sometimes (but not always) express the anatman view. Not only don't I have an immutable, indestructible soul (atman) that constitutes *me*, but I am extremely ephemeral. In some places, there is talk that my self dies at each moment. Expressed this way, the anatman view is stronger than that required by the denial of the atman doctrine. I can be atman-less, and still be a very stable sort of thing, and not an extremely ephemeral sort of thing. More like a plant or an animal than like a cloud of dust.

Aristotle comes in handy here. He wrote before we in the West were in the grip of our own style of soul-based view, which solidified in the West with the spread of the Christian Roman Empire. Insofar as Aristotle has a theory of personhood, it is compatible with the view I claim one gets in the neo-Lockean tradition. But whereas the view I claim to find in the neo-Lockean tradition requires overcoming the soul-based view, when Aristotle wrote he didn't need to overcome that view because it was not in place. Thus the view he expresses (or assumes) is that of common sense, or of one kind of common sense, namely, ancient Greek folk psychology. The neo-Lockean view is not commonsensical for most contemporary Westerners precisely because soulophilia still abounds (remember: 90 percent of Americans think they possess indestructible, incorporeal souls).

But Aristotle's view is that a person is constituted, among other things, by her character. And whatever exactly makes for character, it is decidedly not extremely ephemeral. It has staying power and resiliency, and this is so whether one is a person of virtue or not (i.e., vicious people have characters too). The point I want to emphasize is that one might credibly position the Aristotelian view of the person as a contender conception between the doctrines of atman and anatman, especially if anatman is given the extremely ephemeral interpretation, with the self dying each moment, and a person is conceived as more akin to a cloud of dust than an oak or a horse, and so on.

Once seen as occupying the middle ground between the doctrines of atman and anatman, a plausible argument can be mounted that the Aristotelian view is the best on offer. Why is that? Because, without embracing the illusion of atman, it makes the best sense of how it is that we are creatures with abiding characters and, just as important, with goals, aspirations, and projects that we stick to. Buddhism is big, as I've indicated, on not getting stuck in the past, as well as on being in the present. But isn't it perfectly reasonable to commit myself to relationships and projects, including moral ones, that require a fairly strong degree of personal constancy?

I think the answer has to be yes. Committing oneself to achieving Buddhahood, or taking the bodhisattva's vows, involves committing oneself going forward, to being a certain kind of person, to staying the course, and to reliably living in a certain way.[19] Even if I am atman-less, I am the

kind of creature who, barring the world being erratic, miserly, and uncoop-
erative, has prospects for sticking to my relationships, goals, and projects.
Furthermore, one condition of my doing what I set out to do requires keeping my eye on the prize(s), monitoring my progress, and so forth. Barring
neurological degradation, severe self-deception, and the like, I can hold in
memory and tell you stories about what I am like, what I care about, aim
at, and how things are going in terms of my goals. My self surfaces in narrative. Narratives have beginnings, middles, and up-to-now parts. Perhaps
on my deathbed I'll be able to tell both you and myself how it went and
how it ends.

The point is that accepting and absorbing the anatman view in a way
that is significantly stronger than the Aristotelian folk-psychological view
(or the neo-Lockean view interpreted commonsensically or in an Aristotelian fashion), and thus that makes it a rival to that view by too strongly
emphasizing ephemerality, requires argument to show that it is not itself
metaphysically excessive and thus mistaken.

Imagine that the reply from a Buddhist inclined to push the ephemerality envelope is to claim that the way I have described the Aristotelian view,
or the Lockean view, which I see as close kin, will make me prone—as it
has most of my fellows in this hemisphere—to fall into the stereotypical
pose of the sort of Western individualist who grasps egoistically at success
for his personal projects. The first response is that the view of the person
on offer, the one that doesn't push the ephemerality envelope—Aristotelian anatman—can hardly by itself be thought sufficient to engender the
excessive individualism and egoism that is found objectionable. That has
to have other causes. A second response is simply to say that I won't do my
life that way. I'll avoid the individualistic and egoistic excesses available in
my tradition. A third response is that this is a problem that the Buddhist
also has: there are many Buddhists who avow anatman but who are selfish
creeps by any measure.

The analytic philosopher and scientific naturalist who denies that we
humans are or have atman has his own way to defend anatman, either in
an Aristotelian or neo-Lockean way or possibly both at once, depending
on how close or far away he understands the views. One could imagine,
although there is no necessity, a Western philosopher from our no-self
tradition(s) advising that seeing oneself as a selfless person gives one some
reason to beware egoism and to live compassionately. It is rational for each
of us to proceed to find the best niche for oneself, for a person with one's
talents and interests. Find some worthy goals and projects that suit you,
and get fired up and passionate about them. Sure, work those projects from

the here and now. Don't get ahead of yourself. Delight in the small steps along the way. And don't let the setbacks surprise or defeat you. But always remember, never forget, never lose sight of the fact that once you figure out what sort of worthy projects suit you, nothing less than the meaning of your life turns on doing your best to make them work out. Well, that and being as lovingkind and compassionate and unselfish as possible. Your job is to make sure you choose projects that do not diminish the prospects that when you die the story is one of a wise person who led, as far as possible, an excellent life. If you dedicate yourself to living wisely and compassionately and mindfully, then even if you, for some reason, miss out on knowing when and how the final chapter ends, we will rightly say that you led a good human life and flourished. If there were gods, they'd bless you. But there aren't, so they won't. But we, your fellows who remain alive and on our own personal journeys, will be grateful for who you were and how you were. You flourished, Buddhist style, and you increased our chances for doing the same.

6 Virtue and Happiness

This alone—one's service to sentient beings (*sattvaraddhana*) is pleasing to Tathagatas [Enlightened or Awakened Ones]. This alone is the actual accomplishment of one's goal. This alone removes the suffering of the world. Therefore, let this alone be my resolve.

—Sāntideva, *The Bodhisattva's Way of Life*, VI, 127

Thus, one who has patience should cultivate zeal, because Awakening is established with zeal, and there is no merit without zeal. . . . What is zeal? It is enthusiasm for virtue.

—Sāntideva, *The Bodhisattva's Way of Life*, VII, 1, 2

Upon mounting the chariot of the Spirit of Awakening, which carries away all despondency and weariness, what sensible person would despair at progressing in this way from joy to joy?

—Sāntideva, *The Bodhisattva's Way of Life*, VII, 30

Psychological Laws and Normative Laws

I have offered an analysis of eudaimonia^{Buddha}. Eudaimonia—flourishing, or happy flourishing, or happiness and flourishing, or more likely flourishing that often or usually leads to some sort of happiness of a serene sort— involves reaching a state, better: achieving a way of being, feeling, and acting constituted by wisdom (prajna) and virtue (sila, virtue, or karuna, virtue of the sort where compassion is the highest or master virtue) and mindfulness. Only in wisdom and virtue and mindfulness do we actualize our full potential, our proper function, as human beings and achieve eudaimonia^{Buddha}. In all likelihood we are happy, contented, happy^{Buddha}.

Here I continue the profitable comparative and cosmopolitan conversation between Buddhism, Aristotle's philosophy, and the Hellenistic therapeutic schools, focusing specifically on their respective ethics, to see what happens, what insights about virtue, flourishing, and happiness, if any, turn up. I am not committed to the view that Buddhist and Aristotelian or Stoic or Epicurean ethics are similar or very similar. It is just that they are all worthy participants in a potentially profitable anachronistic, ethnocentric, and cosmopolitan conversation about the good life.

Assume for analytic purposes that we possess Buddhist wisdom and are mindful in the ways Buddhism recommends: What goods does being virtuous in a Buddhist way add? Many think that Buddhism really only requires a certain kind of moral personality and that the threefold chord picture is elitist. Wisdom and mindfulness are luxuries of people with a lot of extra time, the philosophically curious, and so on. The elitism charge is not crazy, so examining Buddhism as if the ethics could stand alone has precedent, even if the view on offer here is the New York pretzel one.

Three issues absorb me: (1) What is the connection between virtue and happiness generally (if there is any general truth in this vicinity), and what in particular is the alleged, and what is different, actual connection between virtue^{Buddha} and happiness^{Buddha}? Is virtue the normal cause of happiness, even a necessary condition? Is the claim that there is strong, possibly necessary, connection between virtue and happiness (either generally or in the Buddhist case) an empirical psychological claim or is the claim a normative one?[1] A descriptive psychological thesis would be that virtue and happiness do go together; a normative claim would say that in a good or just world they ought to go together. (2) Which theory—for the sake of conversation, Aristotle's or Buddha's—provides the best or most defensible conception of virtue? Is it possible that Aristotle's theory is too undemanding, and the Buddha's too demanding? (3) How much work needs to be done, specifically, on moderating, modifying, possibly eliminating destructive states of mind before virtue and flourishing and happiness (conceived by Aristotelians or Buddhists) can take hold?

A Key Difference between Aristotelian and Buddhist Ethics

There are some structural features, a conception of eudaimonia and a certain teleological structure, that allow comparisons of Aristotle's ethics and Buddhist ethics. To a point, Buddhism can be illuminated by viewing it ethnocentrically through our own concepts of the proper function (ergon) and ideal end (telos) of humankind. However, there are also important contentful differences between what could look like an elegant isomorphism between Aristotelian reason and virtue and Buddhist wisdom and virtue.

Reason, insofar as it is relevant to ethics, consists of the practical intelligence (phronesis) to see things as they are, assess a situation for what it is, evaluate means-ends relations, and settle on an appropriate course of action in conformity with the doctrine of the mean.

Buddhist wisdom involves reason plus, as importantly, a deep and abiding recognition that all things—including the self—are impermanent (annica). The doctrine of anatman (Sanskrit; annata, Pali)—no-self—is simply the application of the general doctrine of the impermanence of all things to the self, and what it irrationally and narcissistically seeks to accrue, hold, and keep. Wisdom, conceived this way, is part of, or at least interpenetrates with virtue since it provides the cognitive basis for quelling "thirst," the cause of much suffering according to the Second Noble Truth. How it does this is not entirely clear but has something to do with removing the illusion that what I attain will please me when I attain it because both it and me will be different then. Wisdom, especially as supported by the work of meditation and mindfulness, also provides deep insight into what states of mind and being inhibit and promote happiness.[2]

Virtue also has different content in the two traditions. Buddhists could, I think, go along with Aristotle's definition of a moral virtue (arete) as "a habitual disposition connected with choice, lying in a mean relative to us, a mean which is determined by reason, by which the person of practical reason would determine it" (NE, II, 6,1107a2). But the Buddhist will complain that Aristotle's list of the virtues is incomplete. For Aristotle the list consists of justice, honesty, courage, temperance, generosity, magnanimity, friendliness, and wittiness (NE, III, 6 to the end of bk. IV). Compassion and lovingkindness are major virtues for the Buddhist, so much so that the Buddhist picture of the eudaimon is described often in terms of wisdom (prajna) and compassion (karuna), where karuna is substituted for the more general term for virtue, sila, and is conceived as the master virtue, as well as the closest kin of metta (lovingkindness; maitri, Sanskrit), with the two, in tandem, comprising the heart of Sila—with a capital "S" (Virtue).[3] Neither compassion nor lovingkindness is on Aristotle's list, nor are generosity and magnanimity—which are on his list—conceived of as virtues by him because they embody, express, or are motivated by great compassion and lovingkindness.

The Comparative Ethicist's Predicament

It follows that the Buddhist conception of the virtuous person is significantly different from Aristotle's, as both are different from, say, the Confucian conception. One might say that such differences are to be expected since moral conceptions are developed in response to local ecologies, and thus are dependent on preexisting aspects of the social, economic, and philosophical climates of different places and times. Conceptions of human nature and the human good, on this view, can be understood as part of "the philosophical climate," by which I mean to include much more than the purely theoretical, but something like what is produced and reproduced by the intellectual, aesthetic, political, and economic climate of a place and a time with its own distinctive history.

Arguments for the ecological approach might lead one to think that there might be legitimate plural contenders for a conception of a virtuous life. We might even think that distinctive conceptions of the good are more or less well suited to different times and places, and that this suitability was part of their appeal in their original context.

It is not, however, that the philosopher who takes the ecological insight seriously is stuck with accepting that each moral conception is, in fact, good, noble, or well suited to its original locale, even by standards internal to that tradition. First, it would be naive to overemphasize the functional aspects of a moral code, since despite the fact that there will normally be a tendency to find an orderly equilibrium in almost any ecology, an orderly equilibrium can be produced by the simple power of some elite. Plato discusses this point in numerous dialogs—for example, *Republic* and *Gorgias*—and it has been a major theme in the last two centuries in such thinkers as Marx, Nietzsche, and Foucault. Second, even if a moral conception looks well suited in the functional sense of satisfying the needs of the many rather than the few, there will always be the question of lacunae, hidden implications (e.g., what, if anything, is it about Buddhism that permits/requires sexism?). The philosopher will need to examine whether a particular theory has drawn out all the implication of its stated view from the background philosophical climate. There are questions of good faith—does the recommended conception of virtue bear signs of being disproportionately in the interests of its promoters, rather than in everyone's interest? And so on.

Furthermore, once engaged in comparative philosophical analysis we are operating from a new ecological perspective. In the present case, we are looking for a worthwhile, possibly noble or excellent, conception of virtue based on an examination of Aristotle's ethics and Buddhist ethics (each with its own particular and shared "backgrounds"). The inquiry arises from our own ecological context with its particular problems and needs and utilizes resources gathered and accrued from 2,500 years of philosophical examination of the pros and cons (some internal, some external) of these and many other ethical conceptions. This explains why, when a philosopher, including this one, asks a question such as "Which view of virtue is better?", he need not be read as ignoring the ecological insight, and thus as asking for an answer from "the point of view of nowhere." And the answer that both are good, "each in its own way," is still an option. That said, making comparative judgments, seeking all-things-considered consensus on which of two views is better, involves, indeed requires, close attention to the original ecology of discovery, invention, and defense; the search for lacunae in the drawing out of available, but possibly unseen, logical implications of the original view; and then critically examining them from one's own culturally and philosophically embedded perspective. This is allowed, even embraced. The cosmopolitan, recall, cops to anachronism and ethnocentrism.

A Necessary Connection between Virtue and Happiness?

Assume that reason, if we are an Aristotelian or an heir to Aristotle's philosophy, or wisdom, if we are a follower of Buddha, is in place, so that for, example, we have a person who is practically wise, savvy in knowing what to do, when, and to what degree, or that we have a person who understands impermanence, no-self, dependent origination, and emptiness. But to avoid the elitism charge make this wisdom minimal, not very cognitive, not easily articulated, something felt in the blood and bones of a person who is paying attention to the way the world is, the way it goes and unfolds. And consider an individual who is well on his way to acquiring virtue as conceived by Aristotle or Buddha. Will he then flourish or be happy, both or neither?

Most philosophers, East and West, have thought that there is a strong connection between virtue and happiness. How strong is the connection? How strong is the connection alleged to be? Earlier I proposed that wisdom and virtue and mindfulness cause or constitute eudaimonia[Buddha] and that eudaimonia[Buddha] is a normal and reliable cause of happiness[Buddha]. Now I give a more complete argument that this is, or might be, so. Start with a strong statement of the nature of the alleged connection, and then throughout the discussion, let reasons reveal themselves that suggest that and how it may need to be weakened.

The strongest thesis would be this: Virtue necessarily produces happiness and nothing else can produce happiness. There are counterexamples: good souls whose spirits are crushed by fate, Hecuba for example, and evil persons who enjoy life thoroughly, Plato's Callicles perhaps.

Aristotle advanced one version of a strong, but weaker claim than the strongest claim. I call this version Aristotle's law, henceforth AL.

AL: (1) Virtue is a necessary condition for happiness (along with reason); (2) normally (barring bad luck, including lack of basic necessities and neurochemical imbalances) it is sufficient to cause/produce happiness.

An especially interesting interpretation of AL involves reading it as a claim of empirical psychology, and as such as falsifiable. AL would be an uninteresting claim, or less interesting, if it is understood as analytic; that is, where the meaning or criteria for "virtue" is simply required for an ascription of "happiness"—where, for example, "being virtuous" was defined in such a way that part of its meaning was "being happy," or vice versa. On the interpretation of AL as empirical rather than merely conceptual, it should not be the case that, in practice, a plausible counterexample of a happy person who is not virtuous (like Callicles) is excluded simply because he is said not to be happy in the right way, where the right way is required or stipulated as the kind acquired by virtue.

As I understand Buddhism, AL, or something close enough to it, is commonly espoused. In Śāntideva's *Bodhicaryavatara* (*A Guide to the Bodhisattva's Way of Life*), composed in the eighth century CE and considered a canonical source of Mahayana wisdom, we are told that the virtuous "dwell in the hearts of spacious, fragrant, and cool lotuses," whereas the nonvirtuous soul "cries out in distress" (bk. VII, 44, 45).

Given that I've claimed that the Aristotelian and Buddhist ethical conceptions have important differences while (possibly) nonetheless sharing a belief in AL—that is, that there is a necessary connection between virtue and happiness—a puzzle, actually a set of puzzles, arises. Is the acceptance of AL to be understood as a psychological truth that obtains only when the right conception of virtue is realized (assuming, for the sake of argument, that there is one right one)? Supposing hypothetically that this is the right interpretation, and that in addition, we have to choose between the Aristotelian and Buddhist conceptions, between virtue[Aristotle] and virtue[Buddha]—knowing somehow that one of them is the right one—which one is the right one, the one we ought to choose, and why? This matters because on the assumption that everyone wants to be happy and that virtue is a necessary condition of happiness, then everyone ought to want to be virtuous. And if only one conception of virtue is the right one, we will want to know which it is.

I can state the puzzles, comprising the set, in other ways: If virtue is a necessary connection (almost sufficient) for happiness, does it not matter what the virtues are? Or is it possible that there is a plural set of ways of being virtuous and that realizing any set brings happiness? And if this is so, is it that different sets of virtues produce the same kind of happiness, or that they each produce their own kind of happiness? Even assuming that the character traits called virtues by two distinct traditions are all good as judged from some more expansive, impartial point of view, does it not matter if the lists are judged incomplete—missing or giving insufficient role to some important virtue? That is, if we accept that some recognizably incomplete set of virtues instantiated in character is necessary (almost sufficient) to produce happiness, would such a deficiency rule out the possibility of happiness? And, as before, does the kind of happiness need to be marked in a theory-specific way, as happiness^{Aristotle} and happiness^{Buddha}? Is it possible that some virtues are mandatory—for example, compassion—whereas others, such as wittiness, are optional so far as AL goes? I'll let these puzzles set and use them to complicate the discussion as we proceed.

One who starts to worry about the interpretation of AL in these ways might recommend a reinterpretation, which is like the strongest thesis in certain respects, but marks that it is only True Virtue and True Happiness—assuming there are such things—that we are talking about, and only these that are necessarily connected:

AL': True Virtue necessarily produces True Happiness, and only it does so.

AL' could be read as a linguistic stipulation, as setting out meaning rules for the terms True Virtue and True Happiness. But AL' can be interpreted as empirical and not simply conceptual. If proponents of different theories are willing to define True Virtue and True Happiness in substantive theory-specific ways that do not beg the question, for example, by simply stipulating that "happiness" is linguistically entailed by the meaning of "virtue," then AL' yields testable predictions.

1. AL': True Virtue is that which necessarily produces True Happiness.
2. Dfs.: True Virtue and True Happiness by Aristotle and Buddha.
3. Population A instantiates True Virtue^{Aristotle}; Population B instantiates True Virtue^{Buddha}.
4. Population A is Truly Happy; population B is not (by the standards set by A and B, respectively).
5. Conclusion: AL' receives some corroboration, as does A's conception of virtue but not B's.

So far, so good. This testable situation works so long as each theory claims that the conception of virtue and the (somewhat) independent conception of happiness it favors will satisfy the strong necessity claim in AL'—the claim that true virtue, as it conceives it, necessarily produces true happiness as it conceives it.

But suppose, as is entirely possible, that the empirical result gained in (4) was this:

4'. Population A and B are both "truly happy," where either true happiness is used unequivocally or as happy^{Aristotle} or happy^{Buddha}, where these are different conceptions of happiness.

Then (5) should read this way:

5'. Conclusion: AL' receives some corroboration, as does theory A's conception of virtue and B's conception of virtue.

Here the situation would be one in which each theory correctly predicted that true happiness, as each defined it, accrues from its conception of virtue and it does. Is this possible? Yes. It is bad? Not necessarily. It would require deep ecology to decide whether a particular conception of happiness is deficient by the lights of the wise members of a culture that avow it, or whether some things were missed by the proponents of the view, so that some deficiency in either the conception of true virtue or true happiness was not seen, and so on. Comparative methods with the resources of ideas and tools acquired over two and a half millennia are, of course, permitted to make arguments for weaknesses or deficiencies from their perspective.

I focus on the testability, theory-choice situation as it regards the necessary condition claim in either the form of AL or AL' because it directly relates to the topic under discussion. Aristotle and Buddhism have different conceptions of virtue and of happiness (as does our own liberal common-sense morality, about which more later). And it may be that, although the relevant conceptions of true virtue and true happiness are not intratheoretically defined in question-begging ways, the two respective conceptions are suited and/or designed to co-occur in the relevant ecologies. This may not be due to any mischievous sleight of hand, but rather to deep-seated and defensible ways that local ecological conditions have evolved and are designed to make the co-occurrence happen. I say more about this prospect below.

For now, notice that AL' could lead to theory choice of the sort we sometimes get in science, if while allowing variability in the definition of "True Virtue," we got, or required, the disputants to agree on the same substantive characterization of "True Happiness." In this way we could test whether A and/or B (C to Z, as well) produce it. If only one did, we have found True Virtue! In my experience, at least at this time in the development of moral theory, expecting agreement on a specific conception of happiness, especially the one allegedly produced by virtue, is not in the cards.[4]

The deep and abiding complexity of the situation facing the comparative ethicist is out on the table. It is what I call "the internalist predicament" (Flanagan 2007)—something unavoidable if one acknowledges that anachronism and ethnocentrism are, to a point, themselves unavoidable and not altogether unwarranted. The situation, the predicament, colors the subsequent discussion. Because the problem is ubiquitous I will not be calling constant attention to it. Nonetheless, keep it firmly in mind.

The Therapy of Desire and Delusion

In *The Therapy of Desire* (1994), Martha Nussbaum presents a compelling case for understanding the post-Aristotelian Greek and Roman philosophers as doing much more than simply advancing and refining Aristotle's ethics. Post-Aristotelian ethics advances a view of the good life that is open to everyone, not just the well-bred. Despite the universal access to a life of virtue, the Epicureans and Stoics, especially, paint a more demanding picture of virtue than Aristotle does. This more demanding ethical conception requires much deeper psychic change than Aristotle thought necessary in order to alleviate suffering and possibly to bring happiness in its place. In part, the need for greater direct attention to an individual's psychic economy is due to the fact that Aristotle was insufficiently attentive to the way certain destructive states of mind, like greed and avarice, cause suffering and bad actions, but are nonetheless subject to voluntary control. According to the therapists of desire, more than good socialization, even as supplemented by attending Aristotle's lectures on ethics, or internalizing the lessons contained therein by being raised in an Aristotelian society, is required for virtue. Direct therapy on the minds of adults to quell or eliminate negative desires is needed as well—something akin to mindfulness practice(s). In addition, the expansion of the list of virtues to include great or universal compassion requires work to expand and enhance whatever tendencies of fellow-feeling are rooted in our nature, but that are enhanced insufficiently by local (Aristotelian) moral conventions.

Fortunately, the transformation of the psyche required for true virtue and happiness is possible so long as the philosopher equipped with a more expansive set of instruments than argument alone, plays the role of a trainer or physician for the soul.

The Hellenistic philosophical schools in Greece and Rome—Epicureans, Skeptics, and Stoics—all conceived philosophy as a way of addressing the most painful problems of human life. They saw the philosopher as a compassionate physician whose arts could heal many pervasive types of human suffering (Nussbaum 1994, 3).[5]

The therapists of desire provided, indeed insisted on providing strong—ideally valid and sound—arguments to support their diagnoses, prognoses, and therapeutic practices. In part, like their Indian counterparts, especially Buddhists, this was because they believed that mistaken views (moha, Pali) are often at the root of human suffering—for example, money is widely thought to bring happiness but doesn't.[6] But they also recognized that argument alone does not always produce the necessary change. Even if false belief—what Buddhists call delusion or wrong view (moha)—is lifted at some conscious level ("Okay, money doesn't bring happiness. Now I get it"), there are typically long-standing emotional and conative tendencies and attitudes associated with the false belief (possibly antecedent to it) that in virtue of being deep-seated and partly unconscious may still control the motivational circuits. Even if the false belief is exposed as false, acquisitive desires and behavior may not abate ("I know that money doesn't bring happiness, but I keep trying to accumulate wealth, and I feel vacant, empty, dissatisfied"). Here the therapists of desire rightly saw the need to bring to bear techniques, in addition to arguments, to adjust or change the economy of desire, often working to outright eliminate certain destructive emotions by antidotes that were psychologically incompatible with them. Wishing someone ill and feeling deep love and compassion for him at the same time are psychologically inconsistent—at least they comprise a highly unstable tandem.[7]

Michel Foucault refers to this style of doing philosophy, which involves working to form or restructure the self as utilizing techniques of self-work, as *techniques de soi*. Nussbaum agrees, but warns that, then as now, there were *techniques de soi* that relied on mesmeric force and hocus-pocus without the requirement that sound arguments also be offered warranting soul change of a particular sort by way of a suitable technique.

One of the complaints by early Buddhists against the "Brahmans"[8] was that, in addition to their own self-puffery, they promoted a delusional vision of happiness as involving, indeed requiring, merger of one's own indestructible Soul, Atman, with the cosmos' life-blood (Brahman). The belief in Brahman epistemically overreaches what the human mind can know, wishfully but confidently asserting that that which is beyond all concepts is most True, most Real, and that I (my Atman) will achieve merger with that which is most True, most Real, and that I deserve such merger. The belief in an abiding and indestructible soul falls to powerful arguments for anatman (annata, Pali), the doctrine that the self is an ever-changing stream without the features of permanence, immutability, and so on.

It is part of Buddhist moral psychology that one way a state can be unwholesome is if false view (moha) causally contributes to it. So suppose the beliefs in the reality of Brahman and Atman, as well as the desirability of their merger (three falsehoods), led (as they did) to rituals designed to produce the merger, and that these rituals produced a state of euphoric joy. There would be this problem: achieving the happy state in this way is undesirable, unwholesome. This would be true even if the state produced was the same substantively and phenomenologically as the happy state that practitioners of virtue aim to create. The underlying thought, perhaps it is a principle, is this: even if some state *phi* is the desired end state (telos) of some practice or set of practices, if *phi* is achieved by certain kinds of shortcuts it doesn't count as a bona fide instance of *phi*. The principle is akin to this one: if I make a copy of Van Gogh's *The Starry Night* that is closer to the original than the aged original, it is still a fake, and not worth nearly as much as the real painting.

How harmful would the discovery that happiness can be achieved by means other than virtue be for AL or AL', which claim respectively that virtue is necessary for either ordinary happiness as in AL or true happiness as in AL'? It would be bad, since the situation, as I have imagined it, is one in which happiness is produced by false belief and while virtue is lacking. A magic pill that could directly produce the right happy state would also provide a counterexample to either necessary condition claim.

Aristotle and his Hellenistic heirs did have a response to these sorts of possibilities. But it is not clear that it saves AL or AL'. The only standard of argument accepted by the bona fide therapists of desire—Hellenistic, possibly by Buddhist therapists too if one takes seriously the claim that false belief is bad, period—was one that legitimately showed that, and how, suffering could be alleviated and happiness or contentment won. Insofar as AL or AL' is assumed, all such arguments have the same logical structure revealed by their major premise, which is stated explicitly or assumed as common background: treatment ψ leads to ethical improvement and only ethical improvement leads to happiness. If there were such things as grief or sadness fixes or euphoric joy producers that could do their magic by introducing false belief ("Your loved one is now happy and with God, you will join her later"), they were considered morally wrong. Aristotle's law, either AL or AL', if true, and according to the interpretation on offer, entails that the best such magic fixes can do is introduce a counterfeit of happiness, not the real thing.[9]

But suppose that there are some magic fixes that don't produce detectable counterfeits on the happiness side of the ledger. If so, then the best solution would be (a) to modify the necessary condition claim to some weaker causal claim: Virtue is a usual cause of happiness, and add (b): Only happiness caused by virtue is the right sort to be counted as wholesome or as virtuous happiness. Claim (b) is an explicitly normative, not an empirical, claim. Call the new claim AL".

AL" differs from AL and AL', as I've indicated, by weakening the necessary condition claim between virtue and happiness (or "True Virtue" and "True Happiness") to a claim to the effect that virtue is a normal and reliable cause of happiness. Then it adds what I'll call "the normative exclusion" clause to the effect that only happiness caused by virtue counts as wholesome, virtuous—the kind we are interested in. Defending the normative exclusion clause requires argument. Here are some bases on which one might mount a plausible defense. First, we might think that there are reasons to say that happiness is only deserved if the happy person participates in producing that state, which she does not do if it is simply produced by a magic pill. Or, in the false-belief case, we might say that an epistemic norm, our commitment to truth, excludes cases where happiness is won by delusion. The main point for now is that the strong empirical necessary condition claim with which we began is not so easy to maintain and may need to yield to a more causally and normatively nuanced view.

Anyone familiar with Buddhist philosophy and psychology will see a strong similarity with the post-Aristotelian therapists of desire. Buddhism is a therapeutic philosophy in Nussbaum's sense. It conceives of the sage as a compassionate soul healer. The bodhisattva, familiarly, makes these vows:

Sentient beings are numberless; I vow to liberate them.
Delusions are inexhaustible; I vow to transcend them.
Dharma teachings are boundless; I vow to master them.
The Buddha's enlightened way is unsurpassable; I vow to embody it.

How does the bodhisattva intend to liberate others? By helping them with *techniques de soi* that will bring their hearts and minds into the space of the Four Divine Abodes (brahmaviharas)—also called the "illimitables" or "immeasureables" (appamanna). The four are:

Lovingkindness (metta)
Compassion (karuna)
Appreciative joy (mudita)
Equanimity (upekkha)

A soul lives in the divine abodes only if she has purified her soul of the three poisons: clinging (tanha) or craving (lobha), hatred (dosa), and delusion (moha). Only a person who has gone some distance toward purging her soul of the three poisons and replacing them with the four "divine abodes" overcomes suffering, as much as humanly possible, and finds peace and happiness—or better, is on her way to achieving peace and happiness. It is important to conceive of the process as one of awakening. A person who is waking up is not normally wide awake.

Buddhism and Liberal Commonsense Morality

The Hellenistic philosophies that Nussbaum champions make themselves felt in contemporary Western moral thought and practice. Kant championed a kind of Stoicism, and exhortations to be "stoical" are part and parcel of the spirit of Protestantism. That said, there is no grassroots Stoical or Epicurean movement. Buddhism, however, is a live option in the West. Perhaps its appeal lies in part to its resonance with these other, more familiar Western therapies of desire. Now in the early twenty-first century, Buddhist therapy for destructive mental states, especially emotions that interfere with happiness and virtue, is increasingly available and being utilized by an ever-growing number of Western practitioners. Without overstating a basis for naive hopefulness and without assuming that there is much quality control in the delivery of trustworthy Buddhist wisdom, the growth of interest in Buddhist philosophy in the West means that novel (to us) resources are available as an antidote to a problem some think is prevalent in liberal societies.

What is the problem with liberalism? There is, on the one hand, a belief that happiness is the goal of human life. But it is an essential feature of the liberal outlook that each person is free to determine what is good for her within a system of constraints that, by and large, only sets out an ethical conception that centers on constraints and prohibitions. Liberal morality tells us what we cannot do lest we interfere with the freedom of others to pursue happiness as they wish. Partly, on principles internal to liberalism itself, great caution is shown in explicitly setting out a shared positive vision of a good life. This is to be settled by individuals, each in their own way, or by individuals in communities, often religious, that promote a positive, sometimes even an expansive, conception of the good.

Surprisingly and ironically, in spite of the mantra that happiness is up to each individual, there is, in fact, some sort of shared positive conception of what will bring happiness, despite the idea that each can and should find that in her own way. This shared conception is not, however, the one that one might expect to gain prominence if the messages conveyed in churches, synagogues, and mosques were noble, demanding (neither of which is clear), and also penetrated the hearts and minds of Americans. The shared conception I see in my world (which is chock-full of people who go to Friday, Saturday, and Sunday services), is the one reflected in and reinforced by the media. What are its main ingredients? Wealth, status, romance (usually superficial). There is more, fancy cars, antiaging skin creams, hair dye, lots of drugs, especially antidotes to depression, digestive problems due to rich foods, and soft penises. The point is that most of the things on the list, especially the first short list, are exactly the ones that every ancient tradition, ancient Greek, Chinese, Indian, and Hellenistic, tells us will not reliably bring happiness.

Are AL or AL', the claims that virtue, possibly True Virtue, is necessary for happiness, possibly True Happiness, accepted by contemporary commonsense morality in the West, where by liberal commonsense morality I mean a morality that advocates a minimalist list of mandatory virtues, perhaps only basic fairness and tolerance? Or is AL''—the weaker claim, that virtue usually causes happiness—accepted? That is, does liberal commonsense morality advertise that virtue brings happiness, or that it is a necessary condition of happiness, or at least that the two are tightly connected? My impression is that it does not. Instead what is held is that the practice of liberal virtues is necessary for creating an environment in which each can pursue his or her own kind of happiness. Liberal virtues of fairness and tolerance are instruments of freedom. Living freely, as one chooses, might bring happiness if anything can. According to liberal commonsense morality, the conception of virtue is weaker, less demanding, than Aristotle's—which requires a deep and abiding sense of (local, in-group) justice, honesty, moderation in acquiring stuff, magnanimity—and is much weaker than the Buddhist conception, which requires many of Aristotle's virtues plus compassion and lovingkindness. Generally, it seems safe to say that classical ethical theories such as those of Aristotle, Buddhism, I would add Confucianism, Hinduism, Epicureanism, and Stoicism, endorse some form of the claim that there is a strong necessary link between virtue and happiness—that is, AL or AL'—whereas the link is understood as weaker or more tenuous in liberal commonsense morality. Perhaps liberal morality accepts some version of AL''—the claim that the link between virtue and happiness is normal and reliable but not necessary. I am not sure, and will not fuss over the matter here. It may be that history has shown that claims that there is a necessary condition between virtue and happiness are empirically dubious, and thus that liberal commonsense morality is more psychologically realistic than its ancient brethren.

From Fellow-Feeling to Universal Compassion and Lovingkindness

The Hellenistic compassionate philosophers, the therapists of desire, advanced certain Aristotelian ideas and methods, and thus Aristotle can be thought of as the founder of the therapeutic schools. The Buddha lived a century before Aristotle.[10] Thus Buddhist ideas on the therapy of desire and delusion were hit on independently, but in response to the same universal problems of human life that motivated Aristotle and his heirs (the same could be said even more credibly of classical Chinese *technique de soi* that focus on self-cultivation and appear earlier than the Hellenistic or Buddhist therapies of desire).

Accepting Buddhism as not only a live, but preferred, option for us depends on the credibility of the following two theses. First, we are social animals who actualize our social nature by having some sort of great, or what is different, universal love penetrate, even fill up, our hearts and minds. Second, this conception of virtue uniquely produces happiness, or, what is different, achieving virtue, Buddhist style, normally brings about a unique kind of happiness that is the most desirable kind.

Familiar claims in Plato, Aristotle, and the Hellenistic philosophers that psychological egoism is self-defeating provide a basis for the Aristotelian recommendation of generosity and magnanimity and the Buddhist recommendation of universal compassion and lovingkindness. We are social animals who live well only in community with others. Insofar as there is a credible philosophical reply to the Thrasymachean challenge that we are psychological egoists, it does not come from Socrates when the challenge is laid down in books I and II of Plato's *Republic,* nor does it come from Plato himself in the later books of the *Republic.* All Plato really shows is that we can set up society and socialize individuals so that egoism is suppressed. But the reasons he gives for suppression can be read, for all he explicitly says, as congenial to Thrasymachus's view. That is, suppression of selfishness by state mechanisms of reward and punishment and by educating individuals to put reason in control of appetite and temperament produces an equilibrium that, on the assumption of egoism, is the best compromise for all.[11] Still, this equilibrium, the best compromise, is not individually optimal, because it yields what Freud called "civilization and its discontents." Who are these civilized discontents? The answer: every single one of us who accepts the compromise involved in suppressing, repressing, or ideally, sublimating our first nature (which is egoistic, pleasure seeking) as the price for gaining the other goods (safety, order, and the like) that civilization affords.

It is left to Aristotle, most explicitly in his chapters on friendship in the *Nicomachean Ethics,* to provide a direct response to the psychological egoist. We are both self-loving and fellow-feeling creatures. Even the mother who is unable to care for her own child and who must give her up for adoption continues to care deeply for her child's well-being (NE, 9, 9.53, 1159a–1159b). Fellow-feeling is a fundamental part of our nature. No one, we are told, would accept the offer of all other goods, if she did not have friends (NE, 9.11, 1155a). The virtues involved in true friendship involve loving the other as oneself and thus wanting the best for him for his own sake. The desires for friendship and community are not introduced from the outside. They are components, or rooted in components, of our nature as social animals. We fare well only if those we care about (initially this may consist of a small circle) fare well. Seeing them do so, and contributing to their so doing, results in some sort of happiness, happiness[Aristotle], but not perhaps most other kinds of happiness sought by Aristotle's contemporaries.

Once this much ground is cleared and the harsh reading of Thrasymachus, Callicles, and possibly Hobbes is somewhat neutralized by recognition of the gregarious, fellow-feeling aspects of first nature, a basis is laid for the Buddhist argument (also Hebrew, Christian, Muslim, Hindu, and Jain) for great (maha) love and compassion. Internal to the logic of secular Enlightenment philosophy, the Buddhist argument for great or universal love and compassion has a familiar ring to it because it has resonances with Kantian and utilitarian defenses of similar ideas, that there is a duty to respect all human beings as ends in themselves or that one ought to maximize the greatest happiness altogether, but it is much more focused on the motivational structure, psyche, of the virtuous person.

Here's the Dalai Lama's (1998, 115) rendition of the core idea expressed as Buddhists commonly do:

Genuine compassion is based on the rationale that all human beings have an innate desire to be happy and overcome suffering, just like myself. And just like myself they have a natural right to fulfill this fundamental aspiration. On the basis of the recognition of this equality and commonality, you develop a sense of affinity and closeness with others. With this as a foundation, you can feel compassion regardless of whether you view the other person as a friend or an enemy. . . . Upon this basis, then, you will generate love and compassion. That's genuine compassion.

One finds this warrant, this rationale, this justification for love expressed this way consistently in Buddhist texts. The warrant for the virtue of compassion does not rest on an innate universal desire, although it gains a grip in some natural fellow-feeling for others combined with recognition of the commonality of the human plight and the equal worthiness of all to be free of suffering and, if possible, to find happiness. In the quote it is said that once you recognize *"this equality and commonality, you develop a sense of affinity and closeness with others"* (my italics). This much provides only the foundation, a good start. Next the work of self-cultivation and therapeutic work with caretakers, friends, and teachers—one's community (sanga, Pali; sangha, Sanskrit) are required to erect something of further value on the foundation. No Buddhist accepts the idea that "recognition of this equality and commonality" is sufficient to produce the state of great or universal compassion. It is sufficient, however, to produce the recognition that this is a worthy goal to be pursued and embodied, and thus to produce a desire to reach this worthy goal. Is great or universal love and compassion your duty? Buddhists don't ask the question that way. Living compassionately and lovingly is a way to realize your potential. And if you want—as you do—to minimize suffering and possibly to gain true happiness, then growing the loving, compassionate sides of yourself will gain you that, if anything will.

The Therapeutic Division of Labor

Although Aristotle recommended the virtues of generosity and magnanimity, these were virtues to some significant degree of the great-souled, well-off, person. And in Aristotle's writings there is both an excessively self-satisfied and patronizing caste to them. There is little textual evidence that Aristotle had a conception of wide compassion on his radar, nor does he display much confidence that eudaimonia[Aristotle] can be achieved by those who are not already well-bred. Furthermore, although he does in many places speak favorably of the analogy between the physician who treats bodily ailments and the philosopher who treats soul sickness, it was left to the later Hellenistic philosophers to practically embody the approach.[12] In addition to being well-bred, a person who wishes to become virtuous will do best if she studies and absorbs the arguments laid out in the lectures that comprise the *Nicomachean Ethics*.

But Aristotle makes clear, especially in the *Poetics*, that there are techniques available beyond, but consistent with, rational argument, to assist in flourishing. The tragic plays of his contemporaries deal with universal human problems. By identifying with the characters and their plight we have a catharsis, a purgation of our own pity and fear. In this way our souls are cleansed to some degree, and we are better prepared to deal with the loss, sadness, and grief that are bound, sooner or later, to come our way.[13]

For Aristotle there is something akin to a division of labor between practices that work on one's emotional economy (possibly on emotions that can interfere with virtue) and those that lead to cultivation of virtue. Habituation in virtue insofar as it involves cultivation of certain ways of perceiving, feeling, judging, and behaving will go some distance toward attuning the mind to see and feel, as well as judge and act, in the nuanced ways required by each virtue. But there may be states of mind, powerful and common ones, such as existential anxiety or dread that are not treated directly by training in virtue.

Attending performances of tragic plays will work some, how long is unknown, to arouse feelings of pity and fear, to have you feel the commonality of your plight with others, and to purge yourself of certain, possibly negative, emotions—desires for permanent life or complete immunity to suffering, fear and trembling, and so on.

The Buddhist therapy of desire blends different kinds of work and techniques to transform the heart-mind. Arguments and direct instruction are used for important philosophical ideas, the Four Noble Truths, the Eightfold Path, and the doctrines of impermanence, anatman, and dependent origination. But these forms of direct teaching, akin to attending Aristotle's *Lyceum* and hearing his lectures on ethics, are interwoven with dramatic parables and teachings on meditation that assist in the psychic changes that Aristotle sees falling mostly in the domain of art.

For the Buddhist, ethical practice is partly artful itself. Here is a classic example of the use of a story, a parable, to adjust the heart-mind. It is ancient and is called "The Parable of the Mustard Seed."

A poor woman, Kisa Gotami, had a baby. But when that boy of hers was old enough to play and run hither and about, he died. Sorrow sprang up within her. Taking her son on her hip she went about from one house door to another saying "Give me medicine for my son!"

Wherever people encountered her, they said, Where did you ever meet with medicine for the dead?

Now a certain wise man saw her and thought: This woman must have been driven out of her mind by sorrow for her son.

Said he: "Woman, as for medicine for your son—there is no one else who knows—the Possessor of the Ten Forces, the foremost individual in the world of men and the worlds of the gods, resides in a neighboring monastery. Go to him and ask." Taking her son on her hip to the Tathagata who sat down in the Seat of the Buddhas, she said: "O Exalted One, give me medicine for my son!"

The teacher, seeing she was ripe for conversion, said: "You did well, Gotami, in coming hither for medicine. Go enter the city. Make rounds of every house in the city, and in whatever house no one has ever died, from that house fetch tiny grains of mustard seed." At the first houses she visited, people went to their pantries to fetch mustard seeds. But she remembered that she was not to accept seeds from households where a family member had died. So she left the first, and the second, and the third house—and so on—empty-handed. Finally, she thought: "In the entire city this must be the way! This the Buddha, full of compassion, must have seen!" Overcome with emotion, she went outside the city to the burning-ground, and holding him in her arms, said: "dear little son, I thought you alone had been overtaken by this thing which men call death. But you are not the only one death has overtaken. This is a law common to all mankind." So saying, she cast her son away in the burning-ground. Then she uttered the following stanza:

No village law, no law of market town,
No law of a single household is this——
Of all the world and all the worlds of gods
This only is the Law, that all things are impermanent.

Kisa Gotami moves from being overcome with grief and sadness to gaining some perspective on her plight. To be sure, she has suffered a great loss, but everything is impermanent. And she now knows—what we all easily forget—that she cannot, just as we cannot, find even one household in any neighborhood, town, village, or country where the household has not suffered the loss of a loved one. Gotami's fellow feeling, her compassion for others, her sense of the common condition of humanity are enhanced, and this helps her deal with her awful loss. She takes her beloved son to be cremated with great love, a love that has deepened and expanded from focus only on her own loss, from her incapacitating grief caused, in part, by the mistaken view that she has been singled out uniquely to suffer in this way. Gotami is deepened by wisdom (prajna; panna). He who hears or reads the parable is similarly deepened.

The Buddha's Law

Aristotle's law—in any of its three forms (AL or AL' or AL")—is a psychological generalization to the effect that happiness and virtue necessarily or normally co-occur. More specifically, virtue necessarily or typically causes happiness, unsuperscripted and simpliciter, or more narrowly, virtue[Aristotle/Buddha] causes happiness[Aristotle/Buddha], and nothing else does so.

The Four Noble Truths of Buddhism can be read in such a way that they express similar ideas. Suffering can be alleviated and happiness can take its place only if one's mind is rid of the three poisons of hatred (dosa), avarice (lobha, tanha), and delusion (moha). Treating the process as developmental, the eradication of the three poisons leaves mental space for a consciousness that makes progress toward embodying the four illimitables, the unlimitables, the divine abodes: compassion (karuna), lovingkindness (metta), appreciative joy at the well-being and success of self and others (mudita), and equanimity-in-community (upekkha). A mind constituted by the four divine abodes is the mind of a person who has diligently followed and abided the Noble Eightfold Path. Her heart is dominated by feelings of compassion and lovingkindness. She is a constant self-cultivator—a mindful being—who watches her own motives carefully and works constantly to be free of wishful thinking and delusion. Being dis-ease free she is happy, contented.

Aristotle and the Buddha agree, or can be read as agreeing without too much interpretive mischief, that freedom from suffering and then if possible, being happy, are the initial psychological goals of humans. A life of reason and virtue or wisdom and virtue and meditation, these being different in several important ways, turn out to be the way, the necessary means, or the normal and best means normatively, to achieve freedom from suffering, to flourish, and possibly with luck to be happy. If we think, as we should, that there is a process of moral and cognitive development, then reason (or wisdom), virtue (without or with great or universal love as a component), and happiness (likely construed in theory-relative ways) will admit of degree along the way, with true happiness, understood theory-neutrally or theory-specifically, resulting only for the fully rational, wise, and virtuous—eudaimon[Aristotle] or eudaimon[Buddha].

In the Four Noble Truths, especially the First and the Second, the focus is on the ubiquity of suffering and its cause in acquisitive desire, anger and delusion. The Third and Fourth Noble Truths point to techniques, following the Noble Eightfold Path: right/appropriate/perfect (samma, Pali; samyak, Sanskrit) view, right attention, right speech, right action, right livelihood, right effort, right mindfulness, and right concentration) that extinguish unwholesome desires, and provide remedy from suffering. Once again the question of the relation of relief from suffering to happiness comes up to puzzle us.

Hammalawa Saddhatissa in his *Buddhist Ethics* (2003; also see 1970, 1997), written from a Theravada perspective, treats virtue as a necessary component for the alleviation of suffering. Although Buddha is consistently referred to as "the Happy One," Saddhatissa points the reader to suttas in the Pali canon where neither Siddārtha, nor anyone else, claims to know techniques for achieving happiness, only ones for relieving suffering. Some claim that in the Mahayana tradition a more upbeat view emerges. Thus Damien Keown in *The Nature of Buddhist Ethics* (1992/2001) reads the remedies offered in the Third and Fourth Noble Truths—wisdom, virtue, and mindfulness—as prescriptions for alleviating suffering and bringing happiness to the heart and mind. And he proposes that nirvana can be understood as a state of virtuous enlightenment in this life, not necessarily as a postmortem state in which all craving (the cause of suffering) is extinguished for good (although, of course, there's that too, and not just for enlightened souls but for everyone). Speaking for Tibetan Buddhism, the Dalai Lama says again and again the "the very purpose of our life is to seek happiness," and he typically describes this happiness seeking as involving feelings associated with living in a meaningful ethical manner.

So the psychological motive that Aristotle claims is universal is back in place. For Aristotle it is our nature to seek to be eudaimon, to live meaningfully and purposefully, to flourish. Eudaimonia^{Arisistotle} requires reason and virtue. The Buddhist view is that we actualize our full potential by living in a wise, virtuous, and mindful manner. Our original motives to be free of suffering, possibly to be happy, serve to get us moving on the path to wisdom (prajna; panna) and virtue (sila or karuna) and mindfulness.

We are now positioned to see a substantive difference between the kind of happiness that comes from virtue as conceived by Aristotle and Buddhism, respectively. The happiness that accrues from virtue^{Aristotle} differs in degree and possibly in stability, since ordinary human luck can undermine it, but not in kind, from the sort of good feelings one has in friendship, in familial love, perhaps in good citizenship. Even the sort of settled contentment that comes from being rational and virtuous seems—for all Aristotle says—to be of the same type as one experiences with success at other, nonmoral, worthwhile projects.[14]

Buddhists emphasize that there are different kinds of happiness that come from family relations, material success, and so on. But the kind of happiness that comes from true virtue, given that it involves the "four divine abodes," uniquely pertains to the enlightened state, or being in its vicinity, and seems to differ, or is advertised as differing in kind from other, more mundane, kinds of happiness that come with family, friendship, and citizenship.

On the view that I have been defending, Buddhism is open to an interpretation that there are in fact three necessary conditions for happiness:

virtue and wisdom and mindfulness. Call this claim *Buddha's law*, hence-forth BL. Minimally, accepting BL over AL entails differences in the meth-ods and techniques required to attain virtue and the set of virtues required, namely, Buddhist ones rather than classical Greek ones. Note there are ver-sions of BL, BL' and BL'' that correspond to AL' and AL'' which say that if you are truly virtuous[Buddha]—and wise and mindful—then you will neces-sarily or with high probability be truly happy[Buddha]. Indeed, the best/most plausible version of Buddha's law is BL'', which says that wisdom, virtue, and mindfulness normally and reliably produce a stable equilibrium among themselves and also normally and reliably produce happiness[Buddha].

One more step: it seems wise, at this point, to acknowledge that for reasons that I spoke of above, such as magic pills for happiness, both the Aristotelian and the Buddhist should give up their respective necessary con-dition claims and weaken them in this way: continue to claim that virtue, or virtue and wisdom, or virtue and wisdom and mindfulness combined, are required for happiness, and indeed, normally cause/produce it. This will allow for possible exceptions. Then introduce a *normative exclusion clause* to disallow certain weird cases from counting as morally approved. This will result in a debate between the two theories that revolves around the weaker and more plausible claims, AL'' and BL'', which say:

AL'': Virtue (and reason) is the normal and reliable cause of happiness.
BL'': Virtue (and wisdom and meditation/mindfulness) is the normal and reliable cause of happiness.

To which is added to each a normative exclusion clause, to the effect that cases where happiness is gained by magic pills or is due to false belief do not count because the allegedly happy person must be involved in culti-vating her own virtue and happiness; happy states born of delusion are undeserved, and so on. The problem remains: AL'' and BL'' do not in all probability offer the same kind of happiness but rather happiness[Aristotle] and happiness[Buddha], respectively.

Being Happy That One Is Good

According to Aristotle, eudaimonia is the goal every rational person sensibly seeks. If a person possesses a good character and thus lives virtuously she has reason to judge herself worthy and will, in all likelihood, feel happy. She will experience herself, at a minimum, as worthy and decent. Happi-ness of the sort we aimed at is a settled or semisettled state that involves a positive feel for—a positive sense of—who one is and how one is doing in negotiating relations and affairs that really matter, intrapersonally and interpersonally. Happiness is not a simple state, so it may involve in addition to admixtures of self-esteem and self-respect, such states as contentment, optimism, joy, serenity, and equanimity.

Money doesn't bring happiness, high status doesn't, having only friendships of utility or pleasure won't. But virtue normally does. Why is this? One answer runs as follows: habituation in virtue, as conceived by Aristotle, is designed to bring the co-occurrence about. Each virtue is a disposition to perceive, feel, judge, and act in a way appropriate to the virtue. That is, building virtuous character involves much more than building good behavior. It involves, to a substantial degree, growing, pruning, and maintaining in good health certain perceptual and emotional attitudes and motivational tendencies that are constituents of the virtues. These mental factors motivate good action and are required according to Aristotle for assignments of credit and blame.

In addition, the virtues, as constituents of a good life, are approved of and sanctioned by the wise. Conforming to wisdom, especially when one understands the force of the high-quality (possibly, valid and sound) arguments of the wise, normally makes one feel worthy or good about oneself. But even for one who has not mastered all the intricate analyses and arguments of, say, the *Nicomachean Ethics*, good character normally results in feeling good about oneself, contented, worthy. Why's that? Because virtue involves the amplification of our social nature, an innately attractive and pleasing aspect of ourselves in social relations, which becomes ever more pleasant the more fully it blossoms.

It is not simply that socialization works to produce the relevant feelings, attitudes, and behavior, which would be worrisome since if it did, it would then be merely a social psychological fact that virtue is its own reward. Happiness would follow from virtue, not because one had hit upon true virtue, but because whatever is designated as virtuous around here (this could be awful) is pulled for and rewarded. Mother Nature wired us over evolutionary time to feel positively about being with others and about their well-being, most especially relatives, and those others with whom we share communal projects. Proper moral socialization works by way of inculcating a form of the good life that is abided and lived by the caretakers of the youth, who can produce sound arguments in its defense if called on to do so, and who are dedicated themselves to the project of passing on that form of life by building noble individuals, growing the seeds of fellow-feeling, autonomy, and critical reasoning. Thanks to a certain directionality in our nature, developing and then expressing a well-formed, virtuous character leads to feelings of contentment. Excellent social relations are a source of happiness. And the development of autonomy enables us to become self-cultivators, knowing how, where, and when to apply *techniques de soi* to adjust and develop our own characters more fully.

But one might harbor this reasonable concern: part of the socialization in virtue will include transmitting the idea that if one is good, one ought to be happy (either because you deserve happiness as a natural reward for virtue or because we will treat you well so you will experience your own worth as a social reward for goodness). Suppose then that I feel happy, but am not virtuous. I might mistakenly think I am happy because I am virtuous. If the happiness is the kind that (allegedly) only comes from virtue according to AL or AL', then that thought is false and serves as yet another counterexample to either version of Aristotle's law, which requires that happiness necessarily and only comes from virtue. But suppose I really am good. Then the thought that I am happy (at least partly) because I am good is true or might be true if any among AL, AL', or AL" or BL, BL', or BL" is true.

It is plausible to think that across various virtue traditions because happiness is not simply a feeling state, but has cognitive content, one sort of content it will have, or be tied to in self-ascriptions, is some modest version of an "I am a good person" thought. Furthermore, the social norms governing self- and other-ascriptions of such thoughts will be tied to genuine decency that comes in part from knowing that I was raised well, from having engaged in some reflective scrutiny of my values, as well as from some self-cultivation. This fact that each moral tradition will work to make reliable a dependency relation between happiness ascriptions and being-good ascriptions has two consequences. One consequence is that some simulacra of true happiness, say, that caused by a magic pill, might reveal themselves as a counterfeit, so long as the state possessed every property of true happiness except the relevant contentful surmise that "I am a good person," where this surmise is correctly attributed only if there is actual good moral training and self-work involved (more self-work than simply choosing and swallowing the magic pill!). If the pill produced that thought—that "I am good"—when it was false, we'd need to do some adjustments to our necessary condition claim (whatever form it has, AL, AL', BL, BL'), since something other that virtue produced it.

This is where the normative exclusion clause would come in handy. We stipulate that even the right kind of happiness, phenomenologically speaking, if it is caused by false belief, doesn't count as the right kind, as happiness^{Aristotle} or happiness^{Buddha} or True Happiness^{Aristotle} or True Happiness^{Buddha}. The rationale? Happiness gained by false belief violates our epistemic norms, which interact with our moral norms, but that have their own defensible basis.

The second consequence of the fact that each moral tradition will work to make reliable a dependency relation between feeling-happy ascriptions and "I am good" (by the lights of my tradition) ascriptions, is this: an individual person, be she an Aristotelian, a Buddhist, or a contemporary liberal, will, if she feels happy, likely think it is (at least partly) due to the fact that she is good. The judgment can be mistaken. But that aside, the widespread fact that self-attributions of happiness accompany more or less accurate judgments that one is conforming to the local conception of virtue, is best explained as due to the fact that we are taught, first, that they should accompany each other, because she who is virtuous deserves to be happy; and second, that virtue is the most likely causal suspect (more perhaps than wisdom and meditation if one had to rank these) if we feel happy, contented, and the like.

The point—maybe it is a worry—is that normal socialization encourages, and thus possibly makes self-fulfilling to some degree, ascriptions of happiness when the agent has reason to judge (correctly) that she is in normative conformity. To my mind, this is only seriously problematic when the conception of virtue is not really very worthwhile.[15] But the conceptual linkage between virtue ascriptions and happiness ascriptions might explain some kinds of moral complacency or chauvinism—the sorts where people tend to believe unreflectively that their conception of the good life is better that other contenders. Only it, their own moral conception, as they see and experience things, produces moral contentment, happiness, and so on for them, in them. An alternative conception of virtue might, due solely to the power of socialization, be judged as too demanding, an odd duck, disquieting, creepy, or whatever. This phenomenon of admiring one's own values and norms because one is socialized to believe that they constitute the right way to be and to live is surely sometimes an instance of what psychologists call "the anchoring effect." One can easily see how socialization in the perceived goodness of one's way of life might legitimately come to the service of producing appropriate feelings of self-esteem, self-respect, while, at the same time, enabling certain unfortunate tendencies of moral chauvinism. These tendencies could, I think, be overcome by also teaching about the danger I have just spoken of.[16]

The Work of Meditation

The *Abhidamma* is the classic text of Buddhist philosophy and psychology, and is the third of the three baskets, Tipitaka, of the Pali canon (Tripitaka,

Sanskrit). The *Abhidamma* is composed of seven books. Books 1 and 7 deal with psychology. The prefix *abhi-* means, or suggests, the drawing of distinctions. It is attached to damma (Pali; dharma, Sanskrit), which in this context refers to the teachings about the Way contained especially in the Sutta Pitaka, the middle basket of the three. The first basket (Vinaya Pitaka) consists of wisdom on the life of monks and nuns. The suttas (sutras, Sanskrit) contain Buddha's wisdom for all persons on the path (dharma, Sanskrit; damma, Pali) to Wisdom (panna; prajna, Sanskrit) and Virtue (sila). Sometimes the suttas consist of doctrinal teachings, as well as parables, such as the "Parable of the Mustard Seed" discussed above.

All Buddhists scholars treat books 1 and 7 of the *Abhidamma* as a psychological masterpiece (other books are devoted mostly to Buddhist views on time, causation, etc.) combining at once deep phenomenology, analytic acuity, and classification of mental states in terms of the wholesome and the unwholesome in accordance with how they fit into the Buddhist view of eudaimonia, eudaimonia[Buddha]. This deep respect for the *Abhidamma* exists despite the fact that some, but not all, Mahayana Buddhists see the original manual penned by Theravada monks, as too glowing in its treatment of the monastic life, as well as still embracing remnants of the doctrine of atman because (it is alleged) early Buddhists didn't get the full effect of the doctrine of emptiness (sunyata).[17]

What first catches the eye of the Western reader is the extraordinary number of distinctions drawn among states of consciousness. The book begins with a taxonomy of consciousness (Citta) into conscious mental-state types (cittas*)*. These number 89 initially, and reach 121 after some adjustments. Each type is characterized in terms of the sort of object it takes in (so visual and auditory consciousness differ in an obvious way); its phenomenal feel (e.g., sad and happy); its proximate cause or root (e.g., there is greed-rooted and hatred-rooted consciousness); and its function or purpose—avaricious consciousness is thirsty and aims to suck in or swallow what it desires; jealous consciousness aims to crush, destroy, obliterate one's rival. Citta and the cittas are analytically distinguished from the mental factors (citasekas) that they, as it were, can contain. Joy-Consciousness might contain joy-at-an-infant's-birth-in-my-family or joy-at-a-friend's-success.[18] Joy-Consciousness is a type of consciousness, thus a citta of Citta, whereas joy-consciousness-about-family and joy-consciousness-about-friends would be two subtypes (factor, citaseka). Even the citasekas admit of lower levels: I might be happy that [nephew Jesse got good grades] and that [niece Kendra got good grades]. The feeling is of the same type, it might even feel exactly the same, but the intentional content, marked off by brackets, differs in the two cases. As one studies the *Abhidamma* one gets into the spirit of drawing distinctions upon distinctions, and, indeed one could really start to believe the Tibetan joke that a master phenomenologist might be able to discern 84,000 (the number is akin to us saying "a gazillion") types of anger or craving!

The second thing that strikes the Western reader is that the words *wholesome*, *unwholesome*, and *neutral* are used in the process of classification itself. This provokes the objection that "real"—that is, scientific—psychology describes and explains and predicts, but does not judge the various kinds of sensations, perceptions, emotions, and learning it analyses in normative terms. And indeed, this is our practice in many parts of psychology. But the fact is that clinical psychology and psychiatry texts abound with normative assessment in much the same way anatomy and physiology texts incorporate norms and standards of health, well-being, and good organic function. So one reply to the objection is to conceive of the *Abhidamma* as a psychological treatise that combines descriptive with normative insights gathered from the Buddha's teaching in the first two baskets. Just as we might criticize a psychiatry text on the grounds that it assumes an unwarranted conception of mental heath, any concerns with the ascriptions of wholesomeness or unwholesomeness require showing what is wrong in the Buddha's conception of the good life.

Buddhism starts in the First and Second Noble Truths with the observation that suffering is abundant, that some suffering is self-caused and self-sustained. The Third and Fourth Noble Truths offer a method to work around, overcome, or eliminate suffering and its causes by defeating the poisons in our nature. The three poisons, recall, are hatred/anger/resentment, thirst/craving/acquisitiveness, and wishful-thinking/illusion/delusion. These three, uniquely perhaps, are always bad or unwholesome. The categorical negative assessment of the poisons—one does not usually call something a poison that is good in small doses, even—is one point where questions can be raised. Most naturalists will give evolved aspects of first nature a close look to discover their merits on the grounds that universal phenotypic traits are usually adaptations—that is, traits that evolved because they were fitness enhancing. Insofar as current environments have some of the same properties as the original evolutionary environment, the traits might still be fitness enhancing. One might make a case that my disposition to destroy you if you try to win my mate over is adaptive, good. My anger in such cases is poison to you, not me. It will contribute to my fitness. In this way one might begin to question whether, how, and to what degree the poisons are poisonous and for whom, and by so doing challenge the Buddhist view that the poisons are categorically bad. The *Abhidamma*, despite being pre-Darwinian by two millennia, anticipates this sort of reply and argues that even in local cases where a poison—my jealous rage—seems to get the job done, it ramifies and interacts with other mental states, indeed with one's overall sense of well-being, in ways that always or almost always produce dis-ease, un-ease in me and those with whom I interact. This is an interesting empirical claim that could be tested.

The three poisons are first elaborated as giving rise to "The Six Main Mental Afflictions": Attachment of craving, anger (including hostility and hatred), pridefulness, ignorance and delusion, afflictive doubt, and afflictive views. These in turn are roots for "The Twenty Derivative Mental Afflictions": anger, which comes in five types: wrath, resentment, spite, envy/jealousy, and cruelty; attachment, which also comes in five types: avarice, inflated self-esteem, excitation, concealment of one's own vices, and dullness; and finally, "Four kinds of Ignorance": blind faith, spiritual sloth, forgetfulness, and lack of introspective attentiveness.

Finally, there are six types caused by ignorance + attachment: pretension, deception, shamelessness, inconsideration of others, unconscientiousness, and distraction. The point is that one can go wrong in a lot of ways. The therapeutic tools required for eudiamonia^{Buddha} will need to be abundant and multifarious in kind.

At the other end of the spectrum from the three poisons in first nature are the "Four Divine Abodes" (brahmaviharas)—also called the "illimitables" or "immeasureables" (appamanna). As a reminder, these four are the bodhisattva's virtues:

Compassion (karuna)
Lovingkindness (metta)
Appreciative joy (mudita)
Equanimity (upekkha)

One might think that just as the three poisons are categorically bad, the "divine abodes" are categorically good. There is a caveat. Delusion can mitigate the sublimity of even the "divine abodes." Suppose a person achieves equanimity because she fails to notice certain particulars about her own character, or the character or plight of others, which she ought to be noticing or paying attention to. Here delusion surfaces and might make us question whether the equanimity is warranted. It feels sublime, but it is supported and sustained by failing to see what one ought to see. There is an unwholesome aspect to such equanimity. Similarly one might feel happy about one's friend's successes, but have failed to notice that the successes

were not achieved in an honest way. Whether one would be judged cul-
pable for this sort of ignorance depends on what was in view and what
wasn't. The point is that certain epistemic deficiencies can undermine the
warrant, and thus the sublimity, full stop, of being in an illimitable state of
mind. As I see things, only by introducing the sort of normative exclusion
clause recommended above do we have legitimate grounds for judging such
cases as unwholesome.

And indeed Buddhist psychology pays a considerable amount of attention to the causes of mental states, especially before moral assessment is
made. All states rooted in hatred or greed are unwholesome, as are states
caused by wrong view. The case of the magic pill that makes one happy
is not discussed, but similar cases are. If a seizure causes me to experience
euphoria, it is deemed rootless, and rootless states are unwholesome. Notice
that this means one can be in a state that feels good, has positive valence,
but that is, nonetheless, unwholesome. One reason for judging the state
unwholesome is that it is normative—both psychologically and ethically—
that happiness be produced by genuine decency, goodness, or self-work I
engage in, not by aberrant neural firings. This is not to say that such states
considered narrowly cannot be produced by aberrant neural firings, or pills,
just that they don't count as "good" in some normatively endorsed sense
if they are so produced. This is the work of the normative exclusion clause.

One other point: all four abodes are said to involve states of mind toward
others. One might agree while emphasizing that, at the same time, all four
are in fact states of mind of the individual who has them, and they have a
unique first-personal phenomenological feel for that person. Their object
is, of course, the good of some other. But this analysis seems to run into
trouble with equanimity (upekkha), which might seem to be a pure state of
my soul, and thus not directed at, for, or toward anything outside me. To be
sure, my being calm and serene might make me more pleasant to be around,
but it is not constitutive of equanimity, as we English speakers understand
the state, that it has this aim. But this is not true of equanimity (upekkha),
which means more than serenity and is not just an intrapersonal state. It is
constitutive of equanimity that I feel impartially toward the well-being of
others. If I am in the state of equanimity, interpreted as upekkha, I am in a
state that involves, as an essential component, equal care and concern for
the well-being of all sentient beings. Whereas all the poisons are personally
focused, the four divine abodes are all interpersonally focused; their object
is the well being of others.

The journey to flourishing, eudaimonia[Buddha], and happiness, happiness[Buddha], requires acquiring and then embodying or realizing a set of

conventional virtues plus the four divine abodes. The Buddha was a compassionate soul healer, a therapist of delusion and desire. The aim is flourishing, eudaimonia[Buddha], and it is expected that happiness, specifically happiness[Buddha], comes from or with flourishing, Buddhist style. Just as Buddhist wisdom and virtue involve several components—three or four pieces of deep metaphysical wisdom and eight or ten mandatory virtues (the conventional virtues plus the illimitables)—the mindfulness techniques required for flourishing and happiness are multifarious. Think of the Buddhist soul healer as akin to an old-fashioned general practitioner whose medical kit contains all the different tools to get done whatever needs doing. Sometimes the patient will simply need to understand that because she is very old, say, her aches and pains must be accepted. Perhaps she will be asked to look around at her old friends and acquaintances. She will realize that many have died, and understand that despite her impatience and stubbornness, she will go that way too. But perhaps she, and the therapist together, will focus on the old and happy souls who go on, find meaning and purpose in friends, communal games and projects, listening to music, and arguing about politics, despite the aches and pains, quirky memories, and so on. Objectively nothing changes in her physical condition. But perhaps, as with the "Parable of the Mustard Seed," the old woman sees things differently and feels better. Stories and parables abound in Buddhist texts, each designed for a different mental affliction. There are stories designed to put anger in perspective, to make it wane, to reveal its ultimate fruitlessness. Stories that reveal the empty feelings that accompany relentless acquisitiveness, and so on for every mental affliction starting with the three poisons, moving on to the six main afflictions, and then to the twenty derivative afflictions.

Sometimes the patient will need clear instruction on how to understand her condition for what it is (she doesn't really get it). And she will need to understand how to get better. Such direct soul diagnosis and instruction for alleviating her dis-ease is given for everyone in the Four Noble Truths since they include, especially in the Third where we are instructed to follow the Noble Eightfold Path, the directions to practice virtue and to meditate.

Meditation is a tool like storytelling and direct teaching. There are many types of meditation. Some work to develop attention, one-pointedness. These may help in living virtuously by making one more attentive to the particulars of another's situation. There is meditation on impermanence (annica) designed to help the individual understand the ephemerality, possibly the emptiness (sunyata), of all things including oneself (anatman). Breathing meditation is good for relaxation, as well as serving as an antidote for moha (false belief). How is that? When I attend to the facts "now I am inhaling," "now I am exhaling," I focus on things as they really are, see how fleeting every state is, and so on. Other kinds of meditation work specifically to awaken moral intuitions, possibly innate, that seem directed toward what is virtuous or that encourage us to orient ourselves in the direction of virtue.

Here I provide just two examples. Both examples are based on a type of Tibetan meditation (Tong-len), which is a form of widely practiced "give-and-take" meditation. The first is designed to enhance compassion; the second works first on selfishness, then on empathy and love.

#1: In generating compassion, you start by recognizing that you do not want suffering and that you have a right to have happiness. This can be verified or validated by your own experience. You then recognize that other people, just like yourself, also do not want to suffer and that they have a right to happiness. So this becomes the basis for your beginning to generate compassion.

So let us meditate on compassion. Begin by visualizing a person who is acutely suffering, someone who is in pain or is in a very unfortunate situation. For the first three minutes of the meditation, reflect on that individual's suffering in a more analytical way—think about their intense suffering and the unfortunate state of that person's existence. After thinking about that person's suffering for a few minutes, next, try to relate to that yourself, thinking, "that individual has the same capacity for experiencing pain, suffering, joy, happiness, and suffering that I do." Then try to allow your natural response to arise—a natural feeling of compassion toward that person. Try to arrive at a conclusion: thinking how strongly you wish for that person to be free from suffering. And resolve that you will help that person to be relieved from their suffering. Finally, place your mind single-pointedly on that kind of conclusion or resolution, and for the last few minutes of the meditation try simply to generate your mind in a compassionate or loving state (Dalai Lama 1998, 128–129).

#2: To begin this exercise, first visualize on one side of you a group of people who are in desperate need of help, those who are in an unfortunate state of suffering, those living under conditions of poverty, hardship, and pain. Visualize this group of people on one side of you clearly in your mind. Then, on the other side, visualize yourself as the embodiment of a self-centered person, with a customary selfish attitude, indifferent to the well-being and needs of others. And then in between this suffering group of people and this self representative of you in the middle see yourself in the middle, as a neutral observer.

Next, notice which side you are naturally inclined towards. Are you more inclined towards that single individual, the embodiment of selfishness? Or do your natural feelings of empathy reach out to the group of weaker people who are in need? If you look objectively, you will see that the well-being of a group or large number of individuals is more important than that of one single individual. After that, focus your attention on the needy and desperate people. Direct all your positive energy to them. Mentally give them your successes, your resources, your collection of virtues. And after you have done that, visualize taking upon yourself their suffering, their problems, and all their negativities.

For example, you can visualize an innocent starving child from Somalia and feel how you would respond naturally towards the sight. In this instance, when you experience a deep feeling of empathy towards the suffering of that individual it isn't based on considerations like "He's my relative" or "She's my friend." You don't even know that person. But the fact that the other person is a human being and you yourself are a human being allows your natural capacity for empathy to emerge and enable you to reach out. So you can visualize something like that and think, "This child has no capacity of his or her own to be able to relieve himself or herself from his or her present state of difficulty or hardship." Then mentally take upon yourself all the suffering of poverty, starvation, and the feeling of deprivation, and mentally give your facilities, wealth, and success to this child. So, through practicing this kind of "giving and receiving" visualization, you can train your mind" (Dalai Lama 1998, 213–214).

These two meditations are ripe for philosophical analyses, containing as they do references to natural feelings of empathy, natural intuitions about universal rights to be happy and that impartial good is a greater good than personal good, that mind training works to improve character and behavior, and the idea that moral intuitions are self-validating. Each claim is worth careful examination. In closing I focus on only one claim, the claim that impartiality is morally best. The demand of impartiality is typically met with two responses: First, it is impractical to be impartial because none of us are positioned to promote the good impartially; we normally interact only with friends, family, and close relations. Second, it is unnatural to care as much about the well-being of people I don't know or personally care about as the ones I know and care about.

How Demanding Is Buddhist Ethics?

The charge of excessive demandingness is commonly made against consequentialism, especially against the version of act consequentialism requiring that for each and every action opportunity I have, I should do, or try to do, what will maximize the greatest amount of good for the greatest number of people. The first objection to a theory of this form is that it requires a psychologically impossible amount of attention to each and every action opportunity. What are all my action opportunities now, at this very moment? How many different actions are action opportunities I have at this moment? If an ethical theory requires me to give determinate answers to these questions, even if I am only required to unconsciously compute what all my action options are (before choosing the most "opti-mific"), it asks something impossible, perhaps something that makes no sense (Flanagan 1991b).

There are familiar ways around this serious objection. Most credible ver-sions of consequentialism define the good as that which maximizes welfare impartially construed, but then go on to suggest a variety of psychologi-cally possible ways that the best state of affairs can be brought about. For example, the good will be maximized if people proceed to love their loved ones, extend benevolence to their neighbors, show concern for their com-munity, care about the well-being of all, their nation-state, its neighbors, and the world. In this way, circles of concern will come to overlap, so that each is the beneficiary of an expanding circle of concern. The usual move is to suggest that impartial good will come from the spreading outward of partial concern. It is not clear that this is true. I do not know how to test it. But it is a popular idea, captured most visibly in bumper stickers that read, "Think Globally, Act Locally"—which seems like pretty good advice.

Without resolving the issue of whether there is an adequate way for consequentialism to keep its distinctive character (defining the good impar-tially), without also being judged to be too demanding, it is nonetheless useful for present purposes—which is to decide if Buddhism is too demand-ing—to identify the feature that is consistently seen as the source of the problem of excessive demandingness. It invariably has to do with how much impartiality, and of what kind, is required.

To get quickly to the point, distinguish among these different kinds of impartiality: (1) the belief that everyone has an equal right to flourish; (2) equal love for everyone; (3) impartiality in action.

The belief that everyone has an equal right to flourish is not psycho-logically too demanding. Furthermore, it is a sensible belief (although it is a very Western way of speaking). Here, I repeat the rationale for (1) from meditation #1 above: "In generating compassion, you start by recognizing that you do not want suffering and that you have a right to have happiness. This can be verified or validated by your own experience. You then recog-nize that other people, just like yourself, also do not want to suffer and that they have a right to happiness."

As stated, this rationale is not logically demonstrative. But it can be made so:

• If there is something I desire for its own sake and recognize that everyone else wants the same thing, then I ought to believe that everyone has a right to that thing.

- Whenever I recognize that I ought to believe something, I believe it.
- I desire to flourish (not suffer, be happy).
- I recognize that everyone else wants to flourish (not suffer, be happy).
- I ought to believe that everyone has a right to flourish.
- I believe that everyone has a right to flourish.

This argument is valid. Thus (1) above—that I ought to believe that everyone has an equal right to flourish—now follows necessarily. The conclusion must be true if the premises are. The best point of entry I can see for questioning the argument's soundness would involve taking on the major premise. I'll assume that the argument simply formally (i.e., deductively) restates the rationale for recognizing a universal right to flourish, and is acceptable, indeed that it is proved. But believing that everyone has a right is not very demanding; it involves believing a certain proposition, not actually doing anything.

Next consider (2), *equal love* for everyone. Two questions arise. First, who conceives of commitment to impartiality—now interpreted in accordance with (1)—as believing that everyone has a right (the same right) to flourish—as also entailing (2), equal love for all?

Jesus and Buddha might seem likely suspects. John Stuart Mill tells us that the main message of his essay "Utilitarianism" is summed up in Jesus of Nazareth's Golden Rule. This is helpful since Mill is not, in arguing for utilitarianism, promoting a doctrine that is particularly lovey-dovey. That is, I don't need to love you in one normal sense of the term, to promote your welfare. This brings attention to the second question about (2). What does equal love mean? There are issues about the meaning of both words, *equal* and *love*. I'll be brief.

Mill's Jesus is not asking us to have warm and fuzzy feelings when he tells us to "Love one's neighbor as oneself." Was exactly did Jesus mean? Biblical scholars agree that Jesus best clarifies what the Golden Rule means when a hostile lawyer asks him, "Who is my neighbor?" Jesus's answer comes in the form of the parable of the "Good Samaritan." The Jewish people and the Samaritans were bitter rivals, worshipping different Gods, and so on. The story is that a certain Jewish man is robbed, beaten, and left to die in a ditch. A rabbi first, and then a sort of deacon, a man of lower rank than a rabbi who assists the rabbi in preparation and oversight of Jewish religious services, both pass by, despite seeing the badly injured man. Then a journeying Samaritan comes along "and when he saw him, he had compassion on him," nursed him, bound up his wounds, put him on his own donkey, and took him to an inn where he nursed him overnight. In the morning when it was time to leave he paid the innkeeper and said, "Take care of him and whatever thou spendest more, when I come again, I will repay thee."

Jesus asks, "Which now of these three, thinkest thou was neighbor unto him that fell among the thieves?" And he [the lawyer] said, "He that showed mercy on him." Jesus then said "Go and do thou likewise" (Luke 10:25–37).

Assuming, as everyone does, that the parable clarifies the meaning of the Golden Rule, what does it help us see? It helps us see that hatred (dosa) is a vice, as is indifference, whereas sympathy, empathy, and compassion (karuna) are virtues. Clearly the Samaritan doesn't feel the sort of love toward the injured Jew that he does for his spouse, parents, brothers and sisters, children, fellow community members—toward whom he may feel different kinds of love. Whatever love he feels here is an active but impartial love (he doesn't know the injured man in any way that could make him feel any special emotions toward his character, toward the unique person he is). It is a love born of compassion and mercy that would motivate him to help anyone suffering in the same way.

We have insufficient evidence, but we might think that the Samaritan is someone whose heart is filled with compassion (karuna) and lovingkindness (metta). It needn't have been that way since some weaker form of fellow-feeling could motivate a person to help anyone in such dire straits. A difference would reveal itself when the straits were less dire, or major inconvenience would result from providing assistance.

In any case, the love required by Jesus in the Golden Rule is decidedly not personal love in any of the familiar forms; it is not romantic or sibling or parental or communal love. It is best described as compassion or lovingkindness toward anyone and everyone who suffers. As I understand Buddhism, it recommends the same virtues, the same kind of love.

What makes such love equal or impartial or universal? It is not because one feels the exact same kind of love for the man in the ditch that one feels for one's children or spouse. What one does ideally feel toward both one's loved ones and the man in the ditch is impartial in the sense that one wishes no suffering and happiness for them solely on the basis of their shared humanity. Both because of how one is positioned and because of the special (additional) love one feels for one's loved ones, one might, possibly through the work of meditation, take some of the deeper features of those personal love relationships and feel-them-into-the wider-world. This if possible would be, I take it, a morally healthy type of projection.

Finally consider (3), impartiality in action. A and B are both in equally dire straits, both are drowning, I am equally well positioned to help A or

B, neither of whom I know, but helping one means the other will die. It is obvious I must help one, but which one? The answer is that in this case it doesn't matter. Flip a coin if you wish. But save one.

Suppose A is my child and B is a stranger. I know what I'd do. Critics of consequentialism sometimes say that a consequentialist in virtue of rec-ommending impartiality in action should do the coin toss. The usual and plausible consequentialist reply is that the world will go better—the good considered impartially will be maximized—if people observe the obliga-tions intrinsic to their special, particularistic human relations.

Such, happily rare, dilemmas aside, consequentialists will rightly press us about our chauvinistic tendencies. In a world in which 20 percent of the people suffer in absolute poverty as defined by the World Bank, am I really doing as much good as I can, as I should? Start just thinking about America—although our love ought to eventually extend beyond the bor-ders of our nation-state. Imagine, sounding like John Lennon, that well-off Americans were raised to feel compassion (karuna) and lovingkindness (metta) in the way Buddhism recommends. As I write these words there are forty million working poor in America and perhaps an equal number of unemployed poor. Aristotle taught that you can't lack basic necessities and have prospects for virtue and happiness. Buddhists agree, although they conceive of the basic necessities required as consisting of a more meager basket of goods than Aristotle did. Suppose that in addition to being raised to be compassionate and lovingkind, we also believed in moderation and quelled our avaricious tastes. Being raised this way, the poor and the suffer-ing are on my mind, I want to act so as to alleviate suffering and help such souls become happy. What to do? I could contribute (large sums of now disposable income) to local charities. I could work for political reform, pro-gressive taxes going from say 60 percent for people in my income bracket to 99 percent for Bill Gates. These are kinds of impartial actions, or better impartial strategies for the greater good. The people I am imagining, good Buddhist persons or good consequentialists, don't feel bad that they have less. They feel good that Fortuna's hand in determining the fate of our fel-lows is weakened and that the hands of those whose hearts feel love and compassion are strengthened.

The only sensible conception of impartial action I have ever heard defended runs along these lines. This is true despite the fact that we are sometimes asked to picture individuals looking at their savings ledger ask-ing "What exacting ought I to do at this moment to maximize the impartial good?" And with this picture in mind, the practical impossibility of doing anything sensible, let alone truly good, bears down on us.

I am aware that, in this final section, I have not directly addressed the question of whether Buddhism is too demanding. I have, however, tried to do so indirectly. We ought to believe that everyone deserves to be free of suffering and to achieve some sort of happiness. This is more or less a matter of rational consistency. Working on compassion and lovingkindness, loving our neighbor as ourselves, makes sense. Doing so, possibly uniquely, holds prospects for making us happier than all the money or stuff in the world can. Furthermore, it positions us—in virtue of our belief about what everyone in fact deserves, and our greatly amplified fellow-feeling—to want to actively work for the impartial good.

Being a virtuous Buddhist is certainly not psychologically impossible. It takes work and practice, but these are not so hard. Usually when an ethical conception is charged with being too demanding, the charge revolves around demands it makes that are perceived to be psychologically or practically impossible. Buddhism advocates no states of mind for the virtuous that are impossible to achieve, nor does it advocate any general-purpose algorithm for deciding at each choice point what to do. So it is not subject to either kind of impossibility charge. One worry that might surface or resurface is that Buddhism, for all I have said, is actually very undemanding. It requires a high degree of mental compassion but is very vague about how much compassionate action is expected or required. This is an old debate, which in Buddhism, is highlighted in the relative priority give to the self-purified life of the arahant versus the active life of the bodhisattva. In the West, the debate concerns the quality of holy lives that can seem morally and spiritually self-indulgent but practically inconsequential. In both traditions, think hermits, recluses, cloistered nuns and monks, sages on mountaintops, and so on.

Conclusion

Buddhism presents a vision of human flourishing, eudaimonia^{Buddha}, as involving an active life of wisdom, virtue, and mindfulness. The life of a eudaimon^{Buddha} reliably, but not necessarily, yields happiness^{Buddha}. Buddhism does not tell us that we are obligated or required to follow the way. It does tell us that so doing amplifies, in healthy ways, our most noble natural tendencies, and thus that if we want to find personal happiness and make the world a better place, following the path of dharma (damma, Pali) is wise and noble.

One final point. I've claimed that Buddhism promotes a noble vision for realizing our potential, and suggested by indirect arguments that it cannot be charged with being too demanding. Aristotle provides a picture of virtue that is better and more demanding than liberal commonsense morality. But as judged from the perspective of Buddhism, it is too undemanding. Aristotle saw clearly that our natures contain a healthy dose of fellow-feeling. His vision of the virtuous person is one who grows fellow-feeling. From a Buddhist point of view, what Aristotle failed to see was that growing these seeds even more fully, to the point where compassion and lovingkindness take over our heart-mind, would make us morally better and happier, too. Maybe, maybe not.

Postscript: Cosmopolitanism and Comparative Philosophy

QED. That is what I would like to say. That which was to be demonstrated has been demonstrated. Philosophy is not like that. Demonstration is for mathematics, where if the premises are true, then the conclusion must be true. If the definitions of terms (number, point, line) are rigorous, the axioms self-evident (parallels never intersect), and logical rules are followed, then the conclusion is true necessarily. A theorem states a certainty. In a right triangle, any right triangle, any conceivable right triangle, it is necessary that the square of the hypotenuse is equal to the sums of the squares of the other two sides.

What are the theorems of eudaimonics, the study of human flourishing? What are the relations between wisdom, virtue, and happiness—three sides of a human life well lived, a human life with the right sort of structure? There are some reliable relations among these three components of human life but there are no necessary connections. Spinoza, or so it seems, was wise, happy, and good. But he is exceptional. There are ignorant, unreflective souls who are good and happy, Tolstoy's Christian peasants, perhaps. There are wise and happy *Übermenschen*, like Plato's character Callicles, who are smart and well educated, who live heroically, as strong poets, brilliantly even, but not, in many cases, compassionately. There are tortured souls, like Nietzsche, who see ever so deeply and are as wise as a person can be, but who pay the price of surrendering their prospects for happiness and for finding a stable moral orientation. Empirical inquiry into human well-being—eudaimonics—has never, not once, in the history of human reflection yielded a theorem about living well, not one claim about necessary connections among wisdom, virtue, and happiness. It has made claims about necessary connections, several of which I have discussed. But in every case there are the exceptions. On one side, there are the extraordinarily good souls like Euripides's Hecuba, who despite her great nobility, her enormous decency and reliability, cannot prevent coming undone when fate skewers her again and again, and then eventually, one time too many, at which point the center, which in her case is her beautiful and resilient character, cannot hold, things fall apart, and she becomes a homicidal maniac. And on the other side there are the Calliclean types who despite walking all over more pedestrian souls, consuming their being as necessary, are nonetheless rewarded with the shiny coat of a beast who flourishes.

That said, philosophy has yielded some wisdom about certain typical or reliable connections among the components of a life well lived, a good life, between wisdom, virtue, and happiness. Uncertainty rather than logical surety is life's usual accompanist. Living is risk, a matter of self-expression under uncertainty, a psychopoetic performance with a troupe of other actors who know—to varying degrees—the norms of a tradition, but all of whom are engaged mostly in improvisation. Living is not a matter of executing an algorithm, or if it is, we are clueless as to what algorithm we are executing.

A good life is a matter of living and being a certain way, or more likely, living and being in one of the multifarious ways that are worthy, which lead to flourishing and, if we are very lucky, to happiness. We are heirs and heiresses to the wisdom of the ages, to the results of numerous previous experiments in living. It is natural to wonder: Which ways of being and living are better or worse among the tried and tested ways? If the ways of living that produce flourishing were a subset of all the possibilities, it would be good to know what the good ones are. Here Buddhism turns up on the radar—as do a host of other ways of being and living; indeed most ways that have been tried, most experiments that have been tried and lasted some, have some merits. Perhaps there are several right answers to the question, How ought I to live? Perhaps there are many answers. Perhaps only a few of the best ideas have been tried. This is what I think.

Philosophical reflection such as we have been engaged in here aims for truth and truthful speaking about flourishing, it aims at wisdom, not proof, deduction, or demonstration, not a set of theorem-like recipes for how to live well. So what can I claim to have accomplished in this book? What truthful things have I said?

The book you have just read has two parts, which overlap, intersect, and interweave in what I intend to be useful ways. I call part I "An Essay in Comparative Neurophilosophy." It was devoted to introducing what, if anything, contemporary Buddhism has to offer as a theory of well-being, flourishing, and happiness. Some neuroscientists claim to have shown that the brains of Buddhists reveal their owners to be unusually mentally healthy, exemplars of persons who flourish, actual but rare specimens of extremely well-formed and happy human beings. I do not doubt that Buddhism is a decent and defensible form of life. But I have expressed reasons for skepticism of the claims that it is the right choice if you want flourish, be happy, and the like, and, furthermore, that neuroscience has shown, is in the process of showing, or even could in principle show that this is so. First, there are problems defining and measuring happiness. Big problems. Second, there are problems with neuroscience claiming that it can measure human flourishing in the robust philosophical sense(s) of flourishing by looking at brains. The problem is not that materialism is false. We are material beings living in a material world. Thus neurophilosophy, the approach that conceives of mind and consciousness as embodied, mostly in the brain, is the way to do philosophy of mind. But flourishing, well-being, even happiness, are not (only) in the head. Or to put it another way: insofar as different philosophical traditions recommend that we construct persons in different ways, they call on us to make the mind-brains of different people work—perceive, process information, and act—in somewhat different ways—all obviously within the possibility space allowed by the basic genetic-neural architecture. Buddhist persons are built to see, be, and act in ways that are Buddhist, and not, say, Confucian or Aristotelian or liberal American. Third, all theories of human flourishing, including the Buddhist one, are about ways of being and living, about forms of life, not just, only, or mainly about feeling a certain way—for example, being happy. Assessment of the goods a particular theory promises is a complex matter that involves philosophical analysis of what precisely a particular theory is advertising when it offers a way to live well, when it offers a conception of human well-being or flourishing. It also requires examination of how, as a historical and sociological matter, people who have lived in the recommended way have fared or are faring. Such inquiry involves the tools of comparative philosophy, history, sociology, anthropology, as well as neuroscience. The last two points reinforce the first point: concepts like happiness, positive affect, good mood, wisdom, virtue refer to different psycho-biological-social states in different theories. There is no one state of happiness or well-being or positive mood that all the contenders seek.

Comparative neurophilosophy is a new idea. But its time has come. Insofar as nervous systems are plastic, there is room for making humans in a host of different ways, many of which have never been tried. Culture has been doing this forever. A unified theory of the mind-brain-world permits us to study the phenomena of person construction in increasingly empirically rigorous ways. But again, the study of forms of life, ways of being in the world, involves vastly more than the study of brain states. There is also the Dasein part that isn't in the head, but is still nonetheless in the natural world.

In part II, "Buddhism as a Natural Philosophy," I used the deconstruction of the first part to advance the analysis of Buddhism as a form of life with attractive features for contemporary folk, specifically for members of two tribes I interact with regularly, indeed tribes that I belong to—analytic philosophers and scientific naturalists. Buddhism, I claim, should be of interest to philosophers because it offers a metaphysics that accepts the wisdom of impermanence, no self, the ubiquity of causation, and emptiness, an epistemology that is empiricist, and an ethics that prizes compassion—all of which have some plausibility—and because it claims that there are logical connections between these three. Outside of Plato in the West, I know of no other philosophical theory that draws such intimate connections among metaphysics, epistemology, and ethics.

That said, there are beliefs that many take to be essential to Buddhism, which are not acceptable to members of my tribe(s). We would say that they ought not to be acceptable to contemporary Buddhists either given the commitment to empiricism, the testing of beliefs against the world. These include the beliefs in immaterial spirits, rebirth, and karma (of the untamed variety). Is there Buddhism without these beliefs? I say yes, why not? Others say no. Buddhism is a historical, philosophical entity or kind, like Poland or the Mormon Church, not a natural kind like water, which is H_2O, always has been, always will be. This means that barring institutional decisions about what counts officially as Buddhist, the ways Buddhism develops, what it assimilates with, what traditions it accommodates, remain to be seen. If there is wisdom in Buddhism naturalized, perhaps it is wisdom for everyone. For myself, I am inclined to think that Buddhist metaphysics and epistemology are plausible, credible in their own right, independently of their association with other ideas born in the Indian subcontinent such as rebirth. Buddhist ethics? There are three things that cause me hesitancy. First, Buddhist ethics overrates the virtue of compassion and undervalues justice as fairness. Second, many Western Buddhists I know are not very nice, both more passive-aggressive and more narcissistic than other types I prefer. This may have nothing to do with Buddhism but mainly with the nature of American spiritual seekers; even so, it concerns me. Third, I still do not see, despite trying to see for many years, why understanding the impermanence of everything including myself makes a life of maximal compassion more rational than a life of hedonism. And isn't that the problem that we keep coming back to, the problem or question that doesn't go away? I am not distraught over not seeing this connection, but then again I am not a Buddhist. If I were a Buddhist I would be troubled by not understanding how Buddhist ethics follows from Buddhist metaphysics and epistemology. My own way of dealing with this problem is to be and live as a platonic hedonist, to try to maximize pleasures at the places where what is true and beautiful and good intersect. The comfort associated with living in this space, insofar as there is any, comes from thinking that no answer is the right answer to the question of how one ought to live. Thinking this is compatible with thinking that there is much worthwhile in the wisdom of the ages, including Buddhism.

Perhaps all we can expect of philosophical reflection, especially among those of us who live in multicultural, cosmopolitan communities, is that different ways of being and living, different experiments in conceiving of good lives and of trying to embody the wisdom contained in these different ways, keep many options alive, and allow maximal freedom in finding ways to be well and to live well, and perhaps, if we are lucky, to be happy.

Some will say that platonic hedonism is a form of liberal ironism, and that liberal ironism is the form of life favored among modern cosmopolitans who live their lives at the intersection of many traditions. This seems right. But it is not clear how this is an objection. Cosmopolitans relish the hybridity of their world, the exhilarating anxiety that comes from lacking confidence in any single traditional way of being and living, while at the same time being hopeful and grateful that the wisdom of the ages can accumulate into new ways of being and doing that advance the project of flourishing. Philosophy's contribution is to examine the great traditions of the past for useful insights into what to do now and next. For that purpose, for going forward, Buddhism has something to offer. Is it the answer? Of course not. Nothing is the answer. This is something Buddhism teaches.

Notes

Introduction

1. There is this joke: Q: What do you get when you cross a Unitarian with a Jehovah's Witness? A: Someone who shows up at your door on Sunday morning with nothing to say. There is this downside to fusion. It can produce what is bland and uninteresting, preserving nothing that was interesting or worthwhile in the antecedents. Then again there are the many amazing gourmet dishes served up by chefs influenced by the intersections of French and Asian cuisines.

2. Mark Siderits (2003, xi) writes: "The enterprise of fusion philosophy is meant to be a successor to the practice of what has been called comparative philosophy." The aim is to "use elements from one tradition to solve problems arising in another." Chris Kelley (2010), a wise friend who, like Siderits, has taught me a great deal about doing comparative, cross-cultural philosophy, has drawn attention to Richard Rorty's notion of "abnormal discourse," as akin to what I call cosmopolitan. Cosmopolitan is to be distinguished from what Pascal Boyer calls the "relevant connections method," familiar from some of Rorty's own writings where points are made by telling the reader that Quine, Davidson, Derrida, Dennett, MacKinnon, and Judith Butler don't reject a certain vague philosophical view that Rorty likes—for example, fallibalism. Cosmopolitan isn't that method, which isn't itself really a method; it is a rhetorical style, a flashy learned way of making, or seeming to make, arguments from authority.

3. Buddhism is at least as diverse in terms of sects and denominations as is Christianity. There are some doctrines, however, that are canonical: the Four Noble Truths, the Eightfold Path, dependent origination, impermanence, and the doctrine of no self. When I claim to be trying to understand Buddhism naturalized or flourishing from a Buddhist perspective I aim to understand whether there is a naturalistic concept of flourishing—for example, without afterlives, without the invisible but powerful hand of karmic orchestration of life, as it is depicted in the vicinity of these shared canonical doctrines. The method makes sense since my target audience is not orthodox Buddhists or Buddhologists, but fellow analytic philosophers and philo-

sophical naturalists (these being somewhat different tribes—but lately especially in the United States, joining ranks), as well as intelligent open-minded souls interested in a worthwhile perspective on human flourishing. The reverse project would be to try to explain to my South and Southeast Asian Buddhist friends what, if anything, unifies all the sects, denominations, and traditions that believe that Jesus is the Son of God. This I take it would require staying in the vicinity of the claim that Jesus is God incarnate and espouses the Golden Rule. Such matters as the relative importance of faith versus good acts, the existence of saints and angels, miracles, and such, would require much delicacy. And supposing one got there, explaining eventually how Unitarian Universalists and the Society of Friends fit in the Christian tradition (if they do) is migraine territory.

4. For the naturalist all beliefs that p, including the beliefs espoused by all great world religions that p, are ripe for natural explanations. Beliefs such as that there are tsunamis and that people suffer are best explained by the fact that there are tsunamis and that people suffer. Beliefs such as that there are gods who cause tsunamis, which cause people to suffer, are not caused by the tsunamis and their effects, but by the tsunamis and the suffering *plus* something additional, often motivated by perfectly sensible questions about what caused the tsunami. Sociology, anthropology, history, and psychology of religion are committed to providing natural explanations of both kinds of thinking, cases where p happening explains belief in p, and cases where what happens, p, underdetermines (sometimes radically) what is believed. Sometimes the *plus* part is itself a naturalistic theory about, say, geology or the weather, and really accounts for why the tsunami occurred; other times it is a supernatural theory and seems to account for it, but doesn't, for example, when it asserts that some god or some devil caused the tsunami.

5. It may help the reader unfamiliar with my other work to know that I am an atheist with respect to nonnatural posits familiar from almost every spiritual tradition (unobservables are fine, if natural)—what I call hocus pocus. Some say one should be an agnostic because after all anything is possible. I take up this idea later. For now I say this much: the burden is on the believers to give reasons for believing in their supernatural posits, God, gods, spirits, heaven and hell, and so on. I have never heard true believers provide good reasons to believe in what they believe in—God, gods, spirits, heaven, hell, rebirth, and so on. So I don't take the weak-kneed and polite out of saying, "Well, anything is possible," which although true, doesn't apply in such cases. If I am being asked to consider an argument for some nonnatural posit, if you can't give me good reasons to believe it exists, or is likely to exist, I don't believe in it. Not believing as opposed to remaining in a neutral posture is what distinguishes atheism from agnosticism, and explains why I am an atheist.

6. In a cosmopolitan exchange, on the occasion of a Mind and Life Institute meeting in Garrison, New York, several years ago, Rob Hogendoorn and I came up with the concept of Buddhshit. Every tradition has its bullshit; Buddhists are just lucky to have such a good name for theirs.

Chapter 1

1. I am grateful to Andy Rotman and Mark Siderits for help with sukha and its interpretation. If they are wrong, I am too.

2. Dreyfus (2003, 170) writes: "The Tibetan tradition proposes an inclusive twofold typology of meditation. The first type is 'meditation of stabilization' ('*jog sgom*; lit. 'meditation [in which one] places [the mind on a single object]'). This exercise, which involves cultivating the ability to remain focused on a single object, corresponds to the cultivation of tranquility (*zhi gnas, samatha*). The second type of meditation is called 'meditation of investigation' (*apyad sgom*) and includes all practices in which the mind is not focused on a single point, ranging from motivational contemplations . . . to the cultivation of liberative insight (*lhag mthong, visasayna*)." One other point: several major scholars of religious epistemology, Wayne Proudfoot of Columbia University and Robert Sharf of UC Berkeley, for example, think that the moves in Buddhism and in many other traditions, East and West, to validate religious truths in meditation or other kinds of personal, sometimes private or mystical experience are relatively recent, and come in part from pressure for intersubjective testing from the epistemology of secular science. On this view, the emphasis of meditation as a source of knowledge is part of a religious epistemology witness protection program.

3. There are interesting differences of opinion on handling the poisons, East and West. See Flanagan 2000a, and Goleman 2003.

4. One criticism of my interpretation of Buddhism is that it overemphasizes the wisdom component, and is thus too philosophical, more philosophical than, for example, Zen or Pure Land Buddhism. Pure Land was founded in medieval Japan in part to respond to the problem of Buddhism being too philosophical, elitist, cognitive, and so on, and not open to the proletariat. Three responses: First, it is true that my view emphasizes the wisdom components and that is because I am a philosopher and I am most interested in the varieties of Buddhism that claim that wisdom in addition to virtue and/or meditation is necessary for eudaimonia[Buddha]. Second, the Eightfold Path is avowed across Buddhisms and it does say that wisdom is required. But, third, neither the Eightfold Path, nor my own view, requires that the wisdom be held in a highly explicit cognitive way. It might be that the wisdom about impermanence, no-self, and the like can be known or can get into one's blood and bones as a sort of know-how, rather than know-that, if a person is just immersed in a culture that speaks, thinks, and moves in certain ways, in ways that convey recognition of impermanence, the importance of focus on the present, and so on.

5. I say release from "unwholesome attachment" rather than all attachment to mark a distinction I think important: there is a sense in which some form of wholesome attachment to the attainment of wisdom and virtue is constitutive of the dharma path. See Bhikkhu Bodhi's (2000, 1726–1728) translation of the *Samyutta Nikaya* (SN) for classical textual support for wholesome attachments.

6. Damien Keown (1992/2001), writing from a Mahayana perspective, proposes that nirvana can be understood as a state of virtuous enlightenment in this life, not extinction for good (although, on my naturalist view, there's that too, the extinction of desire due to death, and not just for enlightened persons but for everyone—this is the "one and done" rule that we naturalists say applies to all lives). Masao Abe (1991) promotes the on-this-earth, in-this-lifetime view of virtue, enlightenment, and engagement from a Zen Buddhist perspective. Sayadaw U. Pandita (1991) does the same from a Theravadan perspective.

7. *Bodhicharyavatara*, ch. 1, verse 28, p. 37. I read Sāntideva as claiming that seeking happiness[Buddha] indirectly by seeking enlightenment and virtue and practicing mindfulness = eudaimonia[Buddha] is a winning strategy. Jay Garfield (personal communication) thinks that Shantiveda is best read overall as not recommending any kind of happiness, and that Shantideva's claim that the search for happiness "crushes our joy" is meant to apply to every kind of happiness, including happiness[Buddha]. Searching for or seeking even it guarantees suffering! Relatedly, Stephen Batchelor (personal communication) reminds me that in chapter 6 of *Bodhicharyavatara*, Sāntideva argues that the Buddhas can never be happy because they identify themselves with the infinite sentient beings who suffer, and he points out that the Dalai Lama, who is a fan of chapter 6, never quotes it in his popular work for Westerners on happiness. Garfield reads the Dalai Lama's work on happiness as an appeal to people of all kinds to seek wholesome kinds of happiness that involve compassion. Most of these kinds of happiness will be different from and less than happiness[Buddha], but they will make the world a better place. These last two points seem fair, and help support my overall claim that the kind of Buddhism that is popular in the West advertises itself as offering happiness, perhaps happiness[Buddha], perhaps more usual kinds of happiness. Whether traditional—older and Asian—kinds also do so is a different matter left to Buddhologists. It would seem an ecological oddity if historically the original Buddhisms from 2,500 years ago offered the kind of happiness that appeals to rich white people in Berkeley and Marin County, California (I spend summers there), who tell me they are Buddhists, and that they claim is on offer by Buddhism. I call this Northern California kind "happy because I am nice, happy," which is different from "happy-happy-joy-joy-click-your-heels-happy," which is most common in Southern California, where it coexists with "happy because I am nice, happy."

8. See also Saddhatissa 1970, 1997, 2003, written from a Theravadan perspective. Saddhatissa consistently refers to the Buddha as "the Happy One." But he points the reader to suttas in the Pali canon (sutras, Sanskrit) where neither Buddha nor anyone else claims to know direct techniques for achieving happiness. This, of course, is compatible with there being indirect techniques via wisdom and goodness and mindfulness.

9. See Flanagan 1991, 2007, 2010, for a discussion of the psychological literature on so-called positive illusions. Buddhists should consider the very idea of positive illu-

sions oxymoronic and unwholesome since illusions and delusions involve moha, one of the three poisons. But insofar as contemporary Buddhists really believe in rebirth they are, I claim, in the grip of an illusion or a delusion, where the latter is a belief that is unrevisable no matter what the evidence says. In Thailand I spoke to many professors and medical doctors as well as a few businesspeople and always asked if they really believed in rebirth. The answer was almost always yes. My surmise is that educated Thai Buddhists believe in rebirth more literally (and spend a fair amount of money gaining "merit" for better rebirth from monks) than similar professionals in the West.

10. If one were really trying to study something like compassion or happiness born of compassion, as Buddhists conceive it or them, one would need to study some form of Buddhism and practitioners of that form. If one did that with Tibetans (specifically Geluks), one would find that compassion is considered a mental state that involves the wish that all sentient beings are relieved of suffering. Now this might seem promising since wishes are surely in the head. But notice that the content of the wish is that [all sentient beings are relieved from suffering]. No one knows where in the brain the wishes department is. How and where do wishes hold their contents? Is the wish known by the person who has it or not? There is debate about this. Does compassion depend on knowledge that I am connected to all others in some metaphysically deep way? Is it just a wish or a wish attached to some know-how (e.g., so that the compassionate person just sees suffering and acts to relieve it); or a wish attached to some know-how and know-that (e.g., that all deserve not to suffer)? There is debate about this. Is a very compassionate person, as we conceive them, a social worker for example, compassionate? It depends on whether she has the wish that no sentient being suffers (Dreyfus 2003, 230–231). The point is that there are very difficult problems comparing conceptions of compassion (or any other virtue) or looking in brains for compassion (or any other virtue). Different traditions interpret what counts as compassion differently—primarily a disposition to feel, to act, to feel and to act, to wish, and so on. How the tradition defines or characterizes the compassion will determine where one might look for it, in the head, in bodily (interpersonal) activity, in know-how, in knowing that, and so forth. The lesson generalizes, but it is not acknowledged in the scientific literature that studies happiness among Buddhists.

11. The doctrine of emptiness comes from Nagarjuna, second century CE, and is part of the Madhyamaka development of Mahayana (Garfield 1995, 2002). Weaker forms of the doctrine are akin to Greek atomist views of the physical universe according to which objects bottom out in indestructible—uncuttable—particles, atoms. On the mental side, consciousness might decompose, but then stop with sensation, perception, the emotions, and so on. But then again these might decompose further. In contemporary terms the emptiness of consciousness as we know it would involve reduction of, say, visual perception into the neural networks that

execute it, then these might be reduced to biochemistry, then into physics, and so on ad infinitum. Emptiness according to Nagarjuna is the view that all things are analyzable/decomposable into parts that are further analyzable ad infinitum (this view might be read as akin to certain quantum mechanical and/or string theoretical views). In my experience in Theravadan countries like Thailand, emptiness (sunyata) and no-self (annata) are often treated the same thesis. Compare: many non-Trinitarian Christians—even more so Muslims—think Mary is one of the three persons in God among Trinitarians; or even more common, almost no Christians in my experience (I have been asking for years and think over 90 percent get it wrong) can give the correct answer when asked to distinguish between the immaculate conception and the virgin birth. The first is Mary's being the first human (since Adam and Eve) to be born without original sin; the second is that she didn't get pregnant with Jesus in the usual way.

12. Meditation includes lots of esoterica, some Buddhist, some from antecedent and adjacent yogic traditions. So for example, in Tantric practice, mostly Tibetan, there are all sorts of sexual meditations, which are not at all like Shantideva's techniques for overcoming sexual desire—imagining she who you desire as dead and decomposing—but rather can be used (I am told) to have orgasms without touching (why this is a good idea I am not sure). And there are meditations that adepts claim provide deep insight into the ultimate nature of things such as the nonphysical nature of mind. But here we naturalists object: the production of unusual or hallucinatory experiences no doubt produces experiences of a certain sort. But such experiences are not reliable sources of information about the nature of mind.

13. See Naht Hahn 1987, 2003; Queen and King 1996; Queen 2000. Queen's introduction in Queen 2000 contains an excellent overview of the three vehicles, Theravada, Mahayana, and Vajrayana (Tibetan Mahayana or Tantric Buddhism), as well as an argument that socially engaged Buddhism is sui generis enough to be counted as a new fourth vehicle Navayana ("new vehicle"). The view I favor is that Navayana is continuous with the other Buddhism(s), just the latest accommodation Buddhism has made to changing social conditions.

14. We live, and Buddhist philosophy especially lives, in the age of "fusion philosophy" (Siderits 2003). Thus it is not surprising, or inherently objectionable, when some credible interpretation of Buddhist philosophy meets, for example, Western secularism and they fuse, resulting in the sort of secular Buddhism one sees in Stephen Batchelor's bestseller *Buddhism without Beliefs* (1998; also see his *Confessions of a Buddhist Atheist,* 2010) (Batchelor was a monk). What I call naturalistic Buddhism is what results from a similar interpenetration of modern scientific understanding of the human mind and world with Buddhist wisdom. Obviously, not all traditional Buddhist wisdom will survive such interpenetration. The Dalai Lama calls for adjusting the tenets of Buddhist philosophy, if there are strong scientific reasons for so doing. See chapter 3 for a discussion of the thorny question of whether recent Tibetan Buddhism is science friendly.

15. I reject one all too common way of distinguishing the bodhisattva of Mahayana Buddhism from the arahant (arhat, Pali) of Theravada Buddhism, which involves claiming that the bodhisattva unlike the arahant takes her virtue into the world. Some Mahayanans will complain that although the arahant must work to develop her compassion and lovingkindness, she might in principle do so in nunish or monkish seclusion. I don't see that the Pali *Nikayas*, which contain stories, speeches, and so on about the Buddha and his disciples (suttas, sutras), support such a reading (the three baskets of the Pali canon consist of the *Nikayas*, the *Vinaya*, and the *Abhidamma*). See Bond 1988 and Lopez 1988 for excellent scholarly discussions of the arahant and bodhisattva, respectively. Bond (1988, 159) writes that "arahants are depicted not as silent, self-centered sages but as beings interested in liberating humanity from its predicament." Shantideva's *The Way of the Bodhisattva* (*Bodhicharyavatara*), eighth century CE, is the *locus classicus* on the bodhisattva's path.

16. There are two connected issues here, the development issue and the individual-difference issue. The Buddha regularly called his teaching a "Gradual Training" (Bhikku's Nyanamoli and Bodhi, MN, 1995, 34) and he consistently reveals great sensitivity to individual differences in his students. SN 4.235–237, pp. 1283–1284 indicates that the highest happiness involves gradual training, the gradual destruction of the afflictions, and four levels of awakening, and suggests that the various stages or levels that characterize the happiness of a bodhisattva unfold accordingly. As for the distinctive personality traits and life circumstances of particular individuals, the *Nikayas* show that the arahants surrounding the Buddha had distinctive personality traits. This can be seen clearly in the *Mahagosinga Sutta* (MN 1.212ff. Also see Bodhi, SN, 2000, 4, *Marasamyutta*, (pp. 195–201). In the West, William James's *Varieties of Religious Experience* (1890/1982) remains the deepest and most comprehensive analysis of the many differences of personality and temperament found among saintly types.

17. I know from conversation with the Dalai Lama, high lamas, and other Tibetan Buddhist practitioners that talk of self-esteem, self-respect, and pride makes them nervous. As I understand things, this is because they see a certain kind of puffery in ordinary Western forms of pride. Furthermore, self-esteem and self-respect as well as pride engender worries that these states are normally supported by a false sense of self as a permanent atman. My position is that these states have nondelusional forms that are wholesome, that can assist in overcoming certain negative emotions, and that can be legitimately felt by a person who understands himself or herself as anatman.

18. See Lopez 1988 for an excellent scholarly overview of the bodhisattva's path and stages. The joyous or blissful stage is usually described as occurring at the first or second levels when the opening to the path is first seen and the journey begins. It is not clear that the initial joy or bliss remains continuously as the bodhisattva traverses the full of ten or eleven levels or grounds, many of which are depicted in terms of difficult struggles—for example, fighting off demons through concentra-

tion (fifth ground), or perfecting the understanding of dependent arising (sixth ground), or working to perfect skillful means to help others (seventh ground).

19. According to Sāntideva, even the bodhisattva will sometimes need to overcome inappropriate lust. One way to do this is to imagine the object of one's lust as old and decrepit or covered with shit or dead and decomposing. Even if one judges the use of such antidotes as good, it is hard to imagine that they could make one feel happy on any use of the term.

20. One might think that one of the four divine abodes or illimitables, namely equanimity (upekkha, Pali; upeksa, Sanskrit), automatically secures happiness[Buddha] or brings about one ordinary kind of happiness. In English *equanimity* means tranquil, calm, at ease, not frazzled, or not ill at ease. "Zenlike" is used sometimes to refer to a chilled-out, unflappable person. Because equanimity is a stable state of one's mind, any person who is possessed of the four divine abodes experiences that kind of contentment, namely equanimity, that is a familiar kind of happiness. Thus my imagined bodhisattva who is contented but not happy is not really possible. But equanimity has a somewhat different meaning in Pali and Sanskrit than in English. My Pali dictionary defines *upekkha* as a state midway between sadness and joy. Furthermore, upekkha, like all four divine abodes, involves a state of mind directed toward others. Its aim is the good of others as well as a virtuous regard for oneself. Buddhist equanimity (upekkha) means more than, or something different from, personal serenity. It is constitutive of equanimity that I feel impartially toward the well-being of others. If I am in the state of equanimity, interpreted as upekkha, I am in a state that involves, as an essential component, equal care and concern for all sentient beings. Thus even if I am equanimous, in this sense, I may see, for example, that others are not, or that efforts by myself and others who are virtuous, continuously run into obstacles. Despite being equanimous, this may make me feel low and also keep me from being serene.

21. Steven Collins (1998, 156), speaking about what he calls "the Pali imaginaire," writes: "A number of stories about both Arahants and Buddhas make it clear that they suffer both bodily pain and certain kinds of mental discomfort. . . . So even enlightened Buddhas can sometimes find things irksome, uncomfortable."

Chapter 2

1. William James made the study of exemplary individuals, some of them genuine odd ducks, respectable in his masterpiece *The Varieties of Religious Experience* (1898/1982).

2. Deficit studies are terrific ways to figure out how a complex system works, so looking at areas affected by stroke, tumors, and so on has been very helpful in distinguishing among areas differentially involved in particular types of processing. Damasio's work (especially 1994) has gotten lots of attention. Phineas Gage is widely

taken as an example of someone with a moral deficit, a "moral knockout," due to a brain deficit in the medial frontal cortex. Maybe he is. But the evidence from Gage and contemporary patients involves gross anatomical problems. You knock out a big area and you normally get big problems.

3. Seligman (2002) is exceptional among mind scientists in trying to sort out the constituents and components of our ordinary conception of happiness at the psychological level.

4. Many wise scholars say that Buddhism has always promised many normal kinds of happiness, well-being, and felicity. See, for example, Collins 1998).

5. I take the necessity and sufficiency claims to be more than simply linguistic. The claims direct us to what Buddhist philosophy says flourishing and happiness consist in, what Buddhist philosophy means by the concepts of flourishing and happiness. There are closely related claims that are empirical and testable—for example, being a Buddhist is necessary for happiness, sufficient for happiness, and so on.

6. The meditative technique here, which I myself have used with my dog Kayla, who sometimes annoys me by barking to get me to play fetch when I am reading outdoors, may have gone like this: I know that Kayla will bark to ask me to play fetch (the monk knows a sound as loud as a gunshot is coming); I imagine Kayla is as far away as the other end of a soccer field. When she barks it doesn't seem so loud. Ditto for the gunshot sound.

7. Throughout this book I gloss meditation and mindfulness as equivalent. This is not quite right and here's why: mindfulness is a practice of lived attention that can be taught and then practiced most of the time, as one watches one's behavior and thoughts at work, for example. Meditation as a formal sitting practice is different, and insofar as Buddhists practice prostrations and what we'd call praying, we have yet a third thing. Regarding my claim that Westerners dramatically overstate the identification of Buddhism with meditation practice, see Dreyfus 2003, Sharf 1998, or possibly more enjoyably, visit a Buddhist country.

8. In *Consciousness Reconsidered* (1992), I called the method of triangulating all information sources about mind, brain, and behavior, "the natural method." By the mid-1990s in work on dream consciousness (1995, 2000b), I explained how the natural method could be expanded to include any relevant empirical information source in understanding the nature of persons, their minds, and their social life.

9. There is research that indicates that the paralimbic system of psychopaths is "on the thin side." Seeing this is not of course seeing vice in the brain, it is seeing anatomical structures that are abnormal and can support a kind of psychopathology.

10. For the time being, we might follow Seligman's (2003, 304) attitude toward the scientific status of the terms *happiness* and *well-being*: "The word *happiness* is the overarching term that describes the whole panoply of goals of Positive Psychology.

The word itself is not a term in the theory. . . . Happiness, as a term, is like *cognition* in the field of cognitive psychology or *learning* within learning theory. These terms just name a field, but they play no role in the theories within the field."

Chapter 3

1. A significantly different version of this chapter appeared in *The Really Hard Problem: Meaning in a Material World* (Flanagan 2007).

2. The claim is about science's ability to produce truth, which is not the claim that science produces all goods. Art and music produce beauty, which science may or may not also indirectly produce. Exercise and good nutrition produce health; love and sex produce various kinds of interpersonal and physical pleasures. Truth matters to the present inquiry because normally philosophical and spiritual traditions, like scientific traditions, claim to provide it: The Truth.

3. In his brilliant book, *Buddhism and Science* (2008), the historian Donald S. Lopez Jr. emphasizes the ways Buddhism has not been science friendly, indeed typically since its inception it has been very science unfriendly. After setting the historical record straight, Lopez writes: "This history will give pause to anyone who thought that Buddhism is modern, *au courant*, up-to-date with the latest scientific discoveries" (p. 216). One consequence of Lopez's history for my philosophical purposes is to remind us that until very recently Buddhism may have had less interaction with scientific culture than any other major world spiritual tradition, and when it did interact with science it was not until recently—possibly only or mainly in the hands of the 14th Dalai Lama and a band of his followers—open to or impressed by science.

4. The first statement of this form goes back to 1981. See Cabezon 1988. Indeed, the Dalai Lama gives a remarkable example of what Buddhist beliefs might have to yield: "Buddhists believe in rebirth. But suppose through various investigative means, science comes one day to a definite conclusion that there is no rebirth. If this is definitely proven, then we must accept it and we will accept it" (pp. 20–21). In a private audience with the Dalai Lama in Dharamsala in April 2000, the Dalai Lama and I discussed the Roman Catholic conception of heaven and hell. He expressed concern about my reports of being scared by hell as a boy. "Very bad." I then asked about Buddhist views of the afterlife, including karmic prospects for worse lives. He acknowledged that such an idea of rebirth was common among his people, but expressed personal reservations about his followers' idea of rebirth. I must admit to not probing very deeply—I was in a bit of shock. What is certain is that the Dalai Lama's conception of rebirth is more sophisticated than that of more ordinary Buddhists.

5. The citation is to a book by the Dalai Lama (1990). One gets glimpses of it in other writings. But Jinpa's formulation is very clear and I'll use it as the official statement of the caveat. He himself gives as an example the belief in rebirth. Science has

produced no evidence for it but has not shown its nonexistence. A lot depends here on the logic required in "finding" or "showing." If the demand is deductive proof, then rebirth is not ruled out. If there is a high level of inductive evidence disfavoring it, then it has been ruled out.

6. In graduate school in the 1970s, I was introduced to the problem of demarcation being played out in different ways among the logical positivists in Berlin and Vienna the 1930s. Popper (not officially a positivist)—born in Vienna but living in England—worked on the problem of demarcation in his own critical way. Sometimes the problem was to demarcate in a principled way meaningful discourse that was scientific from meaningful discourse that was not scientific. So scientific assertions were testable, either confirmable or disconfirmable, whereas the expressions of music, visual art, and literature were not testable, or better, not testable in the same way, but nonetheless meaningful. Others were interested in a line of demarcation between sense and nonsense: science would fall on the side of sense because it made testable assertions, whereas (depending on the thinker) religion and parts of Heidegger's philosophy would be designated nonsense. They seem to make assertions about the world, but they don't. Why? Because they are untestable gobbledygook.

7. I would be foolish to deny that the doctrine of rebirth is considered mandatory across many Buddhist sects (see Willson 1987 for an excellent overview of "the logical arguments" the Dalai Lama accepts and advances in favor of the doctrine). Stephen Batchelor (1997, 20), a self-avowed Buddhist atheist, writes that "I do not believe, as is sometimes claimed, that the teaching of Buddha stands or falls on the doctrine of rebirth, and that one cannot really be a Buddhist if one does not accept it." In an exchange with Batchelor, Robert Thurman, a leading Tibetan Buddhist scholar, suggests that it is true that you don't have to believe in rebirth, but that the belief does a huge amount of motivational work in Buddhism. Dostoyevsky's Grand Inquisitor expresses the view that ordinary people need to be given false hope to behave decently, and Marx acknowledged that the powerful typically dispense spiritual Kool-Aid to keep the masses in normative conformity to their will.

8. I have also had contact with Western Buddhism that comes in a very secular form through such people as Stephen Batchelor, Joseph Goldstein, Sharon Salzburg, and Jon Kabat-Zinn.

9. The excellent Dutch scholar Rob Hogendoorn is now undertaking this very important work.

10. The Dalai Lama also mentions warnings he has received that science and spirituality do not make good friends. He thinks that this is a special problem for theistic (Abrahamic) traditions.

11. In Lopez 2005, I learn that Chöpel called himself a "geshe," but never in fact sat for the required exam. This fits his personality. Also in certain circles in exile, Chöpel is a cultural hero or icon of Tibetan modernism (Lopez 2005, 239). Perhaps I am safest saying that he is persona non grata among most orthodox Gelugs.

12. Thupten Jinpa (2003) quotes from Gendun Chöpel's journal, written in the 1930s and 1940s: "Even the Indian Brahmins who regard the literal truth of their scriptures dearer even than their own life, were eventually compelled to accept modern science." To move any recalcitrant Tibetan souls, Chöpel quotes from the revered epistemologist Dharmakirti (seventh century): "The nature of things cannot be cancelled, Through means of falsity, even if attempted, the mind will [eventually] uphold that [truth]." There is a tradition in Tibet among those who take the bodhisattva's vows—to live a life of complete dedication to compassionate and lovingkind action toward all sentient beings—to learn as much as possible about everything (including as many languages as possible), so all claims to knowledge can be tested with a critical eye. Except for unusual thinkers like Chöpel and the 14th Dalai Lama, science was not on the list of things to learn as much as possible about, in large part because there was so little exposure to science among Tibetans until after the diaspora that began in 1959 (see Lopez 2008).

13. I'm betting that if one were to poll ordinary Americans and Europeans about what impels scientific inquiry, most Westerners will say it is the search for truth, power over nature, and profit.

14. Hopefulness is a good thing. But there are worrisome "laws"—really, generalizations such as these: (1) whatever we can do, we will do; (2) whatever can go wrong (with technology) will go wrong (eventually).

15. Not all Buddhists are trained formally to debate. Gelugs are exceptional to the degree that formal debate, and practice thereof, is considered an essential part of their education and practice (Dreyfus 2003). Not even the other Tibetan sects practice debate to the extent that Gelugs do. That is, although there is some room for formal debate within other sects, it pales compared to that of the Gelugs. For Gelugs, debate is integral to scholarship; for others it isn't. All Buddhist sects endorse, in principle, the examination of assumptions. In practice, much depends on how open a sect/school is to critical examination of itself.

16. The oldest *Vedas* date to 1500 BCE and do not include the *Upanishads* and the *Bhagavad Gita*. The *Upanishads* date from the sixth century BCE. The *Bhagavad Gita* is included in the *Mahabharata Epic*, written from the fourth century BCE to the fourth century CE, but the *Bhagavad Gita* is thought by many, perhaps most scholars, to be a late text composed possibly entirely in the Common Era. In any case, the latter are the key texts of what came to be known as Hinduism. Hindus don't typically call their religion *Hinduism* (although they may call themselves Hindus as a sort of ethnic attribution). The name originates most likely in the desire of British colonialists to name their—the Indians'—religion/spiritual practices something. So Buddhism did not come from Hinduism, because whatever exactly Hinduism is or names, it comes after Buddhism. To make matters worse, the English word *Hindu* is almost certainly based on a mispronunciation that relates to the importance of the Indus (not Hindus'!) river. To describe their spiritual practice, Hindus sometimes use

the word *darshana*, which is best translated as "philosophy." Often they refer to their way as *Santana Dharma*, the eternal way of truth. There is no Hindu Pope. It is not a creedal faith with a single orthodox doctrine. There is no Buddhist Pope either. Buddhism is also not a creedal faith with a single orthodox doctrine. That said, every spiritual tradition has some commitments that constitute the minimal conditions of being a member, advocate, and so on. A traditional Tibetan textbook, *Cutting through Appearances,* says, "The definition of a proponent of Buddhist tenets is: a person who asserts that the four seals which are the views testifying that a doctrine is Buddha's. The four seals are: 1. All compounded phenomena are impermanent; 2. All contaminated things are miserable; 3. All phenomena are selfless; and 4. Nirvana is peace."

17. Brahman is the name for the ultimate, self-sustaining source of all creation. But "it" is not a person. Furthermore, many Hindus conceive their elaborate pantheon of gods, even high Gods like Brahma (creator of earth but not everything; that is Brahman's role), Vishnu (loving protector), and Shiva (fierce protector) as "aspects" on the one and only God, Brahman. Hints of Spinoza.

18. The Dalai Lama (2005, 92–93) writes: "Even with all these profound scientific theories of the origin of the universe, I am left with questions, serious ones: What existed before the Big Bang? Where did the Big Bang come from? What caused it? Why has our planet evolved to support life? What is the relationship between the cosmos and the beings that have evolved within it? Scientists may dismiss these questions as nonsensical, or they may acknowledge their importance but deny that they belong to the domain of scientific inquiry. However, both these approaches will have the consequence of acknowledging definite limits to our scientific knowledge of the origin of our cosmos. I am not subject to the professional or ideological constraints of a radically materialistic worldview. . . . And in Buddhism the universe is seen as infinite and beginningless, so I am quite happy to venture beyond the Big Bang and speculate about possible states of affairs before it."

19. Compare: when Descartes vows to doubt everything, he makes it clear that he does not throw his ethical convictions into the mix. As he sees it the epistemological crisis he is in does not require it.

20. I'll assume that something like Ernst Mayr's (2001) judicious account is understood by the Dalai Lama and his colleagues as an accurate representation of neo-Darwinian theory circa 2000.

21. Right now people in Bangladesh are vastly more fit from the point of view of population genetics than the people of Belgium. Why? Because there is a population explosion in Bangladesh and most of South Asia and zero population growth in Belgium. If all humans cared about was fitness, we'd all be trying to maximize the number of our own children, grandchildren, and so on. But flourishing commonly supersedes ordinary biological fitness as our goal (Flanagan 2002). There is a dispositional account of fitness that might say this: your average Belgian person is more fit than your average person from Bangladesh because he/she is generally in better

health and so forth, so if they were trying to reproduce at the same rate, the Belgian would produce more viable offspring.

22. Simple vertebrates first appeared during the Cambrian explosion circa 500 million years ago.

23. The concept of "omniscience" is exclusively Mahayanan. In fact, it's one of the reasons Tibetans think less of "Buddhas by way of Theravada." It is a curious fact (to me) that early Buddhism (Theravadan) is in many respects less metaphysically extravagant, more practical, pragmatic, down to earth, than later Buddhism(s).

24. My diagnosis of what is going on here is this: the idea of rebirth is not played up much in the Dalai Lama's book, although it is mentioned several times. We know enough about Buddhism to know that the idea matters. And the normal way it is described is as follows: karmic causation does not in fact operate in the tame way any naturalist armed with the combined resources of the natural and human sciences can accept and potentially explain. Karmic causation is not simply an innocent way of referring to mental causation and what it gives rise to, to the sum of all good and bad effects that humans create and that affect future generations. These effects are subject to a complex payoff system that involves a cycle of conscious rebirth. If I live well, then I live well in my next appearance. Because Buddhism is atman-less, how and in what form my consciousness survives or lives again is quite mysterious. Hinduism and Christianity have less trouble making sense of the idea of an afterlife that is mine and that is, in addition, a sensible reward or punishment for my karma. Why? Because they hold respectively that each person possesses an immutable atman or soul. Despite, many other problems, such views have a much easier time than Buddhism, which rejects the reification involved in such posits as the self, soul, or atman, when it comes to explaining what it is about me that is reincarnated or that gets to sit at the right hand of God. It is my essence, my soul, my Self. To keep things simple here, I am not going to delve more deeply than necessary into the thorny issue of rebirth (but see chapter 5). For the especially curious, here is a bit of philosophical history and critical analysis of the idea: in his magisterial book *Imagining Karma: Ethical Transformation in Amerindian, Buddhist, and Greek Rebirth* (2002), Gananath Obeyeseker distinguishes between two kinds of rebirth theories, *nonkarmic eschatologies* and *karmic eschatologies*. The first are most common in small-scale societies. There are two typical beliefs: a dead member of the community will circle back into the community; a newborn can be identified as the reincarnation of a specific ancestor. There is rebirth but it is not moralized.

We can understand the appeal of the idea. Grandmother has died and is missed; her grandchildren are bearing children. A newborn daughter is seen as grandmother's reincarnation. Note: In a small society there will be, for now familiar Darwinian reasons, strong physical "family resemblances." One sees the *nonkarmic rebirth* idea with frequency in Amerindian and West African tribes. In larger-scale societies with greater mobility, especially if community members exit or new ones enter, one sees the emergence of *karmic eschatology*: there is rebirth. But it may occur far away.

Sometimes this involves going to heaven or hell for eternity, which involves going very far away (usually to be joined later by one's loved ones). Or it may involve entering a cycle of rebirths, until—according to most schemes—some form of final liberation/release/dissolution/heavenly life is achieved. The key to the "quality" of one's next life is one's good or bad karma in one's current life (adding in perhaps karmic effects of previous ones). Rebirth is moralized in this way. Sticking with the Indic religions, one finds both types of eschatologies. Obeyeseker (2002, 1) writes: "Consider the *Rg Veda*, the oldest stratum of Brahamanic religion [now dated at about 1500 BCE]. The soul at death, driven by a chariot or on wings, takes the route of the Fathers and reaches a place of eternal rest. The *Rg Vedic* notion of heaven is a paradisiacal one; 'there is light, the sun for the highest waters, every form of happiness, the Svadha, which is at once the food of the spirits and the power which they win by it, their self-determination.'" There is music, drink, and merriment.

Outside of the *Rg Veda*, "The association between karma and rebirth is not at all clear in the earliest texts and discourses of Indic religions. There are virtually no references to rebirth or to an ethical notion of karma in the *Vedas* or in the *Brahmanas*, the oldest texts belonging to what became known as the Hindu tradition. The first significant references appear in the early Upanishad, the *Brhadaranyaka Upanishad*, probably composed sometime before the sixth century BCE, followed by the *Chandogya* and the *Kausitaki*. A hundred years or more later these theories appear in full bloom in the so-called heterodox religions—particularly in Buddhism and Jainism—that have karma and rebirth at the center of their eschatological thinking. Soon afterwards these ideas surface in mainstream Hinduism itself and become an intrinsic part of the eschatological premises of virtually all Indic religions" (Obeyeseker 2002, 1).

I get the impulse behind karmic eschatologies. Had I been in charge of the choice between the one life and you go to heaven of the *Rg Veda* option, and the later karmic cycle of rebirths option, I'd have definitely gone for the former. It's much quicker for one thing. For another, there is only paradise. Then again, some evil people don't deserve paradise. From what Obeyeseker says, there is reason to think that no choice was made since the *Rg Vedic* idea—everyone gets paradise—was never picked up in the first place. In fact, he thinks the basic idea was not really ethicized because there was only the paradisiacal outcome, not a punitive one. A workable karmic eschatology requires a sensible system of rewards and punishments. Thus, there was a vacuum and the idea of the karmic rebirth cycle filled it.

In India the idea of karmic rebirth with good and bad outcomes appears and fixes as the dominant meme, no later than 600 BCE—some think it appears as early as 900 BCE—and it spreads in the East like wildfire. (Similar ideas appear in the West in Pythagoras and Plato and eventually in all three Abrahamic religions, in the latter cases in something akin to the *Rg Vedic* idea but ethicized thanks to "hell.") The key feature of all forms of karmic eschatologies is that they moralize life in a specific metaphysical way. There is the normal earthy system of payoffs for living well. But there is, in addition, a metaphysical system of payoffs that operates after death. In orthodox Indic traditions, my identity, my essence is constituted by my atman, my soul. It is not 100 percent clear what or who orchestrates the system of karmic pay-offs, although what happens is pretty straightforward. Depending on the quality of this life, one's atman is reincarnated into a better or worse, higher or lower, human or nonhuman life. Perhaps Brahman, the creative source behind the universe, "makes the decisions" about reincarnations or, more likely, because Brahman is pretty impersonal by Abrahamic standards, the laws of karma work somehow up and alongside ordinary causal laws. How this came to happen is obscure.

Now Buddhism is distinctive in several ways. It is heterodox. First, it is not theistic. It is either atheistic or quietistic on theological matters. Second, there is the denial that I am, or have, an immutable atman. A person is a psychologically continuous and psychologically connected being. But personhood is part of the flux. Without going into the various interpretations of the anatman doctrine (but see chapters 4 and 5), we can see why, if Buddhists are going to talk about future lives, most careful ones will distinguish between reincarnation, where my atman is reborn, and rebirth, which is the view that (maybe) the-conscious-stream-of-being-that-I-am continues on in some way. Think of the idea along these lines: a naturalist might think, using conservation principles, that when I die the stuff I am made of disperses and rejoins the universe. If I am anatman I might believe that the consciousness that constitutes me is immaterial and resurfaces in another living being in a way suited for anatman, rather than for an immutable, indestructible atman. In my experience most Buddhists have serious difficulty explaining how the continuity works and in what way my consciousness continues. One teacher and friend I have sat with at the Kadampa Center in Raleigh, North Carolina, Venerable Robina Curtin—an ordained Australian in the Gelug lineage, well known for her film *Chasing Buddha*—always says that Buddhism falls apart unless you believe that mind is immaterial and also that somewhere between five and seven weeks prior to a human impregnation event, the next "soul" in waiting is in the vicinity of where the conception event occurs! In addition to describing such an improbable event with such precision (how is the time frame known?), she reverts to describing the rebirth in a way that more suits reincarnation. That is, she—and in my experience—many wise and learned Buddhists, have trouble describing how the continuity of anatman works without using the rejected conceptual categories appropriate to atman. It is I—Owen-the-atman—that gets reborn, perhaps in the body of a sewer rat or a bodhisattva, but it's me. Indeed, in Tibetan Buddhism one sometimes hears that enlightened beings, Dalai Lamas, for example, get to plan and/or orchestrate their next rebirth. Actually, this doctrine is easy to find in Tantric teachings.

It is worth pointing out that in the very same inaugural address in which the historical Buddha expressed dismay over the question of God's existence, he claimed to be clueless about whether he (or anyone else) had any sort of afterlife. On the other hand, there is abundant evidence in the suttas/sutras of the Pali canon that the Buddha endorsed the belief in rebirth, even remembering aspects of former lives. One should not underestimate the motivational problem faced by every great spiritual tradition, especially one, such as Buddhism, with perfectionist aspirations. If I only have one life, then my prospects for achieving enlightenment in this very life do not seem that likely (although see Sayadaw U. Pandita, *In This Very Life* (1992), for an exploration of the in-this-life possibilities from a Theravadan perspective). In my 1991 book, *Varieties of Moral Personality: Ethics and Psychological Realism*, I argued that in ethical and spiritual life as in athletics, when traditions set goals too high (unrealistically), there is often a loss of motivational hold on advocates. So by developing the idea that I am responsible for many past and future lives, I may see that I do in fact have enough time to become wise and virtuous, and in addition, this may make me as motivated as possible to try very, very hard. I see this idea, I think, in some of Robert Thurman's writing (see the Batchelor and Thurman debate in 1997).

25. Thus Nāgārjuna's doctrine of emptiness (sunyata) can be read as either or both a theoretical or a phenomenological response to a certain psychic atomism that members of the Madyimaka school see remaining in the descriptions of the *Abidhamma*. "Emptiness" is the thesis that things such as the "mind" or "self" that seem to have an essence, don't. Pre-Buddhist and early Buddhist psychology decomposed mind into familiar sensory and cognitive faculties. Nagarjuna claims to see that these faculties admit to further phenomenological decomposition, as do whatever elements seem to make up the next lower level, and so on, ad infinitum (see chapters 4 and 5 below).

26. The reasons behind the inference are of course much more complex that a straight shot from phenomenology to ontology. There are also the 2,500 years of development of Buddhist philosophy and religion that are only partly dependent on phenomenology. There is the metaphysics of impermanence, dependent origination, karmic causation, rebirth, anatman, emptiness (sunyata), the myriad views about what nirvana is/consists of, and so on.

27. This work, which began in collaboration with the late Francis Crick in the 1990s, is the most philosophically sophisticated and scientifically responsible work on consciousness yet written. Koch, being humble, would be the first to admit—in a Newton-like way—that he has been helped to see as deeply as he does by the work of various underlaborers from James to the present. I had the amazing opportunity to spend the better part of a week at Caltech in the mid-1990s with Koch and Francis Crick discussing consciousness.

28. Koch (2004, 18–19) adds the following judicious thoughts about the exact relation between first-personal experience and the brain: "Along the way, the great debate that swirls around the question of the exact relationship between neuronal and mental events needs to be resolved. Physicalism asserts that the two are identical; that the NCC for the percept of purple *is* the percept. Nothing else is needed. While the former is measured by microelectrodes, the latter is experienced by brains. A favorite analogy is with temperature of a gas and the average kinetic energy of the gas molecules. Temperature is a macroscopic variable that is recorded by a thermom-

eter, while the kinetic energy is a microscopic variable that requires quite a different set of tools to study. Yet the two are identical. Even though, superficially, they appear quite distinct, temperature is equivalent to the average kinetic energy of molecules. The faster the molecules move, the higher the temperature. It does not make sense to talk of the rapid molecular motion causing temperature as if one is the cause and the other the effect. One is sufficient and necessary for the other. . . . At this point, I am not sure whether this sort of strong identity holds for the NCC and the associated percept. Are they really one and the same thing, viewed from different perspectives? The characters of brain states and of phenomenal states appear too different to be completely reducible to each other. I suspect that the relationship is more complex than traditionally envisioned. For now, it is best to keep an open mind on this matter and to concentrate on identifying the correlates of consciousness in the brain."

Chapter 4

1. I leave aside until the next chapter, the question of whether eudaimonia[Buddha], the highest state sentient beings can attain, is the very best, the highest state of all. Many Buddhists will say the highest state of all is attainment of nirvana, at which point one ceases to exist as a desirer and the flame that one was is extinguished forever. This, however, is a matter of controversy. Both ancient Theravada Buddhism and contemporary secular Western varieties go light on some of the more familiar Buddhist metaphysical exotica of rebirth, nirvana, what I call karma[untame] (Flanagan 2007; also chapter 3), and the like.

2. Some, possibly many, Buddhists believe in rebirth. The idea that there is or could be rebirth is unstable in relation to the idea of anatman (according to which there is no atman to be reborn) and in addition looks suspiciously like a piece of consoling delusion (see Flanagan 2007; also chapter 3).

3. When a Western Buddhist, or Budd-impressed person, says she is "practicing," she almost always means she is doing some form of meditation regularly, alone or with others in silence. Whether such a person knows anything about Buddhist wisdom is highly variable.

4. In virtue of the doctrine of anatman, no-self, Buddhism can seem 100 percent antiessentialist. It is not. Or better, perhaps, it may be antiessentialist from the ultimate perspective of basic metaphysics, according to which everything is impermanent and empty. From the conventional perspective, even one might say, across short spans of time—for example, the last four to fourteen billion years if one is doing physics and chemistry, 500,000 years if one is doing primatology, or 250,000 years if one is doing psychological anthropology—certain patterns obtain and aspects of what unfolds can be profitably classified in terms of essential properties. Water is H_2O, salt is NaCl, and so on. Likewise, there is human nature. First nature contains the poisons, the poisons are natural dispositions, part of human nature

that come with the equipment. Second nature designates a constrained possibility space where there is room to overcome the poisons. Even though the poisons are part of the human essence, they are also sensitive to local ecology, so that, for example, thirst for a fancy car occurs only after 1900, when fancy cars appeared.

5. Emptiness (sunyata) is a doctrine that is made explicit in Mahayana. Think of impermanence, dependent origination, and no-self (anatman) as diachronic doctrines that (taken together) say that nothing stays the same, everything is changing, everything is either coming to be or passing out of being. Think of emptiness (sunyata) as the synchronic equivalent claim. If one takes an item, a chair, and asks what it is made of at this time, one will come to parts, a seat, a back, and four legs. What are these made of? Wood. What is the wood made of? And so on ad infinitum. A Zen and Zeno-like paradox. Emptiness is the thesis that mental decomposition can find nothing that is rock bottom. There is ultimately nothing there, or put another way, there is always something further there. In the case of persons, Theravadans (allegedly) claim that a person is made up of mental aggregates, consciousness and the five senses, and that these six faculties or components are rock bottom, metaphysically basic. The Mahayanan response, specifically in Nāgārjuna's Mādhyamaka school, asks what these mental aggregates decompose into, and the answer is that they decompose into other stuff, ad infinitum. So, persons, like chairs, lack essence. In Thailand (a Theravadan country) everyone I asked about emptiness explained it as equivalent to impermanence. Many non-Trinitarian Christians think Mary is one of the three persons in God. And hardly any Christians can differentiate between the Virgin Birth and the Immaculate Conception. The latter pertains to Mary being born without original sin; the former is the fact that Jesus was conceived without Mary having sex with her husband. Do such theological-philosophical confusions undermine saying that the confused persons are genuine Buddhists or Christians? I doubt it.

6. *Buddhist intentionality*: Citta = consciousness, and the cittas = types of consciousness (e.g., consciousness in each sensory modality). The citta, for example, of olfactory consciousness is different from the citta of visual consciousness, and the cittas can be analytically distinguished from the mental factors (citasekas) that they, as it were, can contain, what we call "the content." Buddhist intentionality is pretty much the same as Aquinas- and Brentano-style intentionality. So, olfactory consciousness might contain the smell [of coffee] or [of roses]. Joy consciousness, where I am joyful that each of my children got a good job, might involve the same feeling, while the intentional content, that [A got a good job] and that [B got a good job] are different.

7. There are interesting questions in the philosophy of mind and cognitive science about whether folk psychology is invariably a primitive and superficial way of conceiving mind, to be replaced eventually by neuroscientific descriptions, or whether it carves nature at its joints. Buddhist psychology hardly answers this question, but it is the possibility proof that one might try to refine and sophisticate folk psychology at its own level, as it were.

8. Not suffering ≠ being happy. Antidepressants make people suffer less. But even if they eliminate suffering, they do not also by themselves bring happiness.

9. In 2004, Luol Deng, now a professional basketball player, returned to Duke after losing a Final Four NCAA game to the University of Connecticut. He thanked his teachers (my colleague David Wong and me) and his classmates (Comparative Ethics) for their support, and explained his admiration and happiness for Emeka Okafor and Ben Gordon, two excellent players on the victorious University of Connecticut team. That's mudita. Mudita is the opposite of schadenfreude. It is an interesting question whether schadenfreude might be a normal and expectable natural human emotion, which is, nonetheless, like other poisons in human nature, worth trying to overcome.

10. Although there is no God in Buddhism, there are often gods and other spirits of various sorts in Buddhism. What kind and how many depend on the variety. As I said in the introductory chapter, what is generally true is that Buddhism is officially (or pretty officially) nontheistic in a familiar sense: there is no creator God. In cases where there is, the creator God is not omniscient, omnipotent, and so on. So most varieties of Buddhism are atheistic in the sense that involves denial of the Abrahamic contenders, Yahweh, God, or Allah. But again many, possibly most, Buddhist sects endorse all manner of beliefs in deities, spirits, ghosts, and so on. This kind is not in view here because it is not naturalistic.

11. There is important new work that raises worries about all research based on WEIRD samples of North American college students (Henrich, Heine, and Norenzayan 2010). The claim is that Western Educated Industrialized Rich Democratic kids are the most anomalous, thus unrepresentative, population ever to walk the face of the earth.

Chapter 5

1. Equating the reason-to-be-moral question with the motivational question might seem misleading because there might be no theoretical reasons to be moral but still be practical ones (e.g., life will go better if I am moral). There definitely are such practical reasons. In this chapter, I am interested in the question of whether there are theoretical reasons in Buddhism that might be sufficient to make a rational person want to act morally and even to act morally in an expansive way, like a bodhisattva. To reward footnote readers, my answer is that Buddhist wisdom in the form of the no-self doctrine (anatman) provides insufficient reason to be moral. Hopefully, the reasons for failure will be instructive.

2. Steven Collins (1982), a leading expert on Theravada Buddhism, thinks that the doctrine of "emptiness" that Mahayana claims for its own is pretty obviously there in the Pali canon.

3. Somparn Prompta (2008, especially chap. 5) is a Thai analytic philosopher who explains how a Theravadan defends the arahant's way of life as at least as worthy as a bodhisattva's. The core idea is that if one focuses on suffering as first and foremost a personal problem to be relieved by *techniques de soi*, then self-work is key. And the arahant is an aficionado at self-work. I might bodhisattva-like be able to bring you material things and lessen your material suffering. But what ails you most is mental suffering and can only be cured by you, working on yourself. This is an interesting debate that I will not even try to address here. The main lesson is that the relative worthiness of these two saintly types largely comes down to premises internal to these two kinds of Buddhism, which relate to complexities about the interpretation of dukkha, nirvana, and the like.

4. Mahayana Buddhists reject the notion that the arahant has achieved full prajna or wisdom if she doesn't, in fact, perform good works. But in neither Theravada Buddhist nor earlier Indic traditions is one likely to be designated an arahant if there is only deep feeling of compassion without compassionate action. But the "ideal type" is described in such a way that it is possible.

5. It is important not to think that all the bodhisattva's work is dedicated to helping others achieve enlightenment. The Buddha speaks of many kinds of happiness— kinds that come from worthy work, from economic security, from friendship, from family, and so on. These are all necessary for full blown flourishing. However, the Buddha points out that the sort of happiness won by financial security (acquired by just means) is "not worth one sixteenth part of the happiness that arises from living a wise and compassionate, morally faultless, life" (Rahula 1954/1974, 83).

6. Jean-Paul Sartre also rejects the strong self-view, in his case of Kant and Husserl, in his *Transcendence of the Ego* (1937). The rejection of The Self, transcendental egos, what William James called the "Arch-Ego," and the like, occurs across both the analytic and continental philosophical traditions, where the dialectic often sees that commitment to The Self produces an infinite regress. For Buddhists infinite regresses are logical support for the doctrine of emptiness; in the West, soulophiles stop regresses with regress stoppers: God in the case of the cosmos, The Self or The Soul in the case of persons.

7. *Note for philosophers only*: What I have said so far implies that Buddhism might shed light on debates about is-ought, as well as about internalism and externalism. First, regarding is-ought: there is no clear claim or valid and sound argument in any Buddhist text that proves that seeing-the-way-things-are requires or entails moral action. Nonetheless, seeing how things really are might play a role in providing the right sort of motivational basis for thinking that one ought to do good. Second, is seeing the truth about the self or what is good (even seeing THE GOOD) intrinsically motivational? I think the answer is that it is not and essentially for the reason(s) just given. If I see both that I am a selfless person and that others suffer and would be happier if they suffered less, I still need to adopt a certain attitude toward these twin

facts in order to feel motivated to act morally/compassionately. Perhaps it is just a fact about the way gregarious social animals like us are designed that makes it the case that adopting a moral attitude toward my own and others' well-being might seem like (and, in fact, be) the only attitude/response that holds prospects for flourishing. On this view, it is the treble force of seeing the twin facts that I am a suffering being and so are all other sentient beings plus seeing that one and only one attitude/response to them holds prospects for personal flourishing, that eventually motivates me to choose morality. So we need to see/absorb three external reasons in the right sort of way for them to become sufficiently motivational (at which point they have become internal). Usually the internalism-externalism issue is put to us as the question of whether "moral reasons" are intrinsically motivating. Maybe "moral reasons" are, maybe they are not; for now I claim agnosticism. But knowledge that I am a selfless person and that others (as well as myself) suffer, assuming that it satisfies the necessary conditions to count as a reason, is not, according to the view on offer, intrinsically motivating. Making this knowledge sufficiently motivating such that I choose morality (over, say, amoral indifference) requires some more stuff—most likely the idea I just mentioned, that for certain evolutionary reasons we are designed so that choosing morality is the only policy that affords better-than-average chances for happiness and flourishing. Once all these (external) reasons are seen, I am most likely to choose morality that goes beyond kin altruism and strategic reciprocal altruism. But again even if these three reasons come together they are not likely to be sufficient to make me choose morality, although they seem to add up to strong reasons to so choose. Once I have chosen the moral road, and am, as we say, inside morality—then the situation can persistently recur. What sort of perceptions, observations, and thoughts (even when combined with certain emotions and the like) will, in fact, motivate me to see a certain situation as calling for a moral response? Well, all sorts of features of a situation might move me if I am already attuned in the right way to perceive that sort of situation as a "moral situation," and as begging for the sort of moral responsiveness I've been trained to display in response to such situations. But all this will be contingent on my having been morally developed or educated in a certain way. There will be no necessary connection, no automatic way any set of reasons is intrinsically motivational. The externalist seems to have the more plausible view. But then again I have always thought that this whole internalism-externalism debate is a muddle. The concept of "reason" is typically used differently by the internalist and the externalist, so I'm not clear that they are debating the force of the same thing. And I've yet to see an argument for internalism that meets the amoralist challenge. Yes, once you are "inside morality" some moral reasons will exert some degree of motivational force, but this is analytic. It is part of what it means to say you are "inside morality." I don't see that any internalist has ever said anything deeper, which is the reason I have written absolutely nothing on this debate.

8. If one wanted to pursue this question—I don't—of exactly which kind of ethical theory Buddhism is by using our typologies, one would mark the contrastive space,

on a first pass and speaking ethnocentrically, as made up of E-theories, eudaimonistic theories, which are agent-centered; C-theories, consequentialist theories, which are concerned with maximizing pleasure or welfare impersonally; and D-theories, deontological theories, which are concerned with doing one's duty, impersonally understood. E-theories are normative theories of the content and structure of the hearts and minds of flourishing individual persons, and thus they are agent-centered. Eudaimonistic theories are typically therapeutic—devoted to practices that work or might work to adjust, moderate, and modify our desires and emotions so that virtue and rationality, and thus personal flourishing, can be attained. Furthermore, almost all E-theories so far—perhaps hedonism and libertarianism (moral) are exceptions—focus on at least some interpersonal virtues that a person who flourishes possesses. That is, normally it is taken to be partly constitutive of being a virtuous and happy individual that one is attuned to the flourishing of others. It follows that E-theories typically advance the interpersonal good. Buddhism is a eudaimonistic theory with this sort of structure. But is also has C-features, end suffering, and D-features, because its commandments are often stated as categorical imperatives: Do not kill, Do not lie or gossip, and so on.

9. One might have the thought that all ancient ethical theories are eudaimonistic—that is, that the first problem all ethical theories try to confront is what makes for individual happiness and flourishing. Maybe. But an argument could be made (I won't make it) that Confucianism, the most ancient ethical theory of all, is arguably not agent-centered. Despite advocating certain virtues, the consistent focus of Confucian ethics is on social harmony and coordination. The virtues of individuals are the ones that lead to peace, harmony, and social coordination. Peace and social harmony and social coordination are the ends; good character and well-being contribute to those goals and thus are secondary ends. This, of course, does not preclude social coordination paying off in terms of individual well-being.

10. The focus of Buddhism historically on self-development may help explain why and how, in places like California, so many on both the political left and right say they "practice," code for "meditate in a Buddhist way." Buddhism as a personal way of life is compatible with all sorts of political orientations and political philosophies. Thailand, the most Buddhist country in the world, has a monarch about whom one had better never speak ill or jail awaits; Myanmar (formerly Burma) is governed by a Soviet-style military dictatorship; and Nepal, where Buddhism began, was until recently a monarchy, and now is betwixt and between a democracy, a military dictatorship, and a Maoist state. It may be hyperbolic but it would not be entirely unfair to say that although there are many successful Buddhist communities and Buddhist countries, there has never been a successful Buddhist state.

11. Compassion has typically, indeed commonly, been endorsed in soul-based, atman-based traditions, the orthodox Indic traditions as well as the Abrahamic ones. This is one reason to be suspicious about the claim that compassion has a necessary connection with anatman, no-self, views. Furthermore, the advice not to cling can

work inside an atman metaphysics: Don't cling to good or bad past experiences or invest too much or focus too much energy on the future, because despite the fact that my soul, my self, my atman remains the same over time, what's past is past and what is to be is not yet. So either way, whether one is atman or anatman, being in the past or future is irrational.

12. See Nāgārjuna's "Fundamental Wisdom of the Middle Way" (*Mulamadhaymakakrikia*), especially Jay Garfield's breathtaking translation and commentary (Nāgārjuna 1995)—a philosophical tour de force that provides a reading of Nāgārjuna on his own terms while making contact with Western philosophy in a most illuminating way.

13. Here I am avoiding this heady question: Does the fact that conceptual decomposition seems never-ending mean that things in reality decompose ad infinitum? The real numbers, for example, are an uncountable infinite, but it does not follow that the number of things, elementary particles, strings, bosons, and fermions, whatever there might be, are like the real numbers. Although I am officially neutral on this question, my impression is that the Buddhist doctrine of emptiness is sometimes expressed in such a way that conceptual decomposition is taken to track real-world decomposition and in that way prejudges what physics might say about the ultimate fabric of the universe, namely, that some items or other are basic—strings, say—the way atoms were once thought to be.

14. There is no necessity here. Much modern consequentialism focuses on character and motives, following John Stuart Mill's program. But there is a tendency to divide labor, so Peter Singer and Shelley Kagan are important philosophers who defend consequentialism and do not have much to say about character or about personal happiness (although I hear Kagan teaches about the latter).

15. An earlier version of this section appeared in Narvaez and Lapsey 2009.

16. For neither Aristotle nor Buddha is "feeling happy," a necessary condition of a good human life. Achieving one's proper function is necessary and sufficient for a good life. And happiness is a normal accompaniment of living well. But the connection is contingent, perhaps highly reliable, though it is not necessary. See chapter 6. That said, eudaimonistic theories promote practices and conditions that work to make the contingent connection between flourishing and happiness probable, so that normally the person who flourishes feels good about herself and her life.

17. Kant does provide an underestimated theory of virtue, both in his discussions of imperfect duty in the *Groundwork* and more explicitly in *The Doctrine of Virtue*. But it is hard to argue that he produces the right sort of "virtue-theoretical Kantianism" himself. For one thing, the picture of the virtuous person is on the thin side, and the master virtue, which Kant calls "autocracy," seems a kind of creepy, excessively Prussian, way of conceiving virtue.

18. There is lots of recent work in psychology on so-called positive illusions. It is thought to be good to underestimate (possibly by a lot) the probabilities that one's chance of getting cancer, divorced, in a car accident, and so on, are the base-rate probabilities. It isn't that false optimism will improve my chances of not, for example, getting cancer; it is just that I'll be happier before I get cancer if I think I won't get it than if I think I might or will. See Shelley Taylor, *Positive Illusions* (1988). There is also some recent work in philosophy that takes the attitude that although, for instance, free will is illusory or morality is illusory, it is better not to know or think so. See Saul Smilansky, *Free Will and Illusion* (2000), and Richard Joyce, *The Myth of Morality* (2002). I discuss the psychological literature on positive illusions in *Varieties of Moral Personality* (1991b), in *The Really Hard Problem* (2007), and in 2010.

19. On some readings of Parfit, he seems open to being charged with pushing the ephemerality envelope. There is all his talk of conceiving of persons in terms of stages. Stage talk can be innocent, as when we speak of infancy, adolescence, adulthood, and the like. But Parfit's stages are not those. Since I favor a narrative view, it seems to me a person-by-person decision whether stage talk helpfully explains their lives. Augustine has a famous stage break, marked most clearly by his transformation, a conversion, from a hedonist to a devout intellectual. Among famous Buddhists, Milarepa and Naropa, and probably Siddhārtha Gautama as well, lived lives with certain abrupt and important stage breaks. These lives are best explained (narrated) by marking the stage breaks that essentially constitute them. But many lives don't contain the right sort of stage breaks to be usefully explained (narrated) in self-stage terms, beyond the normal developmental stage transitions.

Chapter 6

1. A strictly causal psychological claim would be something along these lines: Virtue typically causes happiness. Stated this way, happiness might have unusual other causes (e.g., magic pills) that produce it directly. One might impose therefore, what I call a *normative exclusionary clause*, that might say that happiness caused by magic pills or by false belief is not a suitable kind. Below I discuss how one might defend such an exclusionary clause.

2. For Aristotle, reason has a theoretical component (sophia or theoria) as revealed in mathematics and science, and a practical component (phronesis). Practical reason is required for virtue, and thus interpenetrates in similar ways. One might think of Buddhism as claiming that theoretical knowledge of the nature of the self, that it is no-self (anatman), and of psychology, especially of which mental states are wholesome and which are unwholesome, is also essential to virtuous self-cultivation. Aristotle can be read as thinking that sophia similarly contributes to ethics by teaching us what our proper function is. It would still be the case that theoretical wisdom of the sort we get in the elaborate Buddhist psychology presented in the *Abhidamma (Abhidarma)* plays a much larger role in Buddhist ethics than sophia plays in Aristotle's ethics.

3. In Mahayana, compassion (karuna) involves wishing that all sentient beings be free of suffering and its causes and working for this; lovingkindness (metta) involves hoping that all sentient beings are happy insofar as this is possible, and working to produce good kinds of happiness insofar as this is possible. The main point is that the two terms are not synonyms.

4. This point is closely related to points made in chapters 1 and 2. Much of the neuroscientific research on positive mood, affect, and happiness uses one marker (LPFC activity) for all kinds of happiness. But LPFC-measured positive mood is not what any great wisdom tradition promises.

5. See Lawrence Becker's masterpiece, *A New Stoicism* (1998), in which he attempts to show that, and how, Stoicism is a live option for us.

6. These Greek and Roman compassionate philosophers—Epicurus, Lucretius, Zeno of Citium, Chrysippus, Pyrrho, Seneca, Cicero, Epictetus, Sextus Empiricus, Marcus Aurelius, among them—were founders, luminaries, and practitioners of schools that arose after Aristotle's death (in 322 BCE) and that remained highly influential into the second or third centuries CE. In various ways these philosophers retained admirers until the nineteenth century. Descartes, Spinoza, Adam Smith, Kant, Nietzsche, and Marx all engaged the work of one or more of these philosophers. And the American Founding Fathers who had read Plutarch's *Moralia*, which includes his famous "Lives" of the major Hellenistic philosophers, as well as in all likelihood Cicero and Seneca, reveal that influence in well-known ways in the American Declaration of Independence and Constitution.

7. This cognitive and affective instability of loving and hating at the same time is behind mindfulness techniques such as this: if you want your enemy to die a painful death, imagine him as your mother (or child). This could be done in an "as if" make-believe manner, or thought to be guided by recognition of a deep truth: if there is an infinite amount of time, then every being has been, and will be again, in every possible relation (mother/child) to every other being. For example, I am Hitler's mother, he is my father, and so on.

8. The individuals I am calling "Brahmans" were not Hindus (that comes later) but members of a sacrificial cult that followed the ancient *Vedas* and early *Upanishads*, especially the doctrine on merger of Brahman and Atman as avowed in the *Brhadaranyaka Upanisad*.

9. See Robert Nozick's "experience machine" thought experiment in his *Anarchy, the State, and Utopia* (1974). Here is another exam question for the reader who enjoys such things: Suppose that the magic pill did not provide a shortcut to happiness, but rather a shortcut to virtue, so that for example, it could make children with terrible upbringings or born with deficient paralimbic systems, good. The pill was a shortcut to virtue rather than happiness. Would that be bad? Why?

10. In *The Shape of Ancient Thought: Comparative Studies in Greek and Indian Philosophy*, Thomas McEvilley lays out an utterly convincing case that Indian and Greek, Egyptian, and Mesopotamian thought—artistic, religious, and philosophical—interpenetrated as far back as 3000 BCE. We know that Alexander, possibly not the best spokesperson for Aristotle's views despite having been raised at Aristotle's knee, "visited" North India and left Greek settlers among Hindus and Buddhists.

11. The Thrasymachean challenge is also raised in the *Gorgias*, where Callicles argues that the happy man is one who grows his passions and appetites as far as he can and who has the power to fulfill them. This— happiness ^{hedonism}—is what human nature aims at. Socrates repeatedly insists that to do wrong is the worst that can befall a person (worse than being harmed), and that Callicles's egoist will harm others. But the dialog ends, just as the debate in the *Republic* ends, with Socrates declaring that egoism is self-defeating and Thrasymachus, his opponent, arguing that it is natural and the only known route to individual happiness. Arguably in the *Symposium* and the *Phaedrus* where Plato discusses love more headway is made against the Thrasymachean and Calliclean challenge. But love for Plato is so intellectualist, the eyes of a true lover are set on Wisdom, on the *Eidos* (Forms)—and human love expresses less nobility than love of the Forms—that he is kept from appealing to the one idea that might mitigate the force of the egoist's picture, which Aristotle and Hume develop, namely, our natures include a strong dose of fellow feeling.

12. See Nussbaum 1994 for a deep and elaborate scholarly analysis of Aristotle's reasons for hesitancy in fully embracing the analogy.

13. Soul-rousing music works similarly (and thus vicariously) for release of certain emotions. In book II of the *Poetics*, which is lost, Aristotle discusses comedy. Some hints about the sorts of emotional release involved and their value can be found in the *Rhetoric*.

14. Book X of Aristotle's *Nicomachean Ethics*, an anomalous book, explores the idea that some sort of pure contemplative life, although suited more for gods than humans, would be the best for humans because it would produce or involve achieving a kind of eudaimonia that is immune to the vagaries of externalities.

15. Some will say that liberal commonsense morality is an example of a very undemanding morality. I am agnostic on that. A different point would be that it does little to discourage people from seeking their good in very unwholesome activities. This seems true. Nonetheless, as in all traditions, people who believe they are morally decent by contemporary liberal standards think they deserve to be happy.

16. There is a good lesson here from social psychology (Goldman 1987; Flanagan 1991b). When research subjects are duped to believe something false and negative about themselves, the effect does not disappear when they discover that they were duped. They need to be taught about the so-called perseverance effect itself, which

says that false beliefs do not go away simply as a result of being shown to be falsely inculcated. They persevere. Only when one learns this does the false belief yield, and the tendency to acquire false beliefs by perseverative mechanisms wanes.

17. The complaint is that the decomposition of mental states bottoms out in indestructible psychological atoms that themselves should be considered conditioned, and thus that are further decomposable ad infinitum. Mahayana endorses emptiness (sunyata) as the next step in the deconstruction. Some Mahayana say that emptiness is in the Pali canon; others think it is a logical consequence of the philosophy of the Pali canon (e.g., impermanence); still others think it comes later in, for example, Nāgārjuna in the second century.

18. This is a form of Brentano's thesis: All consciousness is consciousness of. As for Brentano, there is the objection that moods—for example, feeling low or anxious—aren't always (or necessarily) about anything. They just are. Also, certain supramundane meditative cittas, familiar to Buddhists, involve (attempting to) reaching a state that is pure, in the sense of contentless. So Buddhist philosophical psychology makes room for intentionality while resisting the stronger claim that all mental states are contentful.

References

Abe, M. 1991. God, emptiness, and the true self. In F. Franck, ed., *The Buddha Eye: An Anthology of the Kyoto School*. New York: Crossroad.

Annas, J. 1993. *The Morality of Happiness*. New York: Oxford University Press.

Annas, J. 2011. Virtue ethics. In *The Oxford Companion to Ethical Theory*, edited by David Copp. Oxford: Oxford University Press.

Anscombe, G. E. M. 1958. Modern moral philosophy. *Philosophy* (London) 33: 1–19.

Aristotle. 1984. *The Complete Works of Aristotle*. Princeton, NJ: Princeton University Press.

Baier, A. 1991. *A Progress of Sentiments*. Cambridge, MA: Harvard University Press.

Batchelor, S. 1998. *Buddhism without Beliefs*. New York: Riverhead Books.

Batchelor, S. 2010. *Confession of a Buddhist Atheist*. New York: Spiegel & Grau.

Batchelor, S., and R. Thurman. 1997. Reincarnation: A Debate. *Tricycle* 6(4): 24–27, 109–116.

Becker, L. 1998. *The New Stoicism*. Princeton, NJ: Princeton University Press.

Blum, L. 1994. *Moral Perception and Particularity*. New York: Cambridge University Press.

Blum, L. 2002. *I'm Not a Racist, But . . . : The Moral Quandary of Race*. Ithaca, NY: Cornell University Press.

Bodhi, B., ed. 1993. *A Comprehensive Manual of Abhidhamma*. Sri Lanka: Buddhist Publication Society.

Bond, G. D. 1988. The Arahant: Sainthood in Theravada Buddhism. In G. D. Bond and R. Kieckhefer, eds., *Sainthood: Its Manifestation in World Religions*. Berkeley: University of California Press.

Bond, G. D., and R. Kieckhefer, eds. 1988. *Sainthood: Its Manifestation in World Religions*. Berkeley: University of California Press.

Brandt, R. B. 1954. *Hopi Ethics: A Theoretical Analysis*. Chicago: University of Chicago Press.

Brandt, R. B. 1970. Traits of character: A conceptual analysis. *American Philosophical Quarterly* 7: 23–37.

Cabezon, J., ed. 1988. *The Bodhgaya Interviews*. Ithaca, NY: Snow Lion.

Carrithers, M., S. Collins, and S. Lukes, eds. 1985. *The Category of the Person: Anthropology, Philosophy, History*. Cambridge: Cambridge University Press.

Chapell, D. W. 1996. Are there seventeen Mayhayana ethics? *Journal of Buddhist Ethics* 3: 44–65.

Chodron, P. 2002. *Comfortable with Uncertainty: 108 Teachings*. Boston: Shambala.

Churchland, P. S. 1986. *Neurophilosophy: Toward a Unified Science of the Mind-Brain*. Cambridge, MA: MIT Press.

Churchland, P. S. 2011. *Braintrust: What Neuroscience Tells Us About Morality*. Princeton, NJ: Princeton University Press.

Clark, C. 1997. *Misery and Company: Sympathy in Everyday Life*. Chicago: University of Chicago Press.

Collins, S. 1982. *Selfless Persons: Imagery and Thought in Theravāda Buddhism*. London: Cambridge University Press.

Collins, S. 1998. *Nirvana and Other Buddhist Felicities: Utopias of the Pali Imaginaire*. Cambridge: Cambridge University Press.

The Connected Discourses of the Buddha. 2000. *SN* Trans. B. Bodhi, Boston: Wisdom Publications.

Conze, E. 1951/2003. *Buddhism: Its Essence and Development*. New York: Dover.

Dalai Lama. 1989. Nobel Acceptance speech. http://nobelprize.org/nobel_prizes/peace/laureates/1989/lama-acceptance.html.

Dalai Lama. 1990. *A Policy of Kindness*. Ithaca, NY: Snow Lion.

Dalai Lama. 1997. *My Land and My People*. New York: Warner Books.

Dalai Lama. 1999. *Ethics for the New Millennium*. New York: Riverhead Books.

Dalai Lama. 2005. *The Universe in a Single Atom: The Convergence of Science and Spirituality*. New York: Morgan Road Books.

Dalai Lama and H. C. Cutler. 1998. *The Art of Happiness: A Handbook for Living*. New York: Riverhead Books.

Damasio, A. R. 1994. *Descartes' Error: Emotion, Reason, and the Human Brain*. New York: Bard/Avon Books.

Davids, T. W. R., and W. Stede. 1993. *Pali-English Dictionary*. Delhi: Montilal Bandarsidass.

Davidson, R. J. 2000. Affective style, psychopathology, and resilience: Brain mechanisms and plasticity. *American Psychologist* 55(11): 1196–1214. doi:10.1037/0003-066x.55.11.1196.

Davidson, R. J. 2003. Affective neuroscience and psychophysiology: Toward a synthesis. *Psychophysiology* 40(5): 655–665. doi:10.1111/1469-8986.00067.

Davidson, R. J. 2005. Well-being and affective style: Neural substrates and biobehavioural correlates. In F. A. Huppert, N. Baylis, and B. Keverne, eds., *The Science of Well-Being*, 107–139. New York: Oxford University Press.

Davidson, R. J., H. H. Goldsmith, and K. R. Scherer, eds. 2003. *Handbook of Affective Sciences*. Oxford: Oxford University Press.

Davidson, R. J., and A. Harrington, eds. 2002. *Visions of Compassion: Western Scientists and Tibetan Buddhists Examine Human Nature*. Oxford: Oxford University Press.

Davidson, R. J., and K. Hugdahl, eds. 2003. *The Asymmetrical Brain*. Cambridge, MA: MIT Press.

Davidson, R. J., and W. Irwin. 1999. The functional neuroanatomy of emotion and affective style. *Trends in Cognitive Sciences* 3(1): 11–21. doi:10.1016/s1364-6613(98)01265-0.

Davidson, R. J., J. Kabat-Zinn, J. Schumacher, M. Rosenkranz, D. Muller, S. F. Santorelli. 2003. Alterations in brain and immune function produced by mindfulness meditation. *Psychosomatic Medicine* 65(4): 564–570. doi:10.1097/01.psy.0000077505.67574.e3.

Doris, J. M. 1998. Persons, situations, and virtue ethics. *Nous* (Detroit) 32 : 504–530.

Doris, J. M. 2002. *Lack of Character: Personality and Moral Behavior*. New York: Cambridge University Press.

Doris, J. M., and S. P. Stich. 2008. Moral psychology: Empirical approaches. In E. N. Zalta, ed., *The Stanford Encyclopedia of Philosophy*. Stanford, CA: Stanford University Press.

Dreyfus, G. B. J. 2003. *The Sound of Two Hands Clapping: The Education of a Tibetan Buddhist Monk*. Berkeley: University of California Press.

Easterlin, R. A. 2003. Explaining happiness. Paper presented at the Proceedings of the National Academy of Science: Inaugural Articles by members of the National Academy elected on April 30, 2002.

Easterlin, R. A. 2004. *Money, Sex, and Happiness: An Empirical Study*. Working Papers, no. 10499. Washington, DC: National Bureau of Economic Research.

Ekman, P. 2003. *Emotions Revealed: Recognizing Faces and Feelings to Improve Communication and Emotional Life*. New York: Times Books.

Ekman, P., ed., 2003. *Emotions Inside Out*. Annals of the New York Academy of Sciences, vol. 1000. New York: New York Academy of Sciences.

Fireman, G. D., O. J. Flanagan, and T. E. McVay, eds. 2003. *Narrative and Consciousness: Literature, Psychology, and the Brain*. New York: Oxford University Press.

Flanagan, O. 1991a. *The Science of the Mind*. Cambridge, MA: MIT Press.

Flanagan, O. 1991b. *Varieties of Moral Personality: Ethics and Psychological Realism*. Cambridge, MA: Harvard University Press.

Flanagan, O. 1992. *Consciousness Reconsidered*. Cambridge, MA: MIT Press.

Flanagan, O. 1995. Deconstructing dreams: The spandrels of sleep. *The Journal of Philosophy* 92 (1): 5–27.

Flanagan, O. 1996. *Self Expressions: Mind, Morals, and the Meaning of Life*. New York: Oxford University Press.

Flanagan, O. 2000a. Destructive emotions. *Consciousness and Emotions* 1(2): 259–281.

Flanagan, O. 2000b. *Dreaming Souls: Sleep, Dreams, and the Evolution of the Conscious Mind*. Oxford: Oxford University Press.

Flanagan, O. 2002. *The Problem of the Soul: Two Visions of Mind and How to Reconcile Them*. New York: Basic Books.

Flanagan, O. 2003a. The colour of happiness. *The New Scientist*, May 24.

Flanagan, O. 2003b. Emotional expressions. In M. J. S. Hodge and G. Radick, eds., *The Cambridge Companion to Darwin*. Cambridge: Cambridge University Press.

Flanagan, O. 2006a. The Bodhisattva's brain: Neuroscience and happiness. In D. K. Nauriyal, M. Drummond, and Y. B. Lal, eds., *Buddhist Thought and Applied Psychological Research*, 149–174. London: Routledge.

Flanagan, O. 2006b. Varieties of naturalism. In P. Clayton and Z. Simpson, eds., *Oxford Companion to Religion and Science*. New York: Oxford University Press.

Flanagan, O. 2007. *The Really Hard Problem: Meaning in a Material World*. Cambridge, MA: MIT Press.

Flanagan, O. 2008. Moral contagion and logical persuasion in the "Mozi." *Journal of Chinese Philosophy* 35(3): 473–491.

Flanagan, O. 2009a. Neuro-Eudaimonics or Buddhists lead neuroscientists to the seat of happiness. In J. Bickle, ed., *The Oxford Handbook of Philosophy and Neuroscience*. Oxford: Oxford University Press.

Flanagan, O. 2009b. Moral science? Still metaphysical after all these years. In D. Narvaez, D., and D. K. Lapsley, eds. *Personality, Identity, and Character: Explorations in Moral Psychology*. New York: Cambridge University Press.

Flanagan, O. 2010. "Can do" attitudes: Some positive illusions are not misbeliefs. *Brain and Behavioural Sciences*. 32(6).

Frank, R. H. 2004. How not to buy happiness. *Daedelus* 133(2): 69–79.

Funder, D. C. 1991. Global traits: A neo-Allportian approach to personality. *Psychological Science* (Wiley-Blackwell) 2(1): 31–39.

Funder, D. C. 2001. *The Personality Puzzle*. 2nd ed. New York: Norton.

Garfield, J. 1995. *The Fundamental Wisdom of the Middle Way: Nāgārjuna's* Mullamadhyamakakarika. New York: Oxford University Press.

Garfield, J. L. 2002. *Empty Words: Buddhist Philosophy and Cross-Cultural Interpretation*. Oxford: Oxford University Press.

Goldman, A. 1987. *Epistemology and Cognition*. Cambridge, MA: Harvard University Press.

Goleman, D. 2003a. *Destructive Emotions: How Can We Overcome Them?: A Scientific Collaboration with the Dalai Lama*. New York: Bantam Books.

Goleman, D. 2003b. Finding happiness: Cajole your brain to lean left. *New York Times*, February 4.

Goodman, C. 2009. *Consequences of Compassion: An Interpretation and Defense of Buddhist Ethics*. Oxford: Oxford University Press.

Griffiths, P. J. 1994. *On Being Buddha: The Classical Doctrine of Buddhahood*. Albany: State University of New York Press.

Grimes, J. 1989. *A Concise Dictionary of Indian Philosophy: Sanskrit Terms Defined in English*. Albany: State University of New York Press.

Guzeldere, G. 1997. Introduction: The many faces of consciousness: A field guide. In N. Block, O. Flanagan, and Guven Guzeldere, eds. *The Nature of Consciousness: Philosophical Debates*. Cambridge, MA: MIT Press.

Gyatso, T. 2003a. On the luminosity of being. *The New Scientist*, May 24.

Gyatso, T. 2003b. The monk in the lab. *New York Times*, April 26.

Gyatso, T., and G. T. Jinpa, eds. 2002. *Essence of the Heart: The Dalai Lama's Heart of the Wisdom Teachings*. Boston: Wisdom Publications.

Harman, G. 1999. Moral philosophy meets social psychology: Virtue ethics and the fundamental attribution error. *Proceedings of the Aristotelian Society*, New Series, 315–331.

Harman, G. 2000. The nonexistence of character traits. *Proceedings of the Aristotelian Society,* New Series, 223–226.

Harrington, A. 2008. *The Cure within: A History of Mind-Body Medicine.* New York: Norton.

Harvey, P. 1990. *An Introduction to Buddhism: Teachings, History, and Practices.* Cambridge: Cambridge University Press.

Harvey, P. 2000. *An Introduction to Buddhist Ethics: Foundations, Values, and Issues.* Cambridge: Cambridge University Press.

Hattori, S.-O. 2000. *A Raft from the Other Shore: Honen and the Way of Pure Land Buddhism.* Tokyo: Jodo Shu Press.

Henrich, J., S. J. Heine, and A. Norenzayan. 2010. The weirdest people in the world?. *Behavioral and Brain Sciences* 33:61–83.

Hemphill, J. F. 2003. Interpreting the magnitude of correlation coefficients. *American Psychologist* 58: 78–80.

Hodge, M. J. S., and G. Radick, eds. 2003. *The Cambridge Companion to Darwin.* Cambridge: Cambridge University Press.

Hodge, M. J. S., and G. Radick, eds. 2009. *The Cambridge Companion to Darwin.*2nd ed. Cambridge: Cambridge University Press.

Homiak, M. 1997. Aristotle on the soul's conflicts: Toward an understanding of virtue ethics. In A. Reath, B. Herman, and C. Korsgaard, eds., *Reclaiming the History of Ethics: Essays for John Rawls.* Cambridge: Cambridge University Press.

Homiak, M. 2008. Character traits. In E. N. Zalta, ed., *The Stanford Encyclopedia of Philosophy.* .

Hursthouse, R. 1999. *On Virtue Ethics.* Oxford: Oxford University Press.

James, W. 1890/1982. *The Varieties of Religious Experience.* New York: Penguin Books.

Jayatilleke, K. N. 1975. The Buddhist attitude to other religions. *The Wheel Publication,* no. 216. Kandy, Sri Lanka: Buddhist Publication Society.

Jinpa, T. 2003. Science as an ally or a rival philosophy: Tibetan buddhist thinkers' engagement with modern science. In A.Wallace, ed. *Buddhism and Science: Breaking New Ground.* New York: Columbia University Press

Johnson, G. 2005. Review of the Dalai Lama's *The Universe in a Single Atom. New York Times,* September 18.

Kabat-Zinn, J. 1994. *Wherever You Go, There You Are: Mindfulness Meditation in Everyday Life.* New York: Hyperion.

Kalupahana, D. J. 1992. *A History of Buddhist Philosophy: Continuities and Discontinuities*. Honolulu: University of Hawaii Press.

Kamtekar, R. 2004. Situationism and virtue ethics on the content of our character. *Ethics* 114(3): 458–491.

Kelley, C. 2010. Empathy, altruism, and buddhist selflessness: The abnormal moral psychology of the Bodhicaryāvatāra. Unpublished ms.

Keltner, D. 2009. *Born to Be Good: The Science of a Meaningful Life*. New York: Norton.

Keown, D. 1992/2001. *The Nature of Buddhist Ethics*. New York: St. Martin's Press.

Keown, D. 2003. *A Dictionary of Buddhism*. Oxford: Oxford University Press.

Kim, J. 2005. *Physicalism, or Something Near Enough*. Princeton: Princeton University Press

Kim, J. 2006. *The Philosophy of Mind*. 2nd ed. Boulder, CO: Westview.

King, S. B., and C. S. Queen, eds. 1996. *Engaged Buddhism: Buddhist Liberation Movements in Asia*. Albany: State University of New York Press.

King, W. L. 1964. *In the Hope of Nibbana: An Essay on Theravada Buddhist Ethics*. LaSalle, IL: Open Court.

Koch, C. 2004. *The Quest for Consciousness: A Neurobiological Approach*. Englewood, CO: Roberts.

Kupperman, J. J. 2001. The indispensability of character. *Philosophy* (London) 76(296): 239.

LeDoux, J. E. 1996. *The Emotional Brain: The Mysterious Underpinnings of Emotional Life*. New York: Simon & Schuster.

Locke, J. 1690. *Essay Concerning Human Understanding*. http://oregonstate.edu/instruct/phl302/texts/locke/locke1/Essay_contents.htm.

Logothetis, N., and J. D. Schall. 1989. Neuronal correlates of subjective visual perception. *Science* 245:761–763.

The Long Discourses of the Buddha. 1987/1995. *DN* Trans. M. Walshe. Boston: Wisdom Publications.

Lopez, Jr., D. S. 1988. Sanctification on the Bodhisattva path. In R. Kieckhefer and G. D. Bond, eds., *Sainthood: Its Manifestation in World Religions*. Berkeley: University of California Press.

Lopez, Jr., D. S. 2005. *The Madman's Middle Way: Reflections on Reality of the Tibetan Monk Gendun Chopel*. Chicago: University of Chicago Press.

Lopez, Jr., D. S. 2008. *Buddhism & Science: A Guide for the Perplexed*. Chicago: University of Chicago Press.

Lutz, A., L. L. Greischar, N. B. Rawlings, M. Ricard, and R. J. Davidson. 2004. Long-term meditators self-induce high-amplitude gamma synchrony during mental practice. *Proceedings of the National Academy of Sciences of the United States of America* 101(46): 16369–16373.

MacIntyre, A. 1981. *After Virtue*. South Bend, IN: Notre Dame University Press.

Mayr, E. 2001. *What Evolution Is*. New York: Basic Books.

McEvilley, T. 2002. *The Shape of Ancient Thought: Comparative Studies in Greek and Indian Philosophy*. New York: Allsworth.

Merritt, M. 2000. Virtue ethics and Situationist Personality Psychology. *Ethical Theory and Moral Practice* 3(4): 365–383.

Miller, C. 2003. Social psychology and virtue ethics. *Journal of Ethics* 7:365–392.

Mischel, W. 1968. *Personality and Assessment*. New York: Wiley.

Mischel, W. 1999. Personality coherence and dispositions in a Cognitive-Affective Personality System (CAPS) approach. In D. Cervone and Y. Shoda, eds., *The Coherence of Personality: Social-Cognitive Bases of Consistency, Variability, and Organization*. New York: Guilford Press.

Nāgārjuna. 1995. *The Fundamental Wisdom of the Middle Way: Nāgārjuna's Mūlamadhyamakakārikā*. New York: Oxford University Press.

Nanamoli, B. 1995. *The Middle Length Discourses of the Buddha*. MN Trans. B. Bodhi. Boston: Wisdom Publications.

Narvaez, D., and D. K. Lapsley. 2009. *Personality, Identity, and Character: Explorations in Moral Psychology*. Cambridge: Cambridge University Press.

Nhát Hạnh, T. 1987. *Being Peace*. Berkeley, CA: Parallax Press.

Nhát Hạnh, T. 2003. *Joyfully Together: The Art of Building a Harmonious Community*. Berkeley, CA: Parallax Press.

Nisbett, R. E., and L. Ross. 1980. *Human Inference: Strategies and Shortcomings of Social Judgment*. Englewood Cliffs, NJ: Prentice-Hall.

Nozick, R. 1974. *Anarchy, State, and Utopia*. New York: Basic Books.

Nussbaum, M. 1994. *The Therapy of Desire: Theory and Practice in Hellenistic Ethics*. Princeton, NJ: Princeton University Press.

Nussbaum, M. C. 1999. Virtue ethics: A misleading category? *Journal of Ethics* 3(3): 163–201.

Nussbaum, M. C. 2000. *Women and Human Development: The Capabilities Approach.* Cambridge: Cambridge University Press.

Nussbaum, M. C., and A. Sen, eds. 1993. *The Quality of Life.* Oxford: Oxford University Press.

Obeyeseker, G. 2002. *Imagining Karma: Ethical Transformation in Amerindian, Buddhist, and Greek Rebirth.* Berkeley: University of California Press.

Ospina, M. B., T. K. Bond, M. Karkhaneh, L. Tjosvold, B. Vandermeer, Y. Liang, et al., eds. 2007. *Meditation Practices for Health* [Electronic Resource]: *State of the Research.* Rockville, MD: Agency for Healthcare Research and Quality.

Pandita, S. U. 1992. *In This Very Life: The Liberation Teachings of the Buddha.* Trans. V. U. Aggacitta. Boston: Wisdom Publications.

Perry, J., ed. 1975. *Personal Identity.* Berkeley: University of California Press.

Petitot, J., ed. 1999. *Naturalizing Phenomenology: Issues in Contemporary Phenomenology and Cognitive Science.* Stanford, CA: Stanford University Press.

Prompta, S. 2008. *An Essay Concerning Buddhist Ethics.* Bangkok: Chulalongkorn University Press.

Queen, C. S., ed. 2000. *Engaged Buddhism in the West.* Boston: Wisdom Publications.

Queen, C. S., and S. B. King, eds. 1996. *Engaged Buddhism.* Albany: SUNY Press.

Rahula, W.. 1954/1974. *What the Buddha Taught.* New York: Grove Press.

Rinchen, G. S. 2006. *How Karma Works: The Twelve Links of Dependent Arising.* Trans. R. Sonam. Ithaca, NY: Snow Lion Publications.

Rosenkranz, M. A., D. C. Jackson, K. M. Dalton, I. Dolski, C. D. Ryff, B. H. Singer. . 2003. Affective style and in vivo immune response: Neurobehavioral mechanisms. *Proceedings of the National Academy of Sciences of the United States of America* 100(19): 11148–11152.

Ross, L. A., and R. E. Nisbett. 1991. *The Person and the Situation: Perspectives of Social Psychology.* Philadelphia: Temple University Press.

Ryle, G., 1949. *The Concept of Mind.* Chicago: University of Chicago Press.

Sabini, J., and M. Silver. 2005. Lack of character? Situationism critiqued. *Ethics* 115(3): 535–562.

Saddhatissa, H. 1970/1997/ 2003. *Buddhist Ethics.* 3rd ed. Boston: Wisdom Publications.

Sartre, J. P. 1937/2004. *Transcendence of the Ego.* Oxfordshire: Routledge.

Seligman, M. E. P. 2002. *Authentic Happiness: Using the New Positive Psychology to Realize Your Potential for Lasting Fulfillment.* New York: Free Press.

Sellars, W. 1960. Philosophy and the scientific image of man. Two Lectures. In *Science, Perception and Reality*. New York: Routledge.

Śāntideva. 1997. *The Way of the Bodhisattva (Bodhicharyavatara)*. Trans. P. T. Group. Boston: Shambala.

Sharf, R. 1998. Experience. In M. C. Taylor, ed., *Critical Terms for Religious Studies*, 94–116. Chicago: University of Chicago Press.

Sherman, N. 1989. *The Fabric of Character: Aristotle's Theory of Virtue*. New York: Oxford University Press.

Siderits, M. 2003. *Personal Identity and Buddhist Philosophy: Empty Persons*. Aldershot, England: Ashgate.

Siderits, M. 2007. *Buddhism as Philosophy: An Introduction*. Aldershot, England: Ashgate.

Smilansky, S. 2000. *Free Will and Illusion*. Oxford: Oxford University Press.

Sreenivasan, G. 2002. Errors about errors: Virtue theory and trait attribution. *Mind* 117:257–266.

Sreenivasan, G. 2008. Character and consistency: Still more errors. *Mind* 111:47–68.

Strawson, G. 1998. Luck swallows everything. *TLS* 4969: 8.

Stroud, M. 2008. Mindfulness of mind. *Shambala Sun*, March.

Swanton, C. 2003. *Virtue Ethics: A Pluralistic View*. Oxford: Oxford University Press.

Taylor, S. 1988. *Positive Illusions*. New York: Basic Books.

Thompson, E. 2007. *Mind in Life: Biology, Phenomenology, and the Sciences of Mind*. Cambridge, MA: Harvard University Press.

Thurman, R., and S. Batchelor. 1997. Reincarnation: A Debate. *Tricycle* 6(4): 24–27, 109–116.

Varela, F. 1999. Neurophenomenology. In J. Petitot, F. Varela, B. Pachoud, and J.-M. Roy, eds. *Naturalizing Phenomenology*. Palo Alto: Stanford University Press.

Varela, F. J. 2004. Intimate distances. *Shambhala Sun,* September, 41–45.

Vranas, P. B. M. 2005. The indeterminacy paradox: Character evaluations and human psychology. *Nous* (Detroit) 39(1): 1–42.

Wallace, B. A. 1993. *Tibetan Buddhism from the Ground up*. Boston: Wisdom Publications.

Walshe, M., trans. 1987/1995. *The Long Discourses of the Buddha*. DN. Boston: Wisdom Publications.

Watson, G. 1990. On the primacy of character. In O. Flanagan and A. O. Rorty, eds., *Identity, Character, and Morality: Essays in Moral Psychology*. Cambridge, MA: MIT Press.

Williams, P. 1989. *Mahâyâna Buddhism*. London: Routledge.

Willson, M. 1987. *Rebirth and the Western Buddhist*. 2nd ed. London: Wisdom Publications.

Wong, D. B. 2006. *Natural Moralities: A Defense of Pluralistic Relativism*. Cambridge: Cambridge University Press.

Index

Abe, Masao, 212n6
Abhidamma (Pali)
  in Buddhist ethics, 233n2
  description, 189–190
  study of, 191
Abhidharma (Sanskrit), 102–104
"Abnormal discourse," 209n2
Abrahamic traditions, 60, 63, 116, 132
ADD (attention deficit disorder), 54, 107
Affect, positive, 18, 38, 41. *See also*
    Mood
  and happiness, 51
  and meditation, 50
Afflictions, Six Main, 105, 194
Afterlife, 222n24. *See also* Rebirth
  Buddha on, 224n24
  for no-selves, 131–134
Agnostics, contrasted with atheists, 210n5
"Allegory of the Cave," 118, 119
Amygdala, and startle response, 46
Amygdala-based emotional system, 56
Anachronism, and ethnocentrism, 1
Analytic philosophy, 5–6
Anatman, 97, 98, 158. *See also* Selfless
    persons
  and being good, 116–117
  continuity of, 224n24
  deconstruction of atman to, 127
  doctrine of, 70, 124–126
  extremism of, 159–163
  and Four Noble Truths, 124

and hedonism, 121
  psychological environment of, 130
"Anchoring effect," 189
Anscombe, Elizabeth, 146, 158
Anthropology, psychological, 55
Anticreationist views, of Dalai Lama, 65
Antidepressants, 228n8
Appearance-reality distinction, 68
Appetite, 155
Arahant, 30
  in Mahayana *vs.* Theravada Buddhism,
    229n4
  motivation of, 119
  of Theravada Buddhism, 215n15
  virtues of, 148–149
Aristotle, xi, 10, 11, 94, 148, 152, 165–
    166, 185, 200
  and anatman perspective, 161
  biology of, 140–141
  and compassion, 181
  ethics of, 166–167, 168–169, 178
  and eudaimonia, 186–187
  folk-psychological view of, 162
  on happiness, 14, 232n16
  on human psyche, 141
  Nicomachean Ethics of, 180, 181, 235n14
  Poetics, 181
  and psychological egoism, 179
  on reason, 155, 156, 233n2
  and therapeutic division of labor, 182
  on virtue, 202

Aristotle's law (AL), 170, 171–172, 175, 176, 183, 186, 188
Art of Happiness, The (Dalai Lama and Cutler), 13, 24
Ascetic, virtues of, 148–149
Assumptions, examination of, 220n15
Atheists
  agnostics contrasted with, 210n5
  Buddhist, 5, 219n7
  naturalist, 64
Atman (unchanging self or soul), 68, 98, 161. *See also* Soul
  and Brahmanic tradition, 124
  nature of, 97–98
  rejection of, 68, 69–70, 222n24
Attachment, 127, 211n5
Attention
  and happiness, 50–51
  meditation for training in, 106
Attentiveness, mental, 106. *See also* Mindfulness
Augustine, Saint, 81, 233n19
Autonomic nervous system control, 10, 37–38
Awakening, 9, 16

Basic science education, 63
Batchelor, Stephen, 212n7, 214n14, 219n7
Beats, 13
Behavior, linking Buddhist phenomenology with, 82–84
Beings-in-time, 98
Bhagavad Gita, 220n16
Bhutan, xii
Big Bang theory, 69, 72, 73, 221n18
"Binding problem," 52
Birth, karma and, 223n24. *See also* Rebirth
Bliss, 14, 33. *See also* Happiness
Bodhicaryavatara (Santideva), 170
Bodhisattva, 30, 116–117
  in Botswana, 33–35

eudaimonia[Buddha] achieved by, 29–30
happiness achieved by, 31–32
ideal of, 30, 31
inappropriate lust of, 216n19
of Mahayanan Buddhism, 119, 215n15
motivation of, 119
path and stages of, 215n18
Plato and, 118–120
psyche of, 107–109
vows of, 161–162, 176
work of, 119, 229n5
Botswana, bodhisattva in, 33–35
Brahmanic tradition, and Buddhism, 124
Brahmans, 174, 221n17, 234n8
Brain
  and differences in thought, 41
  examination of, 56
  first-personal experience and, 88, 225n28
  happiness and, 37, 38–42, 45
  linking Buddhist phenomenology with, 82–84
  neuroscientific assessment of, 52
Brain imagery, 55, 58
Brain science. *See also* Mind science
  and eudaimonia, 112
  leftward activity in prefrontal cortex in, 111
  problem of content in, 54
Breathing meditation, 194–195
Buddha. *See also* Gautama, Siddhartha
  "Gradual Training" of, 215n16
  and happiness, 232n16
  inaugural speech of, 124
Buddha's law (BL), 186, 188
Buddhism, xi, 165–166. *See also* Ethics, Buddhist
  atheistic varieties of, 228n10
  attraction of, 2, 13, 122
  and cognitive science, 81
  compared with proselytizing traditions, xi

concept of happiness in, 14
early, 222n23
Eightfold Path of, 21–22, 28, 29, 30,
    32, 43, 100, 101, 123, 184, 209n3,
    211n4
epistemology of, 70–72, 75
eudaimonistic, 13–14
focus of, 122, 231n10
forms of, xii, 15
Four Noble Truths of, 12, 20, 21–22,
    42, 99, 123, 167, 184, 185, 191, 194,
    209n3
heterodox nature of, 224n24
and influenza, 49–51
metaphysics of, 68, 97, 101, 206
and mind science, 88
and modern moral philosophy,
    158–159
as natural philosophy, 206
Northern California kind, 212n7
origins of, 155
philosophy of, xi–xii, xiii
and problem of excessive demanding-
    ness, 197–201
and science, 61, 218n3
secular, 214n14
study of, 60
supernatural beliefs in, 4
three poisons of, 85, 86, 101–102, 105
three vehicles of, 214n13
Western, 117, 212n7, 219n8
Buddhism and happiness, ix x, 6, 19,
    37, 42–45
and contemporary mind science, 14
hypotheses for, 9–10
research on, 9, 110–111
Buddhism and Science (Lopez), 218n3
Buddhism naturalized, 59, 209n3,
    214n14
epistemic standard and, xiii
explained, xi, 3
as imperative, 4
metaphysics of, 3–5

and morality, 116
Buddhist Ethics (Saddhatissa), 184–185
Buddhists
    brains of, 204–205
    characteristics of, 10
    debating, 65
    frame of mind, 10
    happy, 37
    identification as, 19
    numbers of, xii
    "practicing," 226n226
    virtuous, 201
    Western, 13
    Western vs. Asian, 68
Buddhist tenets, definition of propo-
    nent of, 221n16
Butler, Joseph, 97

Calliclean challenge, 235n11
Caste system, 68
Causality
    karmic, 72–74, 75–76, 77, 78
    natural law of, 77
Causation
    and Darwinian theory, 72
    karmic, 72–74, 75–76, 77, 78
    metaphysics of, 135
    natural law of, 77
    sentient-being, 78
    and virtue, 150
Causes
    "final," 78
    kinds of, 77
Character
    Aristotle's view of, 161
    nonexistence of, 143–152
    and virtue, 187–188
Chauvinism, moral, 189
Chopel, Gendun, 63, 219n11, 220n12
Christianity, metaphysics of, 117
Churchland, Patricia Smith, 83
Churchland, Paul M., 83
Citta and cittas, 190, 227n6

Cognitive-behavioral therapy, 107
Cognitive science, 81. *See also* Mind
  science
Cognitive task performance, measure-
  ment of, 56
Collins, Steven, 99, 216n21
Commonality, 181, 182, 183
Community, desire for, 180
Compassion, 115, 155, 156, 202
  and anatman doctrine, 231n11
  comparing conceptions of, 213n10
  Dalai Lama on, 180
  in Mahayana Buddhism, 234n3
  meditation for, 195
  relation of no-self to, 121, 131
  universal, 179–181
  wisdom and, 120
Concentration, one-pointed, 47
Confirmation bias, 110
Confucianism, xi, xiii, 6, 59, 178, 231n9
Confucius, 148, 152
Conscious (atman), 127. *See also* Atman;
  Consciousness
Consciousness
  in *Abhidamma*, 190
  consciousness of, 236n18
  decomposition of (Citta), 104
  epiphenomenal nature of, 88
  human, 62
  joy, 227n6
  linking phenomenology with brain
    and behavior in, 82–84
  luminous, 52–53, 85, 86
  material basis of, 87
  matter and, 80
  musical, 104
  naturalism about, 62
  and natural laws, 77
  neural correlates of, 85, 86, 87
  ontological independence of, 80
  and ontology of mental states, 84–90
  and rebirth, 133, 222n24
  and role of phenomenology, 80–82

Consciousness criterion, of personal
  identity, 96–97
Consciousness Reconsidered (Flanagan), ix
Consequences of Compassion (Goodman),
  121
Consequentialism
  and chauvinistic tendencies, 200
  and eudaimonistic theory, 142, 159
  and excessive demandingness,
    196–197
  modern, 232n14
Consumptive ego, 100
Contemplatives, 41
Continuity, bodily, test of, 138
Correlation coefficient, 153, 154
Cosmological theories, Buddhist, 75
Cosmopolitan philosophy, 2, 4
Cosmopolitans, 207
Cosmopolitan style, 209n2
Crick, Francis, 87, 225n27
*Cult of Nothingness: The Philosophers and
  the Buddha, The* (Droit), 12
Curtin, Venerable Robina, 224n24
Cutler, Howard, 13
Cynicism, xi

Dalai Lama, xii, 3, 38
  bestsellers of, 13, 24, 65
  on Big Bang theory, 221n18
  on evolution, 78–79
  on fundamental nature of mind, 38
  on genuine compassion, 180
  on happiness, 42, 212n7
  interest in science of, 60, 61–65, 218n4
  on investigation of consciousness,
    81, 82
  on karma and consciousness, 80
  on luminous consciousness, 52
  and natural law of causality, 72–73,
    74, 75–76
  and NCC view, 88, 225n28
  Nobel Peace Prize acceptance speech
    of 1989, 64–65

and reincarnation, 132
on scientific materialism, 71–72
Damasio, A. R., 83, 216n2
Damasio, Hannah, 83
Darwinian theory, 72, 114
Davidson, R. J., 9, 39, 48, 49–50, 83
Deficit studies, 216n2
Delusion (moha), 3, 101
Demarcation, problem of, 219n6
Dennett, Daniel C., 160
Dependent origination of all things,
    doctrine of (pratityasamutpada),
    126, 133–135
Descartes, René, 71, 81, 127, 221n19
Desire
    avaricious greedy (lobha), 101
    Buddhist therapy of, 182
    economy of, 174
    satisfaction of, 98–99
    therapy of, 173–174
    untamed, 113
*Destructive Emotions: A Scientific Dialogue
    with the Dalai Lama* (Goleman), x
Dharmakirti, 79, 220n12
Dharma Life (magazine), 9
Disposition(s)
    activation of, 153
    desired sequence activated by, 151
    nature of, 151–152
    virtues as, 150
Divine Abodes, Four (brahmaviharas),
    107–108, 176, 192, 193
Doris, J. M., 145
Dosa (hatred), 101
Dostoyevsky, Fyodor M., 60, 219n7
Dreaming Souls (Flanagan), ix
Dreyfus, George, 16
Droit, Roger-Pol, 13
Dukkha, 14, 99

Eastern philosophy, flux in, 134–136
Ecological approach, 168, 169
Ego, consumptive, 100

Egoism, 98, 135
Einstein, Albert, 63
Ekman, Paul, 9, 45, 46, 47, 48
Emotions
    destructive, 130
    and face reading, 47
    negative, 57
    nondestructive, 18
Emptiness (sunyata)
    and decomposition of mental states,
    236n17
    doctrine of, 116, 127, 213–214n11,
    227n5, 228n2, 232n13
    Nagarjuna's doctrine of, 225n25
Emptiness move, 126–131
Enlightenment. *See also* Wisdom
    (prajna)
    in analysis of flourishing, 28
    epistemology, 59
    and eudaimonia^{Buddha}, 16
    happiness and, 9, 23–27
    and meditation, 17
    secular philosophy of, 180
Epicureans, xi, 81, 173–174, 177, 178
Epiphenomnalism, 66–68
Epistemology
    Buddhist, 6, 59–61, 70–72, 75
    religious, 211n2
    of science, 70–72, 75
Equality, 181
Equanimity (upekkha), 108, 216n20
Ethical theories, 178
    character traits in, 142–145
    eudaimonistic, 231n9
Ethics
    Aristotle's, 168–169
    and Buddhist psychology, 103–104
    comparative, 167–169
    as human ecology, 156–158
    normative, 146
    post-Aristotelian, 173
    and religion, 59
    traditional Indian, 126

Ethics, Buddhist, 70, 101, 121, 140,
196–201, 206
and Aristotle's ethics, 166–167,
168–169
and justice, 206
practice in, 182
theory, 122, 178, 230n8
and view of no-self, 123
Ethnocentrism, anachronism and, 1
Eudaimon, life of, 12
Eudaimon^Buddha, 201
bodhisattva as, 31
and doctrine of anatman, 130
requirements for, 44
Eudaimonia, x, xiv, 10–11, 186. *See also*
Flourishing, human
Buddhist, 140–143
conceptions of, 112
as final end, 142
happiness^Buddha from, 25, 26
polysemous character of, 11–12
translation of, 141
Eudaimonia^Aristotle, 11, 95, 181, 185
Eudaimonia^Buddha, 6, 37, 94, 104, 112–
113, 114, 169, 193–194, 226n1
and *Abhidamma*, 190
achieving, 121
analysis of, 165
components of, 34
concept of, 19
and four divine virtues, 108–109
and happiness, 43
interpretation of, 32
location of, 45
meaning of, 16
nature of, 95
and nirvana, 132
obstacles to, 105
origins of, 27–28
precepts required for, 100–101
therapeutic tools required for, 192
virtues required for, 107–108
Eudaimonia^Hedonist, 11

Eudaimonics, 18, 56, 109, 203
ethical ecologies and, 155–158
experiments in, 109–113
and "internalist predicament," 110
Eudaimonistic theory, 142–143, 232n16
Euripides, 203
Europe, Buddhism in, 15
Evolution, 65
Dalai Lama on, 78–79
neo-Darwinian theory of, 3, 62, 72–80
sentience in theory of, 77
Excellences, 20, 156
Existence, intrinsic, 129
Experience, location of, 90
Experiments
brain, ix, 38–39
in eudaimonics, 109–113
social psychological, 153, 154
Externalism, 229n7
Extravagant conception, 30–31

Face reading, 10
experiments in, 47–48
and happiness, 38, 49
research on, 45, 46–47, 56
Fairness, liberal virtue of, 178
False beliefs
happiness gained by, 188–189
tendency to acquire, 236n16
Falsifiability, criterion of, 62
Fellow-feeling, 180, 183
Final end (telos), concept of, 155
First nature, 93–95
fellow-feeling aspects of, 180
three poisons and, 113
First-person perspective, 66
Flourishing, human, 6, 57, 94, 193–194,
203. *See also* Eudaimonia
analysis of, 165
and anatman perspective, 160
and biological fitness, 221n21
Buddhist analysis of, 16, 27–29, 122
in Buddhist eudaimonia, 140

in Buddhist philosophy, 217n5
in comparative neurophilosophy, xiv
eudaimonia as, 11
and impartiality, 197–198
individual, 158
interpretation of, 110
and love, 117–118
naturalistic concept of, 209n3
in no-self traditions, 162
polysemous character of, 12
role of philosophy in, 207
as selfless persons, 113
theories of, 205
theory-specific conception of, 57–58
virtues and, 154
and wisdom, 121
Fluxing, 134–139
FMRI magnets, 50
Folk psychology, 26, 228
Foucault, Michel, 103, 168, 174
Frame of mind, Buddhist, 10
Freud, Sigmund, 83, 179
Friendships
  desire for, 180
  and happiness, 187
Frontal lobe activity, 39
Fulfillment, polysemous character of, 12
Fusion philosophy, 2, 209n1, 214n14

Gage, Phineas, 216n2
Garfield, Jay, 212n7, 232n12
Gautama, Siddartha, 4, 55, 130, 155,
  233n19. See also Buddha
Geisteswissenschaften, 73–74, 76, 78
Gelugs (Geluks), 213n10, 220n15. See
  also Tibetan Buddhism
Generosity, 181
Goals, human, 93
God
  belief in, 137
  conceptions of, 5
  rejection of existence of, 68–69
  in Western philosophy, 136–137

Golden Rule, 198–199
Goleman, Daniel, x, 38
Good
  being, 37, 186–189
  definition of, 197
  feeling, 37
  liberal conception of, 177–178
Good life, 204. See also Flourishing,
  human
  assessment of, 154
  conceptions of, 95, 109
  mindfulness in, 102
  multicultural approach to, 207
Goodman, Charles, 121
Goodness, in analysis of flourishing, 28.
  See also Virtue(s)
"Good Samaritan," parable of, 198–199
Greek philosophy, xiii. See also Hellenistic philosophers and philosophies
Gyatso, Tenzin. See Dalai Lama

Happiness, 41, 57, 193–194, 203, 204.
  See also Buddhism and happiness;
  Eudaimonia
  achieving true, 34
  anatman perspective on, 160
  and antidepressants, 228n8
  and Aristotle's law, 170
  brain and, 38–42
  in Buddhist eudaimonia, 140
  in Buddhist philosophy, 217n5
  causes of, 233n1
  colloquial concept of, 57
  in comparative neurophilosophy, xiv
  counterfeit of, 175, 234n9
  Dalai Lama on, 24, 212n7
  economic measurement of, 99
  and ethical ecologies, 157–158
  in ethical theory, 142
  as goal of first nature, 113
  hypotheses, 9–10, 46
  interpretation of, 110
  kinds of, 10–12

Happiness (cont.)
  language standards for, 32, 33–34
  liberal conception of, 177–178
  and LPFC, 111
  money and, 43
  necessary conditions for, 185–186
  in philosophical analysis, 205
  and relationship with God, 41
  research on "authentic," 56
  science of, 44, 217n10
  state of, 188
  study of, 56
  terms translated as, 14
  theory-specific conception of, 57–58
  thick description of, 12
  virtue and, 166, 169–173, 183–184, 233n1
  and wisdom, 43
Happiness^{Aristotle}, 186
Happiness^{Buddha}, 1, 6, 19, 24–25, 26, 37,
    42, 43, 186, 193–194
  of bodhisattva, 31–32
  characteristics of, 44, 54
  and good life, 123
  wisdom in, 43–44
Harman, Gilbert, 144, 145
Hatred (dosa), 101
Hawthorne effect, 18
Health, happiness and, 10
Heaven, 2, 223n24
Hedonism, 11, 13, 142, 206
  classical, 140
  extreme, 121
  platonic, 207
Hellenistic philosophers and philoso-
    phies, 173–174, 177, 179
Hellenistic therapeutic schools, 165–166
Heraclitean selves, 95–96
Heraclitus, 136
Hermits, 11
Hinayana Buddhists, 119
Hinduism, xi, 178, 220n16
Hippies, 13
Hogendoorn, Rob, 63, 219n9

Human nature, and human predica-
    ment, 98–101. See also First nature;
    Second nature
Human persons, first and second nature
    of, 93–95
Human sciences, 73–74
Hume, David, 2, 119, 134, 137, 159

Identity, 69
  personal, 96–97, 139
  theory, 51–52, 90
Illimitables, the, 176, 192
Illusions, positive, 22, 212n9, 233n18
Immaterialism, metaphysical, 84
Immune function
  and happiness, 50–51
  measurement of, 56
  and mindfulness meditation, 49–50
Impartiality
  in action, 199–200
  demand of, 196
  kinds of, 197
Impermanence
  and emptiness doctrine, 227n5
  meditation on, 194
  and no-self, 125
Indic religions, 132, 223n24
Influenza, Buddhism and, 49–51
Intelligent design (ID), 65
Intentionality
  Buddhist, 227n6
  in Buddhist philosophical psychology,
    236n18
  theory of, 67
Internalism, 229n7
"Internalist predicament," 173
Investigation, meditation of, 211n2
Irwin, W., 50
Is-ought, debates about, 229n7

Jainism, xi
James, William, 66, 90, 119, 134, 137,
    159, 216n1, 229n6

Jayatilleke, K. N., xi
Jesus of Nazareth, 198–199
Jinpa, Thupten, 61–62, 79, 220
Johnson, George, 65
Joyce, James, 134
Joy consciousness, 227n6
Judaism naturalized, 5
Justice, in Buddhist texts, 157

Kabat-Zinn, Jon, 49–50
Kahnemann, Dan, 99
Kant, Immanuel, 117, 121, 149, 158,
    177, 232n17
Karma
    and consciousness, 80
    law of, 77, 78
    meaning of, 72
    and rebirth, 223n24
    and sentience, 76
Karma^{untame}, 226n1
Karmic causation, 73, 77, 78, 222n24
Karmic causation^{tame}, 79
Karmic causation^{untame}, 78
Karmic eschatology, 222n24
Karuna (compassion), 108. See also
    Compassion
Kelley, Chris, 209n2
Keown, Damien, 121, 185, 212n6
Kierkegaard, Søren, 5
Knowledge, 64, 213n10
Knowledge-for-its-own-sake school of
    thought, 64
Koch, Christof, 83, 84–85, 86, 88
Kohlberg, Lawrence, 146

Labor, therapeutic division of, 181–183
Laws of Nature, in Western philosophy,
    136–137
LeDoux, Joseph, 46, 83
Leftward activity in prefrontal cortex
    (LPFC), 111
Leibniz's law, 137, 138
Levenson, Robert, 45, 46

Liberalism, problem with, 177
Library of Tibetan Works and Archives
    (LTWA), 63
Life, interconnectedness of all, 64
Lobha (avaricious greedy desire), 101
Locke, John, 70, 96–97, 119, 137, 139, 159
Logothestis, N., 83
Lopez, Donald S., Jr., 218n3
Love
    equal, 198
    and flourishing, 117–118
    justification of, 180–181
Lovingkindness (metta), 108, 115, 202
    in Mahayana Buddhism, 234n3
    and no-self, 131
    universal, 179–181
Luminous consciousness, 85, 86
Lust, antidote for, 106

MacIntyre, Alasdair, 158
Madhyamaka (Middle Path) tradition,
    in Mahayana Buddhism, 126, 127
Madyimaka critique, 129
Magnanimity, 181
Mahayana Buddhism, 3, 28, 116, 229n4
    achieving happiness in, 185
    bodhisattva of, 215n15
    compassion in, 234n3
    and emptiness doctrine, 213–214n11,
    227n5, 236n17
    Madhyamaka (Middle Path) tradition
    in, 126, 127
    Theravada Buddhism compared with,
    118–119, 126–127, 229n3
Malunkyaputta, 130
Marx, Karl, 60, 168
Mathematics, philosophy compared
    with, 203
Matter, and consciousness, 80
Mayr, Ernst, 221n20
Meaning, polysemous character of, 12
Médecins Sans Frontières (Doctors
    Without Borders), 33

Media, and shared conceptions of happiness, 178
Meditation, 101. *See also* Mindfulness
in analysis of flourishing, 28
and cardiovascular health, 110
on compassion, 57
concentration, 106–107
esoterica associated with, 214n12
"give-and-take," 195–196
good effects of, 111, 112
happiness and, 23–27, 105
insight (Vipassana), 48
of investigation, 211n2
kinds of, 106
metta (lovingkindness), 48, 107
vs. mindfulness, 217n7
moral, 107
and positive affect, 50
practice, 17
role of, 20
sexual, 214n12
Tibetan (Tong-len), 195, 211n2
types of, 194
validation of religious truths in, 211n2
Western emphasis on, 106
and wisdom, 20–22
work of, 189–196
Meditators
brain patterns of, 18
Buddhist, 10, 38
experienced, 38, 46–47
Zen, 49
Memory, and no-self, 125
Mencius, 148, 152
Mental events, 86–87, 90
Mental life, thick description of, 81
Mental states
in *Abhidhamma,* 103
in Buddhist psychology, 193
causes of, 53–54
content of, 53–54
decomposition of, 236
destructive, 53, 57

functional links among, 82
and neural activity, 89
neural correlates for, 85
ontology of, 84–90
Metta (lovingkindness), 108. *See also* Lovingkindness (Metta).
Metta meditation, 107
Microexpressions, reading, 48
Milarepa, 233n19
Mill, John Stuart, 149, 198, 232n14
Mind
as immaterial property, 62
metaphysics of, 51–53, 90
Mind and Life Conference, Eighth (2000), ix
Mind control techniques, 105
Mindfulness, 17, 155, 184. *See also* Meditation
in analysis of flourishing, 28
and Buddhist happiness, 43
everyday, 105–107
in good life, 102–103
vs. meditation, 217n7
practice in, 114
techniques, 23
Mind science, 90
Buddhism and, 88
Buddhism and happiness in, 14–20
and neo-Darwinian theory, 76
in West, 82
Mind scientists, 58
Mind-world interaction, 113
Minimalist conception, 30–31
Minsky, M., 160
Mirror Test, 138–139
Mischel, Walter, 144, 153
Moha (delusion; false self-serving belief), 3, 101, 213n9
Money, and happiness, 187
Monk, meditating. *See* Ricard, Mathieu
Monks, Tibetan, 16–17
Mood
effect of meditation on, 18

and mindfulness meditation, 49–50
  nature of, 236n18
Mood, positive, 18
  brain experiments with, 39
  concept of, 41
  and happiness, 51
  in philosophical analysis, 205
  and science of happiness, 44–45
Moral habit, 148. *See also* Virtue(s)
Morality
  content of, 115–116
  liberal common sense, 172, 177,
    235n15
  motivation for, 116, 117, 118, 228n1,
    229n7
  and reason, 229n7
  teaching, 147
Moral personality, theories of, 143–144
Moral philosophy, 144, 158–159
Morals, Buddhist metaphysics of,
    115–118
Motivation
  and morality, 116, 117, 118, 228n1,
    229n7
  and reason-to-be-moral question,
    228n1
Mudita (sympathetic joy), 108, 228n9
Murdoch, Iris, 146, 148
"Mustard Seed, Parable of," 182–183,
    190, 194
Myanmar, xii, 231n10
Myths, death-defying, 22

Nagarjuna, 71, 126, 127–128, 213n11,
    225n25, 236n17
Naropa, 233n19
Narratives, 162
Naturalism, 2, 5–6, 60, 62. *See also* Bud-
    dhism naturalized
Naturalists, beliefs for, 210n4
"Natural method," 217n8
Natural selection, 139
Nature

first and second human, 93–95
  laws of, 136–137
Nature of Buddhist Ethics, The (Keown),
    121, 185
Naturwissenschaften, 74
Nepal, 231n10
Neural correlates of consciousness
    (NCC), 85–86, 87
Neural correlate view (NCV), 52, 55
Neurojournalism, 111–112
Neurons, spiking activity of, 897
Neurophenomenology, 53, 54, 82
Neurophilosophy, comparative, xiv, 6,
    56, 111, 204–205, 205
Neurophysicalism, 3, 27, 89
  defined, 65–66
  and subjective realism, 65–68
Neuroscience, ix, 51–52
  happiness and, xiii–xiv
  limitations of, 27
  LPFC research in, 234n4
  problems with, 205
New Age metaphysics, 13
New Scientist (magazine), 9, 37, 38, 85
Newton, Isaac, 71
New York Times, 38
Nicomachean Ethics (Aristotle), 180, 181
Nietzsche, Friedrich Wilhelm, 5, 13, 60,
    131, 168, 203
Nihilism, of Buddhism, 13
Nirvana, 98, 226n1
  conceptions of, 22, 212n6
  and happiness, 23–27, 42
  interpretations of, 23
  naturalistic view of, 22
  for no-selves, 131–134
  in Pali canon, 133–134
Nisbett, R. E., 153
Normative exclusion clause, 188, 193
Normativity, 104
North America, Buddhism in, 15
No-self traditions, flourishing in,
    162–163

No-selves, 70
  afterlives for, 131–134
  and character traits, 143–152
  and doctrine of impermanence, 167
  and emptiness doctrine, 126–131
  metaphysics of, 123
  nirvana for, 131–134
  two views of, 123–124
  well-being for, 120–122
Nozick, Robert, 234n9
Nussbaum, Martha, 173, 174, 176, 177

Obeyeseker, Gananath, 222n24
Omniscience, 76, 222n23
Operant conditioning, 83
Optimism, false, 233n18
Ospina, M. B., 51

Pagnoni, Giuseppe, 49
Pali canon, 236n17
  Abhidhamma of, 102
  classical, 31
  conceptions of nirvana in, 133–134
  doctrine of emptiness in, 228n2
  overall message of, 131
  three baskets of, 215n15
"The Pali imaginaire," 216n21
Parfit, Derek, 119–120, 135, 136, 137,
    160, 233n19
Peace, 231n9
Perseverance effect, 235n16
Personal identity, 96–97, 139
Personality, moral, 143
Person[Buddha], 95
Personhood, 69
Persons, kinds of, 95
Phenomenological method, 53
Phenomenology, 82
  Abhidhamma as, 104
  Buddhist, 80–82
  and development of Buddhist philoso-
    phy and religion, 225n26
  of virtue and vice, 152–154

Phi-experiences, 138, 139
Philosophers, 174, 234n6
Philosophical analysis, 205
Philosophy
  analytic, 5–6
  Buddhist, xi–xii, xiii, 64, 189
  comparative, x–xi, xiii, 1, 55, 209n2
  empirical evidence of efficacy of, x
  and flourishing, 207
  goals of, 204
  mathematics compared with, 203
  styles of doing, 1–2
Phronesis, virtue of, 156
Plato, xi, 136, 148, 152, 155, 168, 179,
    203, 204, 206
  and bodhisattva, 118–120
  and psychological egoism, 179
Pleasures, kinds of, 10
Poisons, three, 85, 86, 101–102, 177,
    184, 193, 194
  assessment of, 191–192
  moha, 3, 101, 213n9
  and Six Main Mental Afflictions, 192
  special Rx for, 105
Politics, 61, 231n10
Popper, Sir Karl, 62, 219n6
Population genetics, 221n21
Practice, Buddhist. *See also specific*
    practices
  eudaimonia [Buddha] in, 17
  happiness in, 14–15
  meditation in, 19–20
  and states of mind, 51
  and various goods, 55
Prajna (Buddhist metaphysics), 101
Prayer, compared with meditation, 106
Prefrontal cortices, 39, 40–41, 111
Pride, 215n17
*Proceedings of National Academy of Sci-
    ences* (PSNA), Buddhist practitioners
    study in, 18
Prompta, Somparn, 122, 229n3
Pronouns, as epistemic positions, 67

Proper function (ergon), concept of, 155
Psychology
  Abhidamma in, 191
  "anchoring effect" in, 189
  Buddhist, 103, 175, 189, 193
  folk, 228
  moral, 102–104
  personality in, 144, 153
  and virtue talk, 147
Psychology, philosophical
  Buddhist, 94
  first and second human nature in,
    93–94
  first nature to second nature in, 108
Psychopathology, 217n9
Pure Land Buddhism, Japanese, 15, 19,
  29

Queer ideas, 117
The Quest for Consciousness: A Neurobio-
  logical Approach (Koch), 84–85

Rahula, Walpola Sri, 15
Rationality, imperfect, 141
Realism, subjective, 66
Reality, 152, 232n13
Really Hard Problem: Meaning in a Mate-
  rial World, The (Flanagan), x
Reason
  in Aristotle's ethics, 156
  components of, 233n2
  and ethics, 167
  and morality, 229n7
  practical (phronesis), 156
Rebirth, 15, 222n24
  belief in, 2, 79–80, 213n9, 226n2
  Buddhist belief in, 131–133
  Dalai Lama's conception of, 218n5
  distinguished from reincarnation,
    224n24
  and happiness, 23–27
  interpretation of, 22–23
  and investigative science, 5, 218n4

  theories of, 222n24
Recluse, 11
Reductionism, Buddhist, 28
Reid, Thomas, 97
Reincarnation, distinguished from re-
  birth, 224n24
Religion, psychosocial roles attributed
  to, 59–60
Research experiments, limitations of,
  51, 54. *See also* Experiments
Ricard, Mathieu, 9, 38, 40, 47, 48
Rinpoche, Achok, 63
Rorty, Richard, 209n2
Rosch, Eleanor, 136
Ross, L., 153
Russell, Bertrand, 128
Ryle, G., 84

Saddhatissa, Hammalawa, 184–185,
  212n8
Saints, Buddhist, 31
Samsara (cycle of suffering), 21
Santideva, 24, 170, 212n7
Sartre, Jean-Paul, 229n6
Schadenfreude, 228n9
Schall, J. D., 83
Scholars, Buddhist, xii
Schopenhauer, Arthur, 13
Science. *See also* Neuroscience
  Dalai Lama and, 61–65, 218n4
  epistemology of, 70–72, 75
  happiness and, xiii–xiv
  and rebirth, 79
  role of "scriptures" in, 70–71, 76
  and spirituality, 60, 219n10
"Science for Monks" program, 63
Scientific inquiry, 88, 220n13
Scientific materialism, 71–72
Scientific method, 59
Scientific naturalism, 5–6
Scriptures, 70–71, 76
Second nature, 93–95
Secularism, and Buddhism, xi

Self, 98. *See also* No-selves
  dominant view of, 117
  examination of, 127
  immutable, 134
  impermanence of, 101
  kinds of, 95
  rejection of, 222n24
Self-cultivation, 181, 184
Self-esteem, 215n17
Selfishness, 98, 195–196
Self-knowledge, Socratic, 103
Selfless persons. *See also* Anatman
  and atman and anatman, 95
  and first and second human nature,
    93–95
  human predicament and, 98–101
  and mindfulness, 105–107
  and three poisons, 101–102
Self-love, 160
Self-respect, 215n17
Seligman, M. E. P., 217n3, 217n10
Sentience
  emergence of, 77–78
  evolution of, 74–76
  and karmic causation, 75
Sentient beings, 77, 141
Serenity, 14
Siderits, Mark, 28, 209n2
Skeptics, 173–174
Slavery, 157
Social coordination, 231n9
Social harmony, 231n9
Socialization, 187–188, 189
Social psychological experiments, 153,
  154
Socrates, 28, 81, 102, 148, 152, 179
Soul, 98. *See also* Atman
  belief in, 137
  rejection of, 222n24
  in Western philosophy, 136–137
Soulophilia, 137–138, 229n6
Sound of Two Hands Clapping, The (Drey-
  fus), 16

Space of Meaning [Early 21st century], 60–61
Spinoza, Benedict, 71, 203
Spirituality
  and political conflict, 61
  science and, 219n10
Spiritual traditions, motivational prob-
  lem faced by, 224–225n24
Sri Lanka, xii
Stabilization, meditation of, 211n2
Startle response, 45, 46–47
Statistics, for prefrontal activity, 39–40
Status, and happiness, 187
Stem cells, 61
Stich, S. P., 145
Stoicism, xi, 81, 148, 173–174, 177, 178
Subjective realism, 89
"Substantialist illusion," 129
Suffering, 20
  and antidepressants, 228n8
  freedom from, 184
  and happiness, 35
  interpretation of, 99
  natural- *vs.* human-caused, 21
  and no-self, 125
  overcoming, 42–43
Sukha, 14
Superscripting strategy, 94–95
Supervenience relation, problem of, 85
Sympathetic joy (mudita), 108

Taoism, xi
Temperament, 155
Thailand, 231n10
Theology, and science, 60
Therapeutic work, 181
Therapy, of desire and delusion, 179
Therapy of Desire, The (Nussbaum), 173
Theravada Buddhism, 3, 4, 159
  arahant of, 215n15
  emptiness doctrine in, 214n11, 227n5
  Mahayana Buddhism compared with,
    118–119, 126–127, 229n3
Thick description, 56, 81

Third-person perspective, 66
Thirst, unquenchable (tanha), 132
Thompson, Evan, 135–136
Thrasymachean challenge, 235n11
Thurman, Robert, 219n7, 225n24
Tibetan Buddhism, 15, 185, 214n14
Tibetan meditation (Tong-len), 195, 211n2
Tolerance, liberal virtue of, 178
Tolstoy, Leo, 203
Traits
  causal efficacy of, 154
  ontology of, 144
  research in, 146–147
Truth, 59, 218n2
  as goal, 204
  search for, 64
Tsongkhapa, 79
Tsunamis, 210n4

Unconscious, 83, 84. *See also*
  Consciousness
Unity, fundamental, 65
Universals, 93
Universe in a Single Atom, The (Dalai
  Lama), 61, 65
Unsatisfactoriness, 20
Upanishads, 220n16
Upekkha (equanimity), 108, 216n20

Varela, Francisco, 53, 82, 135, 160
Vice, phenomenology of, 152–154
Vipassana retreats, 28
Virtue(s), 102, 203, 204
  in analysis of flourishing, 28
  Aristotelian, 156, 157, 185
  and Aristotle's law, 170
  of bodhisattva stage, 32
  Buddhist, 140, 144, 156
  and Buddhist happiness, 43
  and character traits, 146
  comparative view of, 1
  conception of, 166
  defined, 147–148

  detection of, 55
  as disposition, 150, 151–152
  elements of, 149–150
  of eudaimonia[Buddha], 45
  exceptional, 95
  four conventional, 100
  four divine, 108–109
  four exceptional, 107
  four required, 54–55
  fusion of, 2
  and happiness, 23–27, 43, 166, 169–
    173, 183–184, 187, 233n1
  Kantian conception of, 232n17
  kinds of, 149–150
  liberal, 178
  major, 95
  moral, 167
  phenomenology of, 152–154
  phronesis, 156
  teaching, 149
  theory-specific conception of, 57–58
  and three poisons, 102
  transformation of psyche required for,
    173
Virtue theory, 146, 149

Wallace, Alan, 3, 82
Weil, Simone, 148
WEIRD (white, educated, industrialized,
  rich, developed) sample, 40, 228n11
"Welcome mat" statement, of Dalai
  Lama, 61, 62
Well-being
  and Buddhism, 37
  in ethical theory, 142
  happiness and, 10
  for no-selves, 120–122
  in philosophical analysis, 205
  scientific status of term, 217n10
  theory-specific conception of, 57–58
The West
  Buddhism in, 117
  mind science in, 82

Western philosophy, fluxing in,
    136–139
What the Buddha Taught (Rahula), 15
Whitehead, Alfred North, 128
Wisdom (prajna), 102, 155, 203, 204.
    See also Enlightenment
  in analysis of flourishing, 28
  of bodhisattva stage, 32
  and Buddhist happiness, 43
  and compassion, 120
  components of, 125–126
  elements of, 116
  and eudaimonia, 95
  and eudaimonia^{Buddha}, 16
  gaining metaphysical, 101
  as goal, 204
  and happiness^{Buddha}, 43
  in interpretation of Buddhism, 211n4
  legitimacy of past, 71
  literature on, 109
  meaning of, 122
  and meditation, 20–22
  and reason, 167
  and three poisons, 102
Wittgensteinian concern, 83

Zen (Ch'an), 15
"Zenlike," defined, 216n20
Zen meditators, 49
Zeno-like paradox, 227n5